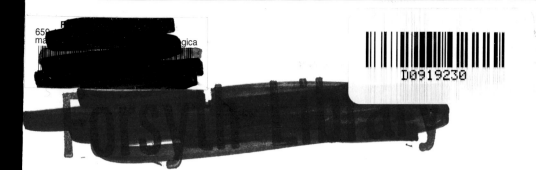

241

PSYCHOLOGICAL PROCESSES
AND
ADVERTISING EFFECTS
THEORY, RESEARCH, AND APPLICATION

List of Contributors

Linda F. Alwitt, *Leo Burnett U.S.A.*
Daniel R. Anderson, *University of Massachusetts at Amherst*
Rajeev Batra, *Columbia University*
Ann E. Beattie, *Columbia University*
John T. Cacioppo, *University of Iowa*
Peter Cushing, *Leo Burnett U.S.A.*
Melody Douglas-Tate, *Leo Burnett U.S.A.*
John A. Fiedler, *Ted Bates Worldwide, Inc.*
Anthony G. Greenwald, *The Ohio State University*
Jonathan Gutman, *University of Southern California*
J. Wesley Hutchinson, *University of Florida*
Clark Leavitt, *The Ohio State University*
Meryl Lichtenstein, *University of Illinois*
Richard J. Lutz, *University of Florida*
Andrew A. Mitchell, *University of Toronto*
Danny L. Moore, *University of Florida*
Richard E. Petty, *University of Missouri at Columbia*
Anthony R. Pratkanis, *Carnegie-Mellon University*
Michael L. Ray, *Stanford University*
Thomas J. Reynolds, *University of Texas at Dallas*
Thomas K. Srull, *University of Illinois*

PSYCHOLOGICAL PROCESSES
AND
ADVERTISING EFFECTS

THEORY, RESEARCH, AND APPLICATIONS

Edited by

Linda F. Alwitt
Leo Burnett U.S.A.

Andrew A. Mitchell
University of Toronto

LEA LAWRENCE ERLBAUM ASSOCIATES, PUBLISHERS
1985   Hillsdale, New Jersey   London

Lawrence Erlbaum Associates, Inc., Publishers
365 Broadway
Hillsdale, New Jersey 07642

Library of Congress Cataloging in Publication Data

Main entry under title:

Psychological processes and advertising effects.

Papers from the Second Annual Conference on
Advertising and Consumer Psychology held in
Chicago, Ill., May 1983.
Bibliography: p.
Includes indexes.
1. Advertising—Psychological aspects—Addresses,
essays, lectures. I. Alwitt, Linda F. II. Mitchell,
Andrew A., 1939-   . III. Conference on Advertising
and Consumer Psychology (2nd : 1983 : Chicago, Ill.)
HF5822.P78   1985   659.1'01'9   84-28773
ISBN 0-89859-515-0

Printed in the United States of America
10 9 8 7 6 5 4 3 2 1

Contents

Preface

The papers in this volume were presented at the second annual Conference on Advertising and Consumer Psychology which was held at Leo Burnett U.S.A. in Chicago on May, 1983, and was sponsored by Leo Burnett U.S.A., the Marketing Science Institute, and the Division of Consumer Psychology of the American Psychological Association.

We sincerely appreciate the efforts of the authors in cooperating with us by participating in the conference and thoughtfully preparing the manuscripts for this volume. We would also like to thank C. W. Park who presented a paper at the conference which is not included in this volume and John Maloney who provided very insightful integrating comments in reaction to the papers presented at the conference. Those comments were inspiring to all participants and were an impetus to advertising professionals to incorporate the ideas presented in the papers in this volume into their practices. We are also indebted to Calvin Gage, Director of Research of Leo Burnett U.S.A. for his support of the conference, to Alden Clayton and Diane Schmalensee of the Marketing Science Institute, who facilitated the participation of academics and advertisers, and to Arch Woodside of the Division of Consumer Psychology of the American Psychological Association, who lent us the benefit of his experience in organizing the first conference on Advertising and Consumer Psychology. We also gratefully acknowledge the assistance of Dian Johnson in preparing the manuscript for this volume.

Introduction

Linda F. Alwitt
Leo Burnett U.S.A.

Andrew A. Mitchell
University of Toronto

Our understanding of how advertising affects consumer behavior is undergoing a dramatic transformation. Recent theoretical and methodological advances in cognitive psychology, social cognition, and artificial intelligence are largely responsible for this transformation. These advances have provided a better understanding of the information acquisition process and how information is stored in memory. Consequently, we have been able to incorporate memory, the processing of visual information and affect into our models of advertising effects. Because of this, richer models of advertising effects are being developed, which include these psychological processes. We also have new methodologies such as the measurement of response times, that are able to provide sensitive tests of these models.

In order to obtain a better understanding of these changes, it is useful to examine the dominant model of persuasion in the early- to mid-1970s, as exemplified by the learning model proposed by McGuire (1968). In this model, an individual has to expend considerable effort in actively processing the information in the message and go through five basic stages before persuasion could occur. These stages are attention, comprehension, yielding, retention of message, and action. Later McGuire (1978) hypothesized that for a given message, there is a certain probability that each stage would occur during exposure to a message. The probability of each stage occurring is independent, so the probability that a given message would be successful is the product of the probability of the occurrence of each stage. Consequently, the likelihood is small that any message would be successful after a single exposure.

1

Modifications of this model stressed the individual's reaction to the message and identified two important mediators of persuasion. These were cognitive responses (Greenwald, 1968; Wright, 1973) and belief formation and change (Fishbein & Ajzen, 1975; Lutz, 1975). Theoretically, cognitive responses, or more specifically, counterarguing and support arguing represent the yielding stage while belief formation and change represent the retention stage. However, it should be noted that this latter mediator is a measure of the retention of *encoded* information from the message as opposed to retention of the message in episodic form.

This class of models might be viewed as a high involvement/verbal response model. It assumes that individuals actively process information from persuasive messages and may resist persuasion through the generation of counterarguments. Although it was rarely explicitly stated, these models are generally interpreted to assume that attitude formation and change is mediated only through verbal responses to the communication or through the product attribute beliefs that are formed or changed. Although there is considerable empirical evidence supporting this assumption, this evidence has been generally obtained from experiments where the experimental stimulus was a single, verbal message on a topic that was highly relevant to the subjects.

Although many researchers questioned whether this high involvement/verbal response model was the only way persuasion might occur, there were few well-defined alternatives to it. One, discussed by Krugman (1965), argued that the viewing of television commercials occurs under conditions of low involvement; however, the psychological processes that would cause persuasion under these conditions were not clearly stated. Perhaps because of methodological problems, little empirical research was directed at understanding the psychological processes underlying persuasion or even determining if persuasion would occur under these conditions. Ray, et al. (1973) also discussed alternative models of how advertising may affect consumer behavior. These alternative models were defined by different orderings of the three attitude components — cognitive, affective, and conative — and the market conditions that may cause these alternative orderings. Under low involvement conditions, for instance, Ray, et al. (1973), hypothesized that conations follow cognition and that affect occurs after conation.

As mentioned previously, there have been many changes in our understanding of advertising effects. These have occurred in four general areas. The first involves the defining of alternatives to the high involvement/verbal response model. Gardner, Mitchell, and Russo (1978) argued that two critical factors affect the information acquisition process. These are the amount of attention devoted to the message and the processing strategy used to process information from the message. Reducing attention levels has been found to reduce the amount of counterarguing or support arguing (Petty, Wells, &

Brock, 1976) which, in turn, either enhances or limits the amount of attitude change.

Two different types of processing strategies were defined by Gardner, Mitchell, and Russo (1978). The first is a brand processing strategy where individuals actively process the information from the advertisement to form an evaluation of the advertised brand. Under full attention, this process is similar to the high involvement/verbal response model discussed earlier. The second is a nonbrand processing strategy which occurs when individuals process information from a persuasive communication to achieve goals other than brand evaluation. Under these conditions they do not form an evaluation of the advertised brand during exposure to the advertisement. They do acquire some information about the advertised brand through incidental learning and a memory trace of the advertisement is retained in memory. At some later point in time, the individual may retrieve this information from memory and form an evaluation.

Chaiken (1980) and Petty and Cacioppo (1981) have also recently discussed alternative information-acquisition processes. These processes were identified by manipulating message relevance. The same message is made either highly relevant or largely irrelevant to the subject population. When the message is highly relevant, the subjects actively process the information from the communication using the high involvement/verbal response process that was discussed earlier. Chaiken refers to this as a systematic process and Petty and Cacioppo call this the central route to persuasion. This process is also consistent with Gardner, Mitchell, and Russo's definition of a brand processing strategy under conditions of full attention. When the message is largely irrelevant, the subjects use other cues, such as the number of arguments (Chaiken, 1980), or the attractiveness of the models used in the advertisement (Petty & Cacioppo, 1981). Chaiken refers to this as a heuristic process, and Petty and Cacioppo call this the peripheral route to persuasion. The nonbrand processing strategy of Gardner, Mitchell, and Russo, while not precisely the same as the heuristic process defined by Chaiken or the peripheral route to persuasion, is similar. The primary difference appears to be that with a nonbrand processing strategy, the individual does not form or change an evaluation of the message topic during exposure to the message.

The second area concerns the conceptualization of involvement. Currently, a number of different conceptualizations of involvement exist in the literature. The first defines involvement in terms of the types of verbal responses made by the individual during exposure to the advertisement. Krugman (1967), for instance, has used the number of linkages made between the advertised product and the individual's life during exposure to an advertisement as a measure of involvement. An alternative conceptualization defines involvement as a motivational state. As such, it has both intensity and direction. Mitchell (1981) has related intensity to the amount of attention devoted to the persuasive communication and direction to the processing strategy that is used. Cohen (1983) uses a similar definition, however, he defines involvement only in terms of intensity and suggests the use of the shared attention paradigm to obtain measures of involvement.

Other researchers have defined involvement in terms of commitment to a particular brand or product category (e.g., Lastovika & Gardner, 1979), while Houston and Rothschild (1977) have discussed three different types of involvement — enduring, situational, and response involvement. Enduring involvement refers to the ongoing relationship between the individual and the product or brand, while situational involvement recognizes transitory factors that may affect this relationship. Finally, response involvement concerns the type of response the individual makes toward the product.

The third area concerns the effect of an individual's affective reactions to the executional elements of the advertisement. Under the traditional high involvement/verbal response model, these executional elements were viewed only as vehicles for communicating the message. However, recent research indicates that the individual's affective reactions to the executional elements of the advertisement also affects persuasion. Mitchell and Olson (1981) showed subjects advertisements that contained photographs that were designed to create positive or neutral affect. The results of their study indicate that the product attribute beliefs that were formed did not mediate all the attitudinal differences that were found; however, the use of a second mediator, a measure of the individual's attitude toward the advertisement, did explain these differences. Mitchell and Olson (1981) suggested that these effects may occur through classical conditioning. Later, Mitchell (1983) presented a model of these effects based on the current research on mood and emotion that included a role for autonomic arousal. Ray and Batra (1983) also discussed how consumers' affective reactions toward advertisements may affect consumer behavior, however, they emphasized the attention-attracting role of these reactions.

The final area involves the processing of visual information. As mentioned previously, most of the research on persuasion has used only written messages; however, most advertisements also contain visual elements. Some of the early work in this area by Rossiter and Percy (1978, 1983) used Pavio's dual coding model (1971) to explain the effect of visual components in advertisements. According to their double loop model, the visual and written elements of an advertisement may create visual imaging that enhance memory and may result in attitudinal differences. Mitchell (1983) has discussed a similar model that differs on a number of important points. Both visual and written elements in advertisements may create or change product attribute beliefs or they may create an emotional response. The product attribute belief effects are mediated through Fishbein's Attitude Model (Fishbein & Ajzen, 1975) while the emotional responses seem to be mediated through attitude toward the advertisement.

In summary, then, although the high involvement/verbal response model is still acknowledged to be a valid model of the persuasion process, it is no longer recognized as the only model. Alternative models of the information acquisition process have been discussed, including heuristic processing (Chaiken, 1980), the peripheral route to persuasion (Petty & Cacioppo, 1981) and nonbrand processing (Gardner, Mitchell, and Russo, 1978). Under these alternative processes, individuals do not fully process all the information in the advertisement — instead, they use other cues such as the attractiveness of the models used in the advertisement or their affective reaction to the advertisement in evaluating the advertised product. These latter processes have been defined as low involvement processes. Consequently, with these alternative processes, verbal responses and the beliefs that are formed or changed do not explain all of the reliable variance in attitude formation or change. In addition, attitude formation and change can occur without full comprehension of the message.

Although these alternative models provide a new perspective for understanding how advertising works, there are still many unanswered questions. Among these are: (1) Exactly what is the relationship between the different mediators of persuasion? (2) How is memory for advertising related to persuasion? (3) What are the theoretical underpinnings of attitude toward the advertisement? (4) What determines the effect of persuasion over time? (5) What factors affect attention to advertising? (6) What psychological processes occur during the watching of a television commercial? and (7) What factors affect individual differences in the processing of advertising messages?

The chapters in this volume provide insights into these questions. They are organized in terms of four psychological processes which contribute to our understanding of how advertising works. These are affective reactions to advertisements, persuasion, psychological processes during television viewing, and involvement. In a sense, this organization forces a Procrustean solution on the order of the papers because those four psychological processes are highly interrelated in advertising. For instance, the effect of the emotional content of advertising and affective responses to it cannot be discussed without also considering the role of involvement. As the chapters in this volume demonstrate, involvement is also closely intertwined with persuasive effects of messages. Persuasion, involvement, and affect in advertising are mechanisms that work most often today within the communication medium of television. Thus, while each chapter emphasizes one of the four psychological processes, it also addresses aspects of the other processes.

The everyday evaluation of effective advertising in the marketplace has been guided by the traditional high involvement/verbal response model of the persuasion process that was discussed earlier. Under this model the advertisement itself was simply a vehicle for presenting the message. Little or no attention was paid to consumer reactions to the advertising itself, yet most advertising professionals would argue that the execution must be inextricably entwined with the message in order to sell the advertised brand. Indeed, for some advertising the execution *is* the message. Recognition of the important role of affective reactions to advertising is the main emphasis of the chapters in Part I of this volume.

In Chapter 1, Batra and Ray, drawing on a long history of advertising research at Stanford University, incorporate affective responses to advertising as a mediating variable into a model of how advertising works. They test this model using data on responses to different types of advertising executions for a number of product categories. According to this model, affective mediating responses are important in influencing brand attitudes, and appear to act through brand familiarity.

Attitude toward the advertisement has been identified as an important mediator of the persuasion process, however, as discussed previously the theoretical underpinnings of this construct are not well understood. Lutz, in Chapter 2, presents a typology of factors that may affect attitude toward the advertisement and discusses situations when attitude toward the advertisement may have its greatest effect on brand attitudes.

In Chapter 3, Moore and Hutchinson review research on the relationship of attitudes toward the advertisement, memory, and brand attitudes. They postulate an immediate direct transfer of advertising affect to brand attitudes as well as a delayed indirect relationship between attitude toward the advertisement and brand attitudes which operates through brand familiarity after exposure to the advertising.

One of the oldest and strongest links between advertising and psychology is persuasion, the theme of Part II of this volume. The mechanisms of persuasion in attitude theory have long influenced theories of how advertising works and how it is evaluated. Petty and Cacioppo (1983) have alerted us to the importance of both the executional elements of advertising and the advertising message as mediators of persuasion in consumers. In Chapter 4, they relate their ideas on central and peripheral routes to persuasion to the issue of message repetition. They offer evidence that repetition of the same message without variation leads rapidly to tedium or advertising wearout. Repetition of a pool of different advertising executions, however, does not. These results are interpreted in terms of the peripheral and central routes to persuasion.

Marketing managers responsible for advertising budgets often rely on measures of how well people recall an advertisement as criteria for evaluating whether and how much to spend on airing a particular advertising execution. Yet there is little evidence that recall of advertising is related to sales of the advertised brand (Gibson, 1983). To the extent that sales can be predicted by persuasion or brand attitudes, the relationship of recall to persuasion is of interest. The next two chapters in Part II are concerned with limits of the relationship between recall and persuasion in advertising. Lichtenstein and Srull, in Chapter 5, demonstrate that recall of product related information for a new product from an advertisement influences purchase intent only when consumers do not form an evaluation of the advertised brand during exposure to the advertisement for a new product. They suggest that consumers who evaluate a product as they watch its advertising (brand processing strategy) will form an evaluation that is stored separately from the content of the advertising. Because it is stored separately, the content will not be readily available when the evaluation is recalled. However, consumers who do not form an evaluation of the product during exposure to the message (nonbrand processing strategy) retrieve the advertisement from memory and construct an evaluation based on that memory.

Like Lichtenstein and Srull, Beattie and Mitchell, (in Chapter 6) also provide evidence that the relationship between recall and judgment is mediated by the type of processing strategy that consumers use during exposure to the advertisement. Beattie and Mitchell showed their subjects a large number of advertisements for hypothetical products so they would not be able to remember all the advertisements. They then examined factors that affect the recall of the advertisement and the relationship between recall and persuasion. Beattie and Mitchell also find that when subjects do not form an evaluation of the advertised product during exposure to the advertisement, there is little relationship between recall of the advertisement and persuasion. However, like Lichtenstein and Srull, they find a relationship when subjects do not form an evaluation of the advertised brand during exposure to the advertisement.

Because there is often a delay between exposure to advertising and the opportunity to purchase the advertised product, the delayed effect of persuasion is of great interest to advertisers. In the 1950s there was some evidence that persuasion is sometimes greater after a delay than immediately after the persuasive message is presented; this is called the "sleeper effect." In Chapter 7, Pratkanis and Greenwald report that the sleeper effect is difficult to produce in the laboratory. An increase in persuasion over time can be found, however, when the persuasive message is immediately followed by another message that disparages the source of the persuasive message. Any increase in persuasion after a delay is really due, Pratkanis and Greenwald hypothesize, to rapidly forgetting the source disparagement over time and more slowly forgetting the persuasive message. The result is *seemingly* greater persuasion after a delay than immediately after the persuasive message.

Although advertising is usually evaluated on the basis of the entire advertising execution — in terms of recall, persuasion, liking of the execution — the executional decisions involved in developing and producing that advertising are made on the basis of scenes, details, and fraction-of-a-second events in the commercials. Part III of this volume is concerned with consumer's reactions to the moment-by-moment flow of events within television commercials.

In Chapter 8, Anderson discusses how people process television programs on a moment-by-moment basis, based on ten years of monitoring people watching television both in the laboratory and in their own homes. He discusses their viewing behavior as well as three principles that seem to determine attention to television.

All of us would agree that a viewer's responses to on-going events in a commercial are controlled by the brain. In Chapter 9, Alwitt relates the electrical activity of the brain (EEG) to the presence of events such as brand mention, zooms, or music in commercials. Despite the complexity of brain activity, individual differences among people's backgrounds and needs, and the limits imposed by a new experimental area of research where there are few guidelines, relationships were found between the commercial content and EEGs.

Involvement of a person with ongoing events, with an object, and with characteristics of an object are aspects of a somewhat vague concept that plays an increasingly central role in theories of persuasion. Indeed, many of the papers in this volume discuss one or another aspect of involvement. Part IV includes three papers that concentrate on different aspects of the concept of involvement. In Chapter 10, Greenwald and Leavitt define involvement in terms of the amount of attention devoted to an advertising message. They argue that involvement with advertising increases as one moves from focal attention to comprehension to elaboration and that different advertising objectives require different levels of involvement in order to be optimally effective.

Another aspect of involvement is how products and brands fit into the lives of the people who buy them. Four types of product users are characterized in terms of how they relate to products by Cushing and Douglas-Tate in Chapter 11. They also demonstrate that these four types of product users respond differently to advertising.

Still another way of considering involvement is how people relate products to their values, motivations and lifestyles in making consumer decisions. Reynolds, Gutman, and Fiedler, in Chapter 12, analyze "laddering," a consumer research methodology for relating product attributes to a consumer's values. By examining product preferences and the perceived importance of reasons for buying a product, they conclude that, because laddering taps basic values as well as attributes and benefits to the user, it has an advantage over techniques such as conjoint measurement or multi-dimensional scaling in developing advertising strategies.

REFERENCES

Chaiken, S. (1980). Heuristic versus systematic information processing and the use of source versus message cues in persuasion. *Journal of Personality and Social Psychology, 39*, 752–766.

Cohen, J. B. (1983). Involvement and you: 1000 great ideas. In R. P. Baggozzi & A. M. Tybout (Eds.), *Advances in consumer research, Vol. X.* Ann Arbor: Association for Consumer Research, 325-328.

Fishbein, M., & Ajzen, I. (1975). *Belief, attitude, intention and behavior: An introduction to theory and research.* Reading, MA: Addison-Wesley.

Gardner, M., Mitchell, A. A., & Russo, J. E. (1978). Chronometric analysis: An introduction and an application to low involvement perception of advertisements. In H. K. Hunt (Ed.), *Advances in consumer research, Vol. V.* Ann Arbor: Association for Consumer Research, 581-589.

Gibson, L. D. (1983). "Not recall." *Journal of Advertising Research, 23,* 39-46.

Greenwald, A. G. (1968). Cognitive learning, cognitive response to attitude change. In A. G. Greenwald, T. C. Brock, & T. M. Ostrom (Eds.), *Psychological foundations of attitudes.* New York: Academic Press, 147-170.

Houston, M. J., & Rothschild, M. L. (1977). *A paradigm for research on consumer involvement.* Unpublished Working Paper. Graduate School of Business, University of Wisconsin, Madison, Wisconsin.

Krugman, H. (1965). The impact of television advertising: Learning without involvement. *Public Opinion Quarterly, 29,* 349-356.

Krugman, H. (1967). The measurement of advertising involvement. *Public Opinion Quarterly, 31,* 583-596.

Lastovika, J. L., & Gardner, D. M. (1979). Components of involvement. In J. C. Maloney & B. Silverman (Eds.), *Attitudes play for high stakes.* Chicago: American Marketing Association.

Lutz, R. J. (1975). Changing brand attitudes through modifications of cognitive structure. *Journal of Consumer Research, 1,* 49-59.

McGuire, W. (1968). The nature of attitudes and attitude change. In G. Lindzey & E. Aronson (Eds.), *Handbook of social psychology,* Second Edition, Vol. 3. Reading, MA: Addison Wesley, 136-314.

McGuire, W. (1978). An information processing model of advertising effectiveness. In H. L. Davis and A. J. Silk (Eds.), *Behavioral and management science in marketing.* New York: Wiley, 156-180.

Mitchell, A. A. (1981). The dimensions of advertising involvement. In K. Monroe (Ed.), *Advances in consumer research, Vol. 8.* Ann Arbor: Association for Consumer Research, 25-30.

Mitchell, A. A. (1983). The effect of visual and emotional advertising: An information processing approach. In L. Percy & A. Woodside (Ed.), *Advertising and consumer behavior.* New York: Lexington Press, 197-217.

Mitchell, A. A., & Olson, J. C. (1981). Are product attribute beliefs the only mediator of advertising effects on brand attitude? *Journal of Marketing Research, 18,* 318-332.

Paivio, A. (1979). *Imagery and verbal processes.* Hillsdale, NJ: Lawrence Erlbaum Associates. Originally published 1971.

Petty, R. E., & Cacioppo, J. T. (1981). *Attitudes and persuasion: Classic and contemporary approaches.* Dubuque, IA: Wm. C. Brown.

Petty, R. E., Wells, G. C., & Brock, T. C. (1976). Distraction can enhance or reduce yielding to propaganda: Thought disruption versus effort justification. *Journal of Personality and Social Psychology, 34,* 874-884.

Ray, M. L., & Batra, R. (1983). Emotion and persuasion in advertising: What we do and don't know about affect. In R. P. Bagozzi & A. M. Tybout (Eds.), *Advances in consumer research, Vol. X.* Ann Arbor: Association for Consumer Research, 543-548.

Ray, M. L., Sawyer, A. G., Rothschild, M. L., Heeler, R. M., Strong, E. C., & Reed, J. B. (1973). Marketing communication and the hierarchy of effects. In P. Clark (Eds.), *New models for mass communication research, Vol. 2.* Beverly Hills, CA: Sage Publications.

Rossiter, J. R., & Percy, L. (1978). Visual imagery ability as a mediator of advertising response.

In H. K. Hunt (Ed.), *Advances in consumer research, Vol. 5*. Ann Arbor: Association for Consumer Research, 621–628.

Rossiter, J. R., & Percy, L. (1983). Visual communication in advertising. In R. J. Harris (Ed.), *Information processing research in advertising*. Hillsdale, NJ: Lawrence Erlbaum Associates.

Wright, P. L. (1973). Cognitive processes mediating acceptance of advertising. *Journal of Marketing Research, 4,* 53–62.

AFFECTIVE REACTIONS TO ADVERTISING

1 How Advertising Works at Contact

Rajeev Batra
Michael L. Ray
Graduate School of Business
Stanford University

INTRODUCTION

It is by now a commonplace that consumers' "low involvement" processing of television ads is different from the initial processing earlier assumed in the advertising literature. Our understanding of these processes, however, is still largely speculative, and certainly incomplete.

Over the last two years, our research has investigated such processing in an attempt to identify situations where advertisers may safely reduce levels of repetition frequency. While this is an applied and managerial objective, it has led us into investigations of the role of different kinds of affect in the processing of advertising messages.

By "affect," we mean here the sorts of feelings towards a stimulus which lead to relative preferences for that stimulus out of a class of similar stimuli. Further, we are concerned only with the kinds of affect involved in preferences, rather than the kinds that constitute emotions such as shame, guilt, etc. (see Zajonc, 1980, p. 152).

Our investigations into the role of affect in such "low involvement" advertising processes have revealed, we believe, some very fundamental insights into how "low involvement" television advertising—indeed, *all* television advertising—is processed on contact. These basic processes are discussed in this chapter. While the research question is posed in terms of "low involvement" advertising processes, the model presented helps to show the different ways in which *all* television advertising works.

We begin with our theoretical development by briefly reviewing the role of different sources of affect in advertising processing, as developed in previous research, and then turn to our extension of currently popular positions. This involves our incorporation, into current models, of two different components of brand attitudes, and of affective, in addition to cognitive, mediating responses. We then develop our operational definition of "message response involvement," and use it in hypothesizing that the two components of brand attitudes make different "percentage contributions" to purchase intentions under different message response involvement conditions.

We then present the empirical evidence, first in reports on two methodological pre-studies, and then in the study to test the theoretical model developed. The final section discusses the results, their implications, and future research.

AFFECT AND INVOLVEMENT:
AN EXPANDED THEORETICAL MODEL

The Sources of Affect across Advertising Situations

Research into the situational role of affect in advertising is, of course, not new. Following Krugman's (1965) initial characterization of most television advertising as being "less involving," research showed that the hierarchy-of-effects typically found in such advertising is such that messages tend to produce behavioral change that precedes, rather than follows, changes in attitudes, or affect (Ray et al., 1973). Within this hierarchy, however, while the effects of behavior on attitude are readily interpretable in terms of attribution (Kelley, 1967) and self-perception (Bem, 1965) mechanisms, the earlier link—that of advertising (awareness) inducing behavioral change—is more puzzling, and has naturally led to much research and speculation about process.

II In earlier research at Stanford, it was found that the major impact of ad exposure in "low involvement" situations was on measures of awareness, which then led (less strongly) to changes in purchase intentions, without attitude change (Ray et al., 1973; Ray & Sawyer, 1971). Krugman's explanations of how "low involvement" advertising works, in fact, sometimes invoke mechanisms of repetition-induced "overlearning" and at other times of "gradual shifts in perceptual structure." To use more recent jargon, the important processes were believed to be brand name "salience" and "availability" (Taylor & Fiske, 1978; Tversky & Kahneman, 1973).*II*

That this initial link is exclusively "awareness-driven" is now less certain, however. Recent research suggests that other mechanisms may be at play as well. In particular, it has been suggested—and our recent studies show—that affect is not absent from this initial link. It is, however, a different *kind* of affect from the one usually studied. The affect invoked here thus differs from the one produced by the sort of active processing of advertising messages that Fishbein and Ajzen (1975) argue leads to changes in component attribute beliefs before leading to changes in attitude, the sort reflected in the "cognitive responses" usually studied.

There have, in fact, been clues for some time that the popular "cognitive response" (Greenwald, 1968; Wright, 1973) explanation of advertising effects does not provide a complete explanation of "low involvement" advertising processing. For instance, Wright's study showed, as have others subsequently (e.g., Petty & Cacioppo, 1979) that the explanatory power of support arguments (SAs), counterarguments (CAs), and source derogations (SDs), in explaining ad-induced changes in attitudes, was noticeably weaker in the "low involvement" manipulation than in the "high involvement" one. In Wright's 1973 study, for instance, attitudinal variance explained dropped from (a maximum of) 43% to (a maximum of) 27%. Some important mediating processes are apparently missing from the set of cognitive responses usually analyzed.

Recent research has indicated what these missing mechanisms might be. Studies indicate that attitude to the advertising itself leads to changes in brand attitudes (Gorn, 1982; Mitchell & Olson, 1981). From social and cognitive psychology have come models of attitude change processes variously labeled as "heuristic" and "peripheral," to reference just two (Chaiken, 1980; Cialdini, Petty, & Cacioppo, 1981). Most such models show that such less involving ing processing typically involves "limited elaboration" of message arguments, with persuasive impact stemming largely from execution cues and source likeability.

Some of these studies, in fact, demonstrate clear interactions between involvement levels and message strategy: Attitude change attempts that use superior attribute arguments are more successful in high involvement situations than in low involvement ones, with the opposite result holding for source (message execution) likeability (Chaiken, 1980; Gorn, 1982; Petty & Cacioppo, 1980; Petty, Cacioppo & Goldman, 1981).

These recent studies show convincingly that the *source* of affect toward the brand may be different in high and low involvement situations. They do not, however, argue for—or attempt to measure—the effect of these sources on two different *kinds* of affect, or the different types of responses that may mediate the effects of these two sources.

We suggest, and here provide evidence for, a model of initial advertising processing that holds not only that attitude change can stem from (broadly speaking) two different *sources* of affect, but also that these two sources act *through* different mediating responses and *on two different components* of brand attitudes. There do seem to be two different "routes" to attitude change. There is more to these routes, however, than just different sources of affect.

Two Kinds of Mediating Cognitive Responses

We have referred to the demonstrated inadequacy of currently studied cognitive responses in explaining how advertising works in "low involvement" situations. To give but two examples, the correlations of the responses studied (support arguments [SAs], counter arguments [CAs], and source derogations [SDs]) with dependent brand attitudes is significantly lower in the low, compared to the high, involvement manipulations (Petty & Cacioppo, 1979; Wright, 1973).

It would seem that some important mediating responses are not being captured by these three response categories. Since recent studies seem to suggest that attitudes to the ad (Aad) mediate brand attitudes, responses mediating this Aad ought to be collected, coded, and analyzed as well.

Such Aad-mediating responses are likely to be very different from the cognitive responses typically studied, because ads are not pallid statements of positions on issues, such as those studied by Chaiken, 1980, or Petty & Cacioppo, 1979. Rather, they are complex messages, combining attribute statements with humor, music, story elements, affectionate vignettes, role portrayals, attractive (or unattractive) visuals, and the like. Some of these elements persuade, others evoke technical appreciation, some irritate, others create a mood of "upbeat" surgency while others create moods that are heartwarming, or just plain relaxing or soothing. Some elements distract; while distraction influences on cognitive response production have been studied before (Festinger & Maccoby, 1964; Osterhouse & Brock, 1970; Petty, Wells, & Brock, 1976), such influences typically have been embedded in the task environment, rather than within the stimulus itself. All of these ad-evoked responses should mediate one's attitude to the ad, and very few of these are captured as SAs or CAs.

There is a clear need, therefore, to collect, code and analyze such affective and distracting responses, in addition to the standard SAs and CAs. Our first pre-study developed a data collection methodology and coding scheme to do just that, and the main study reported here demonstrates clearly their utility in showing how such different responses differently mediate the impact of ad messages and execution elements.

Two Components of Affect Toward the Brand

There has been some interest recently in the existence of a "pure, non-cognitive" affect, distinct from the affect developed on the basis of the cognitive appraisal of a stimulus object (e.g. Abelson, Kinder, Peters, & Fiske, 1982; Zajonc, 1980). Such affect is hypothesized to be, in some sense, "primary and effortless."

Various authors have invoked such affect in speculating on the mechanisms underlying the link between advertising repetition and brand attitudes. Relying largely on the robust results on the "mere exposure" effects in socal psychology (Harrison, 1977; Sawyer, 1981; Zajonc, 1968), these authors have claimed that advertising repetition, especially in "low involvement" situations, influences purchase intentions and brand attitudes through the creation of such exposure-based affect (Batra & Ray, 1983a; Greenwald, Leavitt, & Obermiller, 1980).

At the same time, evidence has accumulated that brand attitudes are not unidimensional.

In the 1970's the model of attitude structure frequently used was that of Fishbein and Ajzen (1975), who argued that attitudes consisted of a unidimensional affect, based on component beliefs evaluated in an "expectancy-value" fashion. Their conception relied heavily on the identification of a primary "evaluative" dimension to concept ratings, as identified by Osgood, Suci, and Tannenbaum (1957). Tests of construct validity were provided by Ostrom (1969) and Kothandapani (1971), using the criteria of Campbell and Fiske (1959).

Recent work has suggested, however, that the Fishbein-Ajzen unidimensional model of attitude structure is wrong. Recent studies by Bagozzi and colleagues (Bagozzi, 1981; Bagozzi & Burnkrant, 1979; Bagozzi, Tybout, Craig, & Sternthal, 1979) have applied the more powerful (Kenny, 1975) Confirmatory Factor Analysis technique to assess the convergent and discriminant validity for the tricomponent and unidimensional models, and have reached dramatically different conclusions. Their analysis suggests quite clearly that attitudes are not unidimensional, but instead have two distinct components, an "affective" and a (multidimensional) "cognitive" one.

In fact, multi-component models have a long history, going back to Rosenberg and Hovland (1960), Katz and Stotland (1959), and others. Going back even earlier, it appears from Osgood, Suci, and Tannenbaum (1957) that while their "evaluation" factor was the first, predominant, and largest factor in "semantic space," as identified through the factor analysis of semantic differential ratings of many concepts, it itself was not unidimensional. Thus they identified clusters of scales within this general evaluative factor, which differentiated between "meek," "dynamic," "dependable," and "hedonistic" goodness (p. 62), and between clusters that were "morally," "aesthetically," "socially," and "emotionally" evaluative (p. 70). Another study of theirs, which factor-analyzed only the 34 items found to load heavily on their evaluative factor, found evidence for 5 factors within it (p. 71).

Further, in a little noticed study, Komorita and Bass (1967) factor-analyzed student attitudes to various issues and found clear evidence for three factors: "functionally evaluative," "affective-emotional," and "moral-ethical." Triandis (1971, 1977), relying on their study as well as on others, has argued that behavioral intentions are a function not of a unidimensional attitude construct, but instead of "expectations of consequences" (measured on "good-bad" and "valuable-harmful" scales) and of "affect" (measured on scales of "enjoyable," "interesting," and "pleasant").

Despite such evidence, however, studies of attitude formation and change continue to use a unidimensional operationalization of attitudes, usually a "good-bad" semantic differential item (or a few very similar items). This is true even for recent studies investigating the two different "routes" to attitude change (e.g., Chaiken, 1980; Gorn, 1982; Mitchell & Olson, 1981; Petty & Cacioppo, 1980). We believe that, taken together, the studies reviewed strongly suggest a two-component model of brand attitudes (affective predispositions to brands), and call for their separate modeling and measurement.

We hypothesize that one component, here called "utilitarian affect," would be based on an appraisal of the product's instrumentality in delivering physical attributes. The other, here called "hedonic affect," would be an approach-avoidance feeling—a "hedonic tone"—towards the product as a whole. While the utilitarian component should be based on physical brand attributes, the hedonic component, on the other hand, should be created by the classical conditioning of affect from ad executions, from ad frequency "mere exposure," etc., and would be "brand specific" instead of being based on component attributes.

Using such a two-component structure model, therefore, we suggest that the "two routes" of attitude change probably work on two different components. Testing such a hypothesis, however, calls for the measurement of these two components. Our second pre-study supported the hypothesis of two components of attitudes, established that they can be discriminated using semantic differential items, and identified specific items to use in such measurement. When used in the study reported here, these scales (despite heavy "concept-scale" interaction) offer some support for our hypothesis that the two routes to attitude formation and change do work differentially through two components, though major measurement problems remain.

Message Response Involvement

Thus far, we have used the term "involvement" rather loosely. It is not our objective here to add to the voluminous literature on what that concept implies, or how it should be operationalized. What follows is a brief restatement of a position we have previously advanced (Batra & Ray, 1983b). Reviews of the involvement literature may be found in Houston and Rothschild (1978) and Mitchell (1979).

We argue that in using the term "involvement" we need to make a crucial distinction between *product class involvement* and *message response involvement,* for the two are qualitatively different phenomena.

Product class involvement refers to the care with which a brand choice is made. This should be a motivational construct, a function of the level of perceived risk or brand differentiation in the relevant product category. It is an enduring predisposition, though there could be temporal differences in its intensity. Such product class involvement could be measured, perhaps, by the importance of a brand choice being correct, across product categories.

Message response involvement, on the other hand, refers (conceptually) to the "depth" of processing for a particular message, by a particular recipient, at a particular time. Such "depth of processing" is conceptualized as message processing involving greater "cognitive elaboration," leading to greater persistence of message effects (cf. Anderson & Reder, 1979; Craik & Lockhart, 1972). This is a situational state, not an enduring predisposition (see Mitchell, 1979). Most importantly, this construct is not purely motivational in origin. Such processing "depth," however operationalized, would be a function not just of the viewer's motivation to respond "deeply," but also of his/ her *ability* to do so, as a function of prior usage and knowledge, and of the *opportunity* to do so, caused by message pace and distraction, for instance (See Wright, 1981.)

This three part conceptualization of the antecedents to message response involvement is supported by a great deal of research at Stanford, which has been concentrated on the various modes (or hierarchies) of initial processing (cf. Batra & Ray, 1983a; Ray, 1976; Ray, 1979; Ray, 1981; Ray et al., 1973). In this research series it has been repeatedly found that greater "depth of processing" (or the "learning" hierarchy of response as opposed to the "low involvement" one) occurs when there is: (1) "involvement," defined somewhat as we would define the *motivational* product class involvement here; (2) perceived or known differentiation between brands with respect to attributes, reflecting both the *ability* and *motivation* antecedents; (3) experience in purchasing in the product category, again reflecting *ability*; and (4) communication in media that allow depth of processing such as print or word-of-mouth, obviously similar to the *opportunity* antecedent posited here.

This past conceptualization both provides refinements to and also falls short of the present one. In terms of refinements, the past research suggests that the three antecedents would act in a multiplicative way to lead to depth of processing or message response involvement. Thus if a person has a high level of the motivational product class involvement, but low ability or opportunity, depth of processing is unlikely. This explains why many schemes to explain communication response behavior on the basis of product class involvement alone have failed (Ray, 1979).

Another refinement suggested by this past research tradition is that there may be interactions among these antecedents. For instance, there may be a point where very high experience-ability would lead to diminished motivation, as in mature product categories where consumers have so much experience in purchasing the product that they are no longer motivated to seek detailed information from advertising.

The past conceptualization falls short of the present one primarily in regard to the opportunity antecedents. The previous studies had not examined carefully the variation in opportunity within an advertising medium, as does the research reported in this paper.

Note, therefore, that we are drawing a distinction between the *antecedent conditions* (the motivation, ability and opportunity to respond), and message response involvement, which is the *state* actualizing some degree of this type of "involvement". Note also that product class involvement is simply one of the determinants of the motivation-to-respond antecedent factor, one of three such antecedent factors for message response involvement.

The conceptualization of motivation, ability and opportunity as antecedent conditions for depth of processing still leaves the question of how such depth of processing or message response involvement is to be operationalized. Our operationalization is somewhat arbitrary but, we believe, useful in the ad processing situation.

The depth of processing or message response involvement definition suggested here is based partially on Chaiken's (1980) evidence that increased viewer motivation-to-respond increases the proportion of cognitive responses dealing with the message (versus the communicator), with the total number of thoughts remaining the same. We therefore believe that the degree of message response involvement could usefully be characterized by the number, or proportion, of ad-elicited cognitive responses that deal with the brand (physical) attribute assertions in the ad (instead of dealing with the ad execution). A similar cognitive-response based definition (Webb, 1978) received preliminary "nomological" validation in the advertising clutter situation. This definition would also be consistent with the cognitive response literature showing the production of such cognitive responses to be a function of enhanced ability, opportunity and motivation (see Roberts & Maccoby, 1973).

However, as in the cognitive psychological area, operationalizations such as this cognitive response one for "message response involvement" are still somewhat arbitrary (see, for instance, Baddeley, 1978). The problem arises because "involvement" has dimensions of both intensity *and* direction (Mitchell, 1979). What one is doing here is equating intensity *with* a certain direction; as we have pointed out earlier (Batra & Ray, 1983), one still has situations where the viewer intensely processes those aspects of the stimulus — such as elements of ad execution — which are, by arbitrary definition, "less involving." While our definition of "involvement" is a reasonable one for this problem context, it is therefore still not unique.

This research, then, is concerned not with product class involvement, but only with message response involvement. Such involvement is defined as "the degree to which the cognitive responses evoked by the ad deal with the brand attribute assertions in the ad, for reasons of motivation, ablility, or opportunity." And the question being asked is: In message reception situations where such brand attribute processing is minimal, how does television advertising work on contact?

The Percentage Contribution Model

We have referred earlier to the recent studies that show that source or ad likeability influences on purchase intentions are significant in low, but not in high, involvement situations (Chaiken, 1980; Gorn, 1982; Petty & Cacioppo, 1980; Petty, Cacioppo, & Goldman, 1981). If, then, it is true that (as we have hypothesized) source (ad execution) likeability evokes "affective" mediating responses, and if these responses then influence one of the two attitudinal components, it should then also be true that the influence of this particular attitudinal component on purchase intentions is much stronger in low, rather than high, involvement situations.

The *percentage contribution model* (Batra, 1982) therefore hypothesizes that, given the definitions developed earlier for low involvement situations, the relative contributions of the two attitude components to purchase intentions should differ across situations with different levels of (message response) involvement. In low involvement situations, compared to high involvement ones, the contribution should be lower for the attribute-based utilitarian component and higher for the advertising execution-based hedonic component.

The ad execution-based hedonic component should thus be the major contributor to purchase intentions in those low involvement situations where the degree of attribute processing is low, for reasons of either motivation (e.g., attribute differences considered trivial), or ability (low familiarity or discrimination competence), or opportunity (not enough time to process attribute information, attributes not presented, etc.). In high involvement situations, on the other hand, the major contributor would be the attribute-based utilitarian attitude component. Note that these contributions refer to strength, not valence. Note also that the model's structure is not necessarily additive.

It is also important to note that the percentage contribution model is here being posited for communication situations only, not decision-making ones. In these latter types of situations, for instance, the hedonic component could play major roles in "elimination phase" (Wright & Barbour, 1977) decisions, decisions before actual product trial, or "tie-breaker" decisions at the "last node" in a hierarchial, "elimination-by-aspects" type choice model (Tversky, 1972).

In addition to hypothesizing these relative influences of the two attitude components in communication processing, the model also argues (based on research reviewed previously) that the influence of brand familiarity, on purchase intentions, should be far greater in low involvement situations than in high involvement ones. Brand familiarity is conceptualized here as an index of differential brand awareness, reflecting degrees of experiences with the brand (ranging from weak, indirect experiences like past exposure to advertising, to strong and direct ones like current usage).

The model also argues that, in their *indirect effects* on purchase intentions, both attitude-to-the-ad and brand familiarity should work more through the execution-based hedonic attitudinal component than through the utilitarian one. This is based on the assumption that both attitude-to-the-ad and brand familiarity (the latter reflecting, in part, "mere exposure" influences) represent "classical conditioning" mechanisms of changing brand attitudes.

In summary, existing process ("two routes") models show that the source of affect in low involvement situations is primarily execution likeability. Our extensions argue first, that such sources generate important "affective" mediating responses; second, that such responses work more through one of two attitudinal components; and third, that this differentially-affected attitudinal component then "drives" purchase intentions in such low involvement situations.

These extensions to the current "two routes" process model also imply extensions to the alternative hierarchies of communication with which we began our review. They suggest the following contrast among the hierarchies of interest.

In a learning hierarchy, detailed cognitive processing about brand attributes should lead to changes in utilitarian attitudes, before modifying purchase intentions and action. In a low involvement hierarchy, on the other hand, changes in brand familiarity (and a liking for the ad) should lead to changes in hedonic attitudes, before modifying purchase intentions and action; such usage experiences would then modify utilitarian attitudes. In this latter hierarchy, brand familiarity would also affect purchase intentions directly.

These hierarchies are discussed and illustrated in the concluding section of this chapter, after the empirical evidence has been presented.

Having now derived our theoretical model, we proceed to the empirical evidence. First, in the next section, we present the summary results of two methodological pre-studies. The first was designed to develop an improved data collection and coding scheme for the cognitive and affective responses which we believe mediate advertising effects, and the second to validate and operationalize the two component model of attitude structure. We then turn, in the following section, to the results of our first major study itself, designed to test the model just developed. In the concluding section, we discuss implications and future research.

METHODOLOGICAL PRE-STUDIES

Pre-Study I: Verbal Protocol Testing and Coding

We have argued that non-attribute based "hedonic affect" plays a major role in preference formation and change in those message response situations where, for various reasons, attribute-based cognitive responses are few. It therefore becomes crucial that the cognitive response measurement methodology used to test this hypothesis be able to measure not only the degree of attribute-based responses, but also those "feeling," "mood," "ad evaluation" and other responses that may influence the degree of "hedonic affect."

There are reasons to believe that current cognitive response measurement methodologies may be inadequate in such a task; we have discussed some of these reasons already. There is, in particular, a need to code the affective, emotional responses that may mediate the formation of the "hedonic affect" component referred to earlier. We attempted to include in this coding scheme, therefore, the results of prior research on emotional response categories (Izard, 1977; Nowlis, 1965; Pribram, 1980) and of advertising "viewer response research" (Schlinger, 1979; Wells, Leavitt, & McConville, 1971).

This methodological pre-study was therefore concerned with (1) the identification of a data collection methodology that encourages the reporting of such "feeling" and "irrelevant" responses, provided such responses are natural and "valid," and (2) the development of a coding scheme using logical, mutually exclusive, and collectively exhaustive categories that go beyond current coding schemes in their use of feeling responses, responses to ad execution, and "distractor thought" data.

To conserve space, we are not reporting here the variations in data collection methods tried to find the one that best encouraged the reporting of feeling and irrelevant, distractor responses. As reported briefly in Batra and Ray (1983b), we found that in terms of quantity, face validity, and sensitivity of results, the "best" method (of the 8 tried) seems to involve fairly non-directive opening instructions, a sample of previously obtained cognitive responses to a commercial, a practice trial with feedback, and a standard open-ended cognitive response question (adapted to stress feeling responses).

The coding scheme eventually developed (after extensive reliability improvement iterations, and a separate collection of coding or sorting responses from naive, non-research respondents drawn from the same universe) for the first study used nine "macro" categories, for which two-judge intercoder reliability was 83%. In essence, this coding scheme distinguishes between four major categories of verbalized responses: brand-related thoughts; ad execution-related thoughts; irrelevant (distractor) thoughts;

and playback of ad content. The first three are then further divided. Brand thoughts split into support and counter arguments, each of which again is (at a micro level) either based on personal experience (connection-like) or not. Ad execution thoughts include source discounting (credibility and derogation) and source bolstering, and moods/feelings induced by the ad (coded separately as three kinds of feelings: upbeat "activation and surgency," relaxed "deactivation," and heartwarming, moving "social affection"). See Table 1. 1 for the scheme.

Pre-Study Two: Scale Development for the Two Components of Brand Attitudes

The theoretical model developed earlier argued that there were two components to brand attitudes, here called "hedonic affect" and "utilitarian affect," and that they made different "percentage contributions" to purchase intentions in situations of differing message response involvement.

In previous work (e.g., Bagozzi 1981) it has been suggested that semantic differential measures of affect can be reliably used to measure the hedonic component, while the utilitarian one could be measured through belief-based Likert, Guttman, or Thurstone attitudinal scales. There is reason to believe, however, based on the studies of Osgood, Suci, and Tannenbaum (1957), that the two components can both be measured through semantic differential scales, which are more easily administered.

This pre-study, therefore, dealt with the identification of semantic differential scales to measure these two components, and the use of such data to demonstrate the convergent and discriminant validity of the two-component model of attitude structure from such data. It also examined whether these measurement properties hold across four different brands (in different product categories) and for both users and non-users of three of these brands.

Sixteen semantic differential items were selected for use in this study from the battery used by Osgood, Suci, and Tannenbaum (1957); all loaded on the "evaluation" factor identified by them. Four brands were chosen, somewhat arbitrarily, for the rating task: Pepsi, Listerine, Comet (Cleanser), and Cadillac. Using these 16 items, information on brand attitudes (and usage) was obtained from 59 women. The data were analyzed for all brands individually, all brands together (treated as 236 observations), and across two collapsed usage categories ("most frequently" + "sometimes" = "users"; "rarely" + "once before + "never" = "non-users").

For these sub-samples, initial analysis consisted of (exploratory) Common Factor analysis, both orthogonal and oblique, using all 16 items. This analysis was done to provide indications of which items to retain further in the development of these two scales. Ten of the highest-loading items were then

TABLE 1.1
Coding Scheme Used for Verbal Protocols

No.	Name	Inclusions
0	Other	Ad Content Playback; subsequently generated thoughts
1	Support Arguments	Reasoned/Simple Affirmations (connections and non-connections coded separately); Trial thoughts (brand + generic)
2	Counter Arguments	Reasoned/Simple Disaffirmations (Conn. + Non-Conn.)
3	Execution Discounting	Execution Credibility; Execution Derogation; Negative "Editorial" Judgments
4	Execution Bolstering	Positive references to elements, style, realism, etc.
5	Feelings: "S.E.V.A."*	Feelings of *Surgency, Elation, Vigor, Activation—upbeat feelings from music, humor, other elements
6	Feelings: "Deactivation"	References to ad elements being soothing, relaxing, pleasant
7	Feelings: "Social Affection"	Refs. to the ad being warm, touching, etc.
8	Distractor Thoughts	Thoughts irrelevant to message, evoked by the message; execution-based curiosity or surprise; refs. to other commercials or viewing occasions

used in initial "confirmatory" factor analysis, in tests of measurement models with three, four, and five variables per factor. Since the three-indicator model fit best, these were finally used in testing for the convergent and discriminant validity of one- and two-factor models using three indicators per factor. Because sample sizes were small, incremental fit indices (Bentler & Bonett, 1980) were used to assess adequacy of fit.

To conserve space, detailed results are not reported here. The exploratory factor analyses showed that in almost all cases (Cadillac and "users" were exceptions) there appeared to be a clear two factor structure; one factor loaded heavily on pleasant/unpleasant and related items, the second on useful/useless and related items. The tests of "convergent and discriminant" validity (Bagozzi, 1980), using the method of restricted maximum likelihood factor analysis (not really "confirmatory" here), with three items per factor, provided convincing evidence that the two scales were, in fact, different. The six items used were: for the first factor, pleasant/unpleasant, agreeable/disagreeable, and nice/awful; for the second, useful/useless, beneficial/harmful, and important/unimportant.

Cronbach alphas were computed for the three item hedonic and utilitarian scales identified here, and for all two-item subsets within each, and these were found to be in the 0.75–0.91 range; utilitarian component reliabilities were lower than for the hedonic one, and improved slightly if "important/unimportant" replaced "harmful/beneficial" in a two-item scale. For pragmatic reasons, two-item scales of each of these two factors were used in the study reported in the next section, eliminating "harmful/beneficial" and "nice/awful" from their respective scales; these two-item scales had a correlation in this pre-study of 0.44 ($p = .00, n = 236$).

While a multiple groups test (Joreskog & Sorbom, 1981, Chapter 5) confirmed that the four brands shared similar two-factor structures, the data did make apparent at the exploratory factor analysis stage that some items loaded on different factors for different products. While we attempted to minimize this problem at the item deletion stage, the study reported in the next section makes clear that we were not successful. Further, and as a consequence, it should be noted that while these tests established the convergent and discriminant validity of a two factor structure, they do not, by themselves, establish construct validity for the hedonic and utilitarian affect constructs, since nomological validity is still lacking. We know we have two components, but we don't yet know what they measure. Based on the end-points of the scales, however, we obviously presumed that the "pleasant/unpleasant" item factor was "hedonic" and the "useful/useless" one was "utilitarian."

A TEST OF THE THEORETICAL MODEL

The objective of the study reported here was to trace the process through which a single advertising exposure creates an impact on brand purchase intentions, thereby testing the process model developed earlier. The results presented here are only preliminary, and are greatly condensed.

This study exposed 120 housewives to 40 test ads, using a half-factorial design to vary the three antecedents of message response involvement — product category involvement (motivation), brand usage and knowledge (ability), and the attribute "intensity" of the ad execution (opportunity). To accomplish this variation, the study ads represented ten different categories, two brands each, and two different ad executions per brand. Measures included prior brand awareness, attitudes, and usage; category involvement and knowledge; post-exposure attitudes (using two components), brand familiarity, and purchase intentions; cognitive and affective responses; ad liking measures; and delayed 2-component attitude measures.

In testing the model, the objectives were to test whether the "affective mediating responses" (as opposed to purely cognitive non-affective ones) collected here were significant mediators of brand attitudes; whether they were primarily the consequences of "source or ad likeability"; whether they affected one attitudinal component more than the other; and whether the attitudinal component affected by them influenced purchase intentions more strongly in low involvement situations than in high involvement ones. The other hypotheses constituting the percentage contribution model, such as the differential role of familiarity, were also tested.

Method

Stimuli

In order to create the maximum variation in the antecedent conditions that were believed to influence message response involvement levels, a pool of over 60 TV commercials was obtained from various companies and advertising agencies. All were fully produced commercials, and most had been run nationally before. From this pool, 40 selected ads were then judged as being either high or low in product category involvement (defined in the earlier section on involvement), as featuring a brand that was a market leader or follower, and as having an execution which stressed attribute superiority ("rational") or relied on likeability ("affective").

The data used in these classification judgments are not described here. It must be stressed, however, that these a priori classifications were made merely to create the maximum variance in the antecedent conditions of message response involvement: the motivation to respond to attribute elements (through product category involvement levels), the ability to do so (through prior knowledge and usage, reflected in market share), and the opportunity to do so (through the creative execution style). As will become apparent, the analysis itself did not assume experimental orthogonality. Further, the analysis, conducted at an individual level, used data on these variables obtained from each individual respondent.

Design

To further maximize, tactically, the variance in these antecedent factors, the ads were assigned to respondents using a half-factorial (balanced incomplete block) experimental design. It has been mentioned that the ads were classified into two product category involvement levels (high, low); two brand share levels (dominant, follower); and two execution style levels (affective, rational). Factorially, this leads to eight combinations.

A half-factorial design was used to create two within-subject blocks of four ads each, such that each block had two ads on each level of each of the three factors, with no product category being repeated within a block. (For example, two of the four ads in each block were "affective," two were "high category involvement," two were "dominant share," etc.) Since the 40 ads comprised five replications of each of the eight factor combinations, five replications were created of each of the two four-ad blocks. See Table 1.2.

In total, therefore, the stimuli covered ten product categories (five each of high, low category involvement levels), 20 brands (ten each of dominant, follower) and 40 executions (20 each of affective, rational).

Within the ten blocks (five replications to two blocks), the four ads within each block were randomized with respect to exposure sequence. Each block was shown to 12 respondents (assigned randomly to one of the ten blocks) in four sessions of three respondents per session. The position of the four ads within a block, after initial randomization, was rotated across the four sessions, to equalize primacy and recency effects. The four sessions were also balanced across the four different times-of-day when the sessions were conducted. Over 40 sessions were held in all, over a two-week period.

Procedure

A total of 120 respondents were used, 12 per replicated block. These were housewives and working women, age 20 through 60, from Palo Alto and

TABLE 1.2
Design of Study

Motivational product category involvement	Brand share status (Ability)			
	Dominant (D)		Follower (F)	
	Attribute intensity of execution (Opportunity)			
	Affective (A)	Rational (R)	Affective (A)	Rational (R)
High (H)	HDA (5 replicates)	HDR (5 replicates)	HFA (5 replicates)	HFR (5 replicates)
Low (L)	LDA (5 replicates)	LDR (5 replicates)	LFA (5 replicates)	LFR (5 replicates)

Half-Factorial (Balanced Incomplete Block) Design:

Block type 'A' (5 replications):
    1. HDA 2. LFA 3. HFR 4. LDR

Block type 'B' (5 replications):
    1. HFA 2. LDA 3. HDR 4. LFR

nearby areas, who volunteered their time in return for a ten dollar donation to a local non-profit organization of their choice. This sample of women is certainly not representative of women generally. They could probably be characterized as being more affluent and educated than the average. Their assignment to different blocks, however, was randomized, as mentioned earlier.

The respondents were contacted by telephone approximately one week before their experimental sessions. At this time, they were assigned to a block and session, and were asked pre-exposure questions on prior brand awareness and attitudes, for each of the four test categories (embedded in other categories) for which they would see ads.

At the experimental session itself, the women were asked to first read a description of the study. This described the study as one, not of advertising effectiveness, but of trying to understand "what thoughts and feelings people naturally have when they see ads." After reading and signing a consent form, respondents were shown each of the four commercials once and asked to indicate prior familiarity with each ad. This exposure also had another purpose, however; since it seemed likely that some respondents had not seen some of the ads before, this exposure ensured that the mediating response data — collected after a subsequent exposure — would reflect responses to an ad seen at least once before, thus reducing the possible effects of a qualitative difference between a first and subsequent exposures (cf. Krugman, 1972).

Respondents then read instructions for the verbal protocol task, which stressed the need to be natural, to not deliberately attempt to memorize content, and to report exhaustively on both thoughts and feelings. They were then shown an "example" commercial, and read samples of reported verbalizations to this commercial. Next, they saw a "practice" commercial, wrote their thoughts and feelings in response, and were given standardized feedback on their responses to ensure they understood the purpose of the study.

They were then shown the four test ads in their replicated block, in the randomized and rotated sequence appropriate for their session. After each advertisement, they were asked to write out their responses to the question "What thoughts and feelings went through your mind while you were looking at the commercial?" They were given a full blank page, and no time limit was imposed, though almost every individual protocol was completed in under four minutes.

After the four protocols had been filled in, respondents answered questions, in sequence, on product category involvement; category knowledgeability; brand familiarity; brand attitudes (four semantic differential scales representing the two components); brand purchase intentions; and prior brand usage. The protocols themselves were coded by two judges, using the scheme developed from the first pre-study (see Table 1.1). As mentioned earlier, their inter-judge agreement, at the level of the nine macro categories, was 83%.

After these questions, respondents were shown the commercials once again, each ad exposure being followed by scales rating the ad on emotional impact, liking for the ad, how informative the ad was, and the degree to which their attention had been on the product claims or the execution while they watched the ad.

The sessions lasted, on average, between 50–60 minutes. Approximately one week later, respondents were contacted by telephone, and asked to rate their attitudes to the test brands on the two attitudinal components. These delayed measures were collected from approximately 100 of the 120 respondents.

Analysis and Results

Analysis was done to investigate three issues: (1) the importance of affective mediating responses (2) the hypothesized differential relationship between affective mediating responses and the two attitude components and (3) the viability of the percentage contribution model. The following three subsections deal with these issues in turn.

Are "Affective Mediating Responses" Important?

The data show that effective mediating responses — feelings of upbeat surgency, pleasantness, or heartwarming tenderness — are important for at least two reasons.

First, it would appear that these "affective" responses do represent the mediators evoked by ad execution likeability. This is apparent when the frequency of different mediating responses is related to those measures developed to rate the execution style of the ad.

In addition to the (classificatory) dichotomous "affective-rational" classification of ad executions, three judges further rated each ad on various related executional scales. The creative elements thought to reflect an "affective" (non-attribute) orientation were developed into a checklist; the number of items checked yielded an "A-score" for that ad. These items, included, for example, the use of mothers with children (weighted twice); humorous visuals; the presence of music; a message stressing emotions; high spokesperson likeability; etc. Similarly, an "R-score" was developed to reflect the degree of "attribute sell" orientation. In addition, the three judges also rated the ad on the number of attributes explicitly mentioned in the ad, and gave a three-level score on the "arousal level" of the music in the ad. Though unidimensionality is not claimed for these measures, inter-judge agreement ranged between 70–90%.

Correlational results showed that the frequency of feelings of upbeat "surgency, elation, vigor, activation" correlated significantly with an ad's A-score ($r = 0.23, p = .0$), and with the arousal level of the music ($r = 0.21$,

$p = .0$). This music arousal level, however, does not correlate significantly or highly with evoked feelings of (heartwarming, moving) "social affection," which correlate highly, instead, with an ad's net A minus R score ($r = 0.42$, $p = .0$). Also consistent with a mediating responses to ad execution link is the finding that a high A-score is negatively related to the frequency of counter argumentation ($r = -0.16, p = .0$), while a high R-score is positively related to counter argumentation ($r = 0.24, p = .0$) and negatively related to "social affection" feeling responses ($r = -0.40, p = .0$).

A second indication of the importance of affective mediating responses is that some of these feelings do represent strong mediating influences on brand attitudes. When the items measuring post-exposure brand attitudes are combined into one scale (Cronbach alpha = 0.91), ignoring (for the moment) possible differences between the two components, regressions of this scale on the frequency of different individual mediating responses show that the only responses having a significant effect are (at a significance level of 0.05) source derogations (standardized beta -0.129), feelings of heartwarming "social affection" (beta 0.128), and counter arguments (beta -0.122).

That relaxed deactivation feelings have no impact in the aggregate is not surprising—they are believed to be of importance only in select product categories such as cosmetics, according to Wells, Leavitt, and McConville (1971). It would also appear that feelings of surgency are not, in these data, of significant attitudinal consequence. Still, studying such affective mediating responses is clearly very important. They represent the mediators of the execution likeability "route" of attitude change, and significantly, if selectively, affect brand attitudes. It is not enough to measure just the support arguments, counter arguments, and source derogations that prior research has tended to stick to.

Do "Affective Responses" Influence the Two Attitudinal Components Differently?

The answer to this question is a very equivocal yes. When the two attitudinal components are regressed individually on the production frequency of the different mediating responses, the mediating responses which are significant at a level of $p = 0.05$ are, in fact, different for the two components. Since the two components were very highly correlated in this study ($r = 0.77, p = .00, n = 480$) prior to adjustment for measurement error, these regressions on each component also included the other component as an independent variable, to partial out shared variance.

In these regressions, one component responds significantly (at $p = .05$) only to counter-arguments (highest standardized beta, at 0.074) and support arguments (beta 0.052); the other responds significantly only to feelings of "social affection" (highest beta, at 0.066).

However, the components in question turn out to be the opposite of those expected to so respond. The feelings of "social affection" turn out to influence the "utilitarian" component ("useful" and "important" semantic differentials), while counter-arguments and support-arguments determine the "hedonic" component ("pleasant" and "nice" semantic differentials). This is obviously non-intuitive. Further analysis was therefore done, to relate aggregates of these affective and cognitive responses to the two attitudinal components, but at the level of the ten individual product categories used in the study.

What emerges is a picture of tremendous "concept-scale interaction" (Osgood, Suci, and Tannenbaum, 1957, p. 176). Given the smaller sample sizes, many relationships were insignificant; it appears, however, that in some cases affective associations increase perceived utility (e.g., some services), while in others attribute superiority leads to enhanced feelings of pleasantness towards the product (e.g., some foods and drinks).

Such interactions have, in fact, been reported before in the literature: see Calder and Sternthal, 1980; Komorita and Bass, 1967; and Osgood, Suci, and Tannenbaum, 1957, pp. 176–188. It was hoped during the second prestudy that the deletion of inconsistent-loading items would remove this problem, but the realities of differential attitude response overwhelmed the initial item analysis. Had only one or two brands from a single product category been used in this study (as opposed to the 40 ads actually used) the richness of concept-scale interaction and differential feelings responses to ads would have been impossible to detect.

In any case, given such interactions at the individual category level, the "properties" of the two attitude components at the 10-category aggregate level are simply a function of the mix of categories in this data set. For reasons of sample size, analysis has to continue at this aggregate level; the scales must, therefore, be recognized for what they measure in this data set, regardless of what they were intended to reflect in the first place.

For subsequent analysis, therefore, the two attitude scales were renamed: the scale sensitive to counter and support argumentation, but not to feelings, was rechristened as the "attribute sensitive" component, while the component sensitive to the affective mediating responses, but not to attribute argumentation, was called the "execution sensitive component." The test of the percentage contribution model was therefore done using these rechristened scales.

Testing the Percentage Contribution Model

Briefly restated, this model argues that the relationships of the execution-sensitive attitudinal component and the attribute-sensitive component, to purchase intentions, will differ in situations of high and low involvement.

The importance of the execution-sensitive component is expected to increase, and that of the attribute-sensitive one to decrease, as the level of involvement decreases. In addition, the effect of brand familiarity across these two conditions is expected to differ as well; theory and previous evidence suggest that such differential familiarity should be more imporant in low involvement situations. Finally, the theoretical development earlier suggests that both brand familiarity and the attitude to the ad (Aad) should, in their *indirect* effects on purchase intentions, work more through the execution-sensitive than through the attribute-sensitive component.

Given the de facto attitude scale properties discussed, the test of the percentage contribution model was transformed to a test of the relative contributions (path coefficients) of these two attitude scales (one sensitive to attribute argumentation in the ad, and the other to ad execution elements) to purchase intentions, in situations of differing message response involvement. Such involvement was operationally defined, for the purposes of this test, as the number of support arguments or counter arguments generated during the viewing episode. A post-hoc split was made in the data to create samples where no support or counter argumentation was generated (low involvement) versus where it was (high involvement).

It becomes crucial, however, given the "category-scale" interactions observed, to ensure that tests of the percentage contribution model across involvement sub-samples not be confounded by different distributions of product category observations across these two sub-samples.

Differences in path coefficients across the test samples should be unambiguously attributable to the differences in involvement across those samples, and should not be confounded with differences in scale properties across the two samples. Since scale properties appear to depend on the product category, the scales could mean different things in the two samples if the samples also have differing "mixes" of product categories.

For this reason, the distribution of cases across the 10 product categories was examined for the involvement sub-samples which would have been used for the test. Chi-square tests indicated that the two involvement level sub-samples were also significantly different ($p < .05$) on product category membership; differences in involvement levels were confounded with differences in product category membership distributions.

Since three of the ten product categories appeared to account for most of this difference in category memberships across involvement level sub-samples, they were dropped, reducing sample size from 480 observations to 336. When the involvement level sub-samples for the remaining seven categories was tested, chi-square indicated non-significantly ($p = .85$) different distributions. In order to allow for a stringent test of the model, therefore, further analysis for the test was restricted to these seven category aggregate sub-samples only.

The test was conducted through the structural equations "causal" modeling of the relationships between these dependent measures, using the methodology and algorithms (LISREL-V) developed by Joreskog and Sorbom (1981; Bagozzi, 1980).

Various models were estimated that hypothesized different relationships between the two attitude components, attitude toward the ad (operationalized through respondents' scores on ad liking, ad emotional effect, and net positive valence of source derogations, source bolstering, social affection, and SEVA responses), brand familiarity, and purchase intentions. In all these models, prior usage and/or prior attitudes were used as covariates. The different models tried are not reported here; as in all such model fitting, of course, it can only be claimed that the model finally chosen was not disconfirmed by the data. Though this was the "best fitting" of the many tried, other equally plausible, or even better fitting, models may still be possible. Despite these standard caveats, the model selected is both theoretically and statistically defensible.

The selected model is given in Figure 1.1, using the notation of Joreskog and Sorbom (1981); the circles represent constructs, the rectangles their operationalizations.

In this model, the two attitudinal components and brand familiarity are modeled as directly causing purchase intentions. In addition, however, both brand familiarity, and attitude to the ad, are modeled as also influencing both the attitudinal components. Further, attitude to the ad is modeled as contributing to brand familiarity (cf. Moore & Hutchinson, this volume). The error terms of the two attitudinal components are modeled as covarying; a test of reciprocal causality between them, while desirable, is not possible for identification reasons. In order to allow the modeling of covariate relationships among the error terms of the exogenous and endogenous variables, they were all run as dependent variables, though attitude to the ad and brand familiarity are actually exogenous to the system.

It was found necessary to model two correlated errors among the measures (see notes to the figure); the model achieved a satisfactory fit with a p-value of 0.124 (the conventional critical level is 0.10) for the overall sample (chi-square = 29.76, df = 22). The correlation between the two attitude factors (now corrected for measurement error) in this model was 0.49. Further, this two attitude-factor model fit marginally but significantly better than a model constraining the relationship between these two factors to unity (chi-square = 36.31, df = 23, chi-square difference significant at $p < .05$, p of model = 0.039).

The model was then run on the two involvement sub-samples defined earlier. Since the variances of the variables are likely to differ across samples, it is appropriate only to compare unstandardized path coefficients across

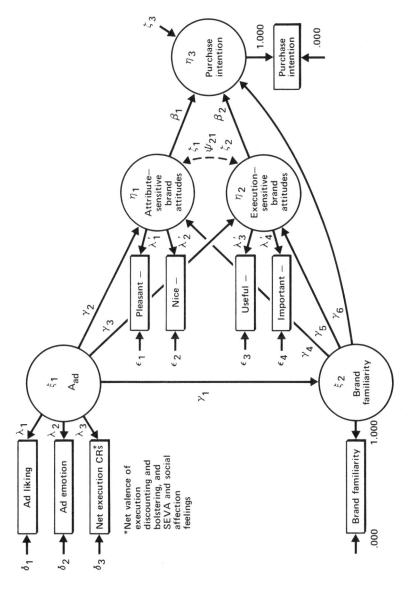

Notes: 1. Covariate relationships between prior usage and these five constructs were modeled by running all variables as dependent variables, and are not shown here for simplicity.

2. Also not shown: correlated errors between (i) ad emotional impact and prior usage and (ii) important – and pleasant –.

FIG. 1.1. Test of "percentage contribution model": causal model of dependent variable relationships.

35

them. The standardized estimates, however, are more interpretable within any individual sample.

The unstandardized statistics show that, in the high involvement sample, while the ad execution sensitive attitudinal component has a zero and non-significant relationship with purchase intentions, the attribute sensitive component has a highly significant ($p < .01$) path coefficient of 0.82. In the low involvement sample, on the other hand, the relationships are reversed: the ad execution sensitive component has the stronger (0.434, $p = .158$) causal influence on purchase intentions than the attribute sensitive component (0.275, $p = .370$), though neither reaches conventional significance. Most importantly, the difference between the coefficients of the execution sensitive component (effect on purchase intentions) across the two samples approaches significance at $p = 0.106$ (one-tail).

The major determinant of purchase intentions in the low involvement sample is brand familiarity. Though its direct path coefficient is a significant 0.23, its total effects — including its causal effects through both the attitude components — are 0.52. Interestingly, it does appear overall that familiarity works (though only directionally) more through the component reflecting ad execution effects, than through the attribute-sensitive component, paralleling the earlier theoretical expectations for its relationships with these two components.

The coefficients for the effects of attitude to the ad on purchase intentions in the low involvement case show that its impact on brand purchase intentions seems to occur most through its impact on brand familiarity (0.380). Further, its effect through the two attitude components does not work exclusively, or even primarily, through the ad execution sensitive one, but rather through both about equally. This is not as hypothesized; other analysis showed that this occurs because attitude to the ad is a function not merely of execution-oriented and feeling-type mediating responses, but also of support and counter argumentation.

An answer to the question, "How do different dependent measures of advertising effect influence purchase intentions, in low involvement situations?" may be found in the standardized path coefficients for the low involvement sub-sample. In descending sequence, the path coefficients are highest for ad execution-sensitive brand attitudes, followed by brand familiarity and then by attribute-argumentation based brand attitudes. In high involvement cases, however, the dominating coefficient is for attribute-argumentation based brand attitudes, with brand familiarity a distant second.

In summary, then, it does appear that the crucial proposition of the "percentage contribution model" is not disconfirmed: brand attitude scales reflecting ad execution effects do appear to mediate brand purchase intentions far more strongly in low involvement situations than in high involvement ones, with the opposite relative contribution for those brand attitude scales responsive to attribute argumentation. Because of the severe "product category-scale" interactions found, however, it cannot be claimed that brands have two stable components to their attitudes, hedonic and utilitarian, *as operationalized* through the semantic differential scales used here, and that ad execution characteristics work only through the hedonic component. Such a test awaits further clarification of the measurement issues made evident by these data. We discuss these issues in the concluding, discussion, section.

CONCLUSIONS AND IMPLICATIONS

We believe this research program makes various contributions to the study of how television advertising works.

First, it measures mediating *affective* responses to ads, in addition to the "cognitive responses" usually collected, and shows that such responses play important roles in determining the effect of advertising executions on brand attitudes. Such affective responses appear to be evoked by more likeable ad executions, and appear to influence brand attitudes significantly. Such responses have not been explicitly measured before; this program indicates not only that such responses ought to be measured, but also provides guidelines in how they may be collected, and coded.

Second, it incorporates the measurement of two separate dimensions of brand attitudes. We have more to say below on their measurement. The results do show, however, that these two components related differentially both to the affective mediating responses measured, and to brand purchase intentions across different involvement conditions.

Third, it would seem from these data that the major impact of attitude to the ad occurs through brand familiarity. The study shows that almost all the mediating cognitive and affective responses measured appear to determine the levels of this attitude to the ad construct.

Fourth, there appears to be directional evidence that familiarity works more through that brand attitude component which develops "classically conditioned" affect from ad executions, than through that component responsive to counter argumentation. More importantly, we show the dominating role of familiarity in driving purchase intentions in low involvement conditions.

In addition to confirming this role of familiarity in the low involvement hierarchy, however, these data show that affect is not absent (prior to purchase intentions) from this hierarchy, as previously supposed. Affect does play a major role — but the kind of affect implicated here is not one based primarily on the considered evaluative processing of brand attributes, as it is in the high involvement "learning" hierarchy. Instead, it stems primarily from the effects of ad execution likeability.

Together, we believe these contributions provide a more comprehensive window into how advertising works on contact, than was available previously. We can now suggest a more detailed view of how the "two routes" differ: from two types of sources, through two types of mediating responses, via two types of attitudes, on purchase intentions. In addition, we can now integrate these (expanded) "two routes" with the alternative hierarchies of effect with which we began this paper.

This expanded and integrated view is illustrated in Fig. 1.2. The heavy lines and dotted lines in the figure indicate pathways of major and minor influence, respectively.

As can be seen, high levels of antecedent motivation, ability, and opportunity lead to high levels of message response involvement, leading to the predominance of an expanded learning hierarchy of effects. In this hierarchy, message argumentation evokes detailed cognitive processing about brand attributes, leading to changes in attribute argumentation-sensitive attitudes and then to changes in purchase intentions and action.

In low message response conditions, however, the primary route is one where execution likeability and exposure frequency lead to changes in execution-sensitive attitudes (after affective response generation) and then to intention and action, with such usage experiences then modifying argumentation-sensitive attitudes. Brand familiarity, however, in this latter hierarchy, also influences purchase intentions directly, in addition to its influence through the execution-sensitive attitudinal component.

Like any study, this one has limitations. Innovation in measurement is never risk free, and the most problematic and also interesting aspect of this study, clearly, is the large amount of interaction discovered between the scales originally developed to measure the two attitude components, and the different product categories used in this study. While the analysis presented here regarding the percentage contribution model used de facto scale correlations, in the aggregate, to see how attitudes based differentially on different affect sources impacted purchase intentions under different involvement levels, the ambiguity regarding scale interpretation makes this a less than satisfactory test of that model.

Such interactions are, of course, not new. Osgood, Suci, and Tannenbaum (1957) devote a full 12 pages (pp. 176–188) in their book to the concept-scale interactions they discovered in their use of evaluative semantic differential scales.

The severe magnitude of these problems in our data may suggest that future studies be confined to single product categories — but that would be dangerously short-sighted. Just as these problems would probably not have emerged had we used just one product category, neither would we have dis-

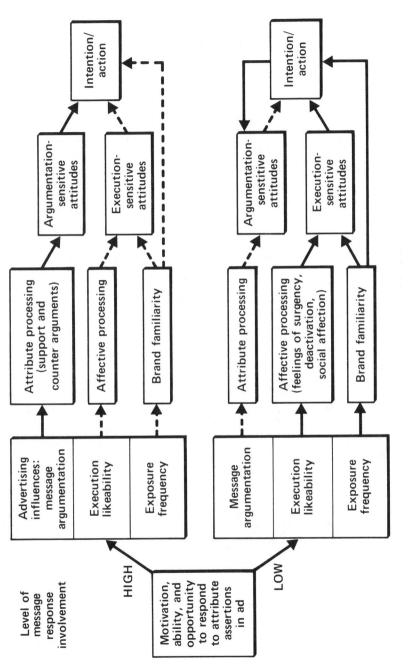

FIG. 1.2.   Alternative routes of advertising influence.

39

covered these interactions, which have clear implications for the use of evaluative semantic differentials in any research, especially in cross-product research. Clearly, the search must go on instead for better, more stable measures of the two attitude components.

Our research program is now proceeding to test alternative measurement scales. We will also test whether the processes traced here — and predictions flowing from them — find support in a situation when respondents view test ads in an embedded program environment, without potentially reactive verbal protocol tasks imposed on them. While we can claim to have fully understood how TV advertising works only when we understand such "natural" processing, we do believe we are already somewhat better informed now than before.

ACKNOWLEDGMENTS

Financial support for this project was provided by the Marketing Science Institute and by the Marketing Management Program at the Stanford Business School. We gratefully acknowledge the helpful comments made by Profs. Richard Bagozzi, Lynn Phillips, V. Srinivasan, and Peter Wright, and the cooperation of the many companies and ad agencies who made available the commercials used in this project, but prefer anonymity.

REFERENCES

Abelson, R. P., Kinder, D. R., Peters, M. D., & Fiske, S. T. (1982). Affective and semantic components in political person perception. *Journal of Personality and Social Psychology, 42,* 619–630.

Anderson, J. R., & Reder, L. M. (1979). An elaborate processing explanation of depth of processing. In L. S. Cermak & F. I. M. Craik (Eds.), *Levels of Processing in Human Memory.* Hillsdale, N.J.: Lawrence Erlbaum Associates.

Baddeley, A. D. (1978). The trouble with levels: A reexamination of Craik and Lockhart's framework for memory research. *Psychological Review, 85,* 139–152.

Bagozzi, R. P. (1980). *Causal models in marketing.* New York: Wiley.

Bagozzi, R. P. (1981). An examination of the validity of two models of attitude. *Multivariate Behavioral Research, 16,* 323–59.

Bagozzi, R. P., & Burnkrant, R. E. (1979). Attitude organization and the attitude-behavior relationship. *Journal of Personality and Social Psychology, 37,* 913–929.

Bagozzi, R. P., Tybout, A. M., Craig, C. S., & Sternthal, B. (1979). The construct validity of the tripartite classification of attitudes. *Journal of Marketing Research, 16,* 88–95.

Batra, R. (1982). Consumer preference formation under low involvement message reception conditions: Processes and advertising implications. Unpublished thesis proposal, Graduate School of Business, Stanford University, Stanford, Calif.

Batra, R., & Ray, M. L. (1983a). Advertising situations: The implications of differential involvement and accompanying affect responses. In R. J. Harris (Ed.), *Information processing research in advertising.* Hillsdale, N.J.: Lawrence Erlbaum Associates.

Batra, R., & Ray, M. L. (1983b). Operationalizing involvement as depth and quality of cognitive response. In R. P. Bagozzi & A. M. Tybout (Eds.), *Advances in consumer research* (Vol. 10). Ann Arbor: Association for Consumer Research.

Bem, D. J. (1965). Self-perception theory. In L. Berkowitz (Ed.), *Advances in Experimental Social Psychology* (Vol. 6). New York: Springer.

Bentler, P. M., & Bonett, D. G. (1980). Significance tests and goodness of fit in the analysis of covariance structures. *Psychological Bulletin, 24,* 163–204.

Calder, B., & Sternthal, B. (1980). Television commercial wearout: An information processing view. *Journal of Marketing Research, 17,* 173–186.

Campbell, D. T., & Fiske, D. W. (1959). Convergent and discriminant validation by the multitrait-multimethod matrix. *Psychological Bulletin, 56,* 81–105.

Chaiken, S. (1980). Heuristic versus systematic information processing and the use of source versus message cues in persuasion. *Journal of Personality and Social Psychology, 39,* 752–66.

Cialdini, R. B., Petty, R. E., & Cacioppo, J. T. (1981). Attitude and attitude change. *Annual Review of Psychology, 32,* 357–404.

Craik, F. I. M., & Lockhart, R. S. (1972). Levels of processing: A framework for memory research. *Journal of Verbal Learning and Verbal Behavior, 11,* 671–684.

Festinger, L., & Maccoby, N. (1964). On resistance to persuasive communications. *Journal of Abnormal and Social Psychology, 68,* 359–366.

Fishbein, M., & Ajzen, I. (1975). *Belief, attitude, intention and behavior: An introduction to theory and research.* Reading, Mass.: Addison-Wesley.

Gorn, G. J. (1982). The effects of music in advertising on choice behavior: A classical conditioning approach. *Journal of Marketing, 46,* 94–101.

Greenwald, A. G. (1968). Cognitive learning, cognitive response to persuasion, and attitude change. In A. G. Greenwald, T. C. Brock, & T. C. Ostrom (Eds.), *Psychological foundations of attitudes.* New York: Academic Press.

Greenwald, A. G., Leavitt, C., & Obermiller, C. (1980). What is low consumer involvement? In G. J. Gorn & M. E. Goldberg (Eds.), *Proceedings of the Division 23 Program, 88th Annual Convention of the American Psychological Association,* Montreal, Canada.

Harrison, A. A. (1977). Mere exposure. In L. Berkowitz (Ed.), *Advances in experimental social psychology* (Vol. 10). New York: Academic Press.

Houston, M. J., & Rothschild, M. L. (1978). *A paradigm for research on consumer involvement.* Unpublished manuscript, Graduate School of Business, University of Wisconsin, Madison.

Izard, C. E. (1977). *Human emotions.* New York: Plenum Press.

Joreskog, K. G., & Sorbom, D. G. (1981). *LISREL V: Analysis of linear structural relationships by Maximum Likelihood and Least Squares methods.* Chicago: National Education Resources.

Katz, D., & Stotland, E. (1959). A preliminary statement to a theory of attitude structure and change. In S. Koch (Ed.), *Psychology: A study of science* (Vol. 3). New York: McGraw-Hill.

Kelley, H. H. (1967). Attribution in social psychology. In D. Levine (Ed.), *Nebraska Symposium on Motivation.* Lincoln, Neb.: University of Nebraska Press.

Kenny, D. A. (1975). An empirical application of confirmatory factor analysis to the multitrait-multimethod matrix. *Journal of Experimental Social Psychology, 12,* 247–252.

Komorita, S. S., & Bass, A. R. (1967). Attitude differentiation and evaluative scales of the semantic differential. *Journal of Personality and Social Psychology, 6,* 241–244.

Kothandapani, V. (1971). Validation of feeling, belief and intention to act as three components of attitude and their contributions to prediction of contraceptive behavior. *Journal of Personality and Social Psychology, 19,* 321–333.

Krugman, H. E. (1965). The impact of TV advertising: Learning without involvement. *Public Opinion Quarterly, 29,* 349–356.

Krugman, H. E. (1972). Why three exposures may be enough. *Journal of Advertising Research, 12,* 11–14.

Mitchell, A. A. (1979). Involvement: A potentially important mediator of consumer behavior. In W. G. Wilkie (Ed.), *Advances in consumer research* (Vol. 6). Ann Arbor: Association for Consumer Research.

Mitchell, A. A., & Olson, V. P. (1981). Are product attribute beliefs the only mediator of advertising effects on brand attitude? *Journal of Marketing Research, 18,* 318–332.

Nowlis, V. (1965). Research with the mood adjective check list. In S. S. Tomkins & C. E. Izard (Eds.), *Affect, cognition and personality: Empirical studies.* New York: Springer.

Osgood, C. E., Suci, G. J., & Tannenbaum, P. H. (1957). *The measurement of meaning.* Urbana: University of Illinois Press.

Osterhouse, R. A., & Brock, T. C. (1970). Distraction increases yielding to propaganda by inhibiting counterarguing. *Journal of Personality and Social Psychology, 15,* 344–358.

Ostrom, T. M. (1969). The relationship between the affective, behavioral, and cognitive components of attitude. *Journal of Experimental Social Psychology, 5,* 12–30.

Petty, R. E., & Cacioppo, J. T. (1979). Issue involvement can increase or decrease persuasion by enhancing message-relevant cognitive responses. *Journal of Personality and Social Psychology, 37,* 1915–1926.

Petty, R. E., & Cacioppo, J. T. (1980). Effects of issue involvement on attitudes in an advertising context. In J. G. Gorn & M. E. Goldberg (Eds.), *Proceedings of the Division 23 Program, 88th Annual Convention of the American Psychological Association.* Montreal, Canada.

Petty, R. E., & Cacioppo, J. T., & Goldman, R. (1981). Personal involvement as a determinant of argument-based persuasion. *Journal of Personality and Social Psychology, 41,* 847–855.

Petty, R. E., Wells, G. L., & Brock, T. C. (1976). Distraction can enhance or reduce yielding to propaganda: Thought disruption versus effort justification. *Journal of Personality and Social Psychology, 34,* 874–884.

Pribram, K. H. (1980). The biology of emotions and other feelings. In R. Plutchik & H. Kellerman (Eds.), *Emotion: Theory, research, and experience: Vol. 1. Theories of emotion.* New York: Academic Press.

Ray, M. L. (1976). Attitude as communication response. In D. Johnson & W. D. Wells (Eds.), *Attitude research at bay.* Chicago: American Marketing Association.

Ray, M. L. (1979). Involvement and other variables mediating communication effects as opposed to explaining all consumer behavior. In W. L. Wilkie (Ed.), *Advances in consumer research* (Vol. 6). Ann Arbor: Association for Consumer Research.

Ray, M. L. (1981). *Applications of a marketing communication research system* (Research Paper No. 617). Stanford: Stanford University, Graduate School of Business.

Ray, M. L., & Sawyer, A. G. (1971). Repetition in media models: A laboratory technique. *Journal of Marketing Research, 8,* 20–30.

Ray, M. L., in collaboration with Sawyer, A. G., Rothschild, M. L., Heeler, R. M., Strong, E. C., & Reed, J. B. (1973). Marketing communication and the hierarchy of effects. In P. Clarke (Ed.), *New models for communication research.* Beverly Hills, Calif.: Sage Publications.

Roberts, D. F., & Maccoby, N. (1973). Information processing and persuasion: Counterarguing behavior. In P. Clarke (Ed.), *New models for communication research.* Beverly Hills, Calif.: Sage Publications.

Rosenberg, M. J., & Hovland, C. I. (1960). Cognitive, affective, and behavioral components of attitudes. In C. I. Hovland & M. J. Rosenberg (Eds.), *Attitude organization and change.* New Haven: Yale University Press.

Sawyer, A. G. (1981). Repetition, cognitive responses, and persuasion. In R. E. Petty, T. M. Ostrom, & T. C. Brock (Eds.), *Cognitive responses to persuasion.* Hillsdale, N.J.: Lawrence Erlbaum Associates.

Schlinger, M. J. (1979). A profile of responses to commercials. *Journal of Advertising Research, 19,* 37–46.

Taylor, S. E., & Fiske, S. T. (1978). Salience, attention, and attribution: Top of the head phenomena. In L. Berkowitz (Ed.), *Advances in experimental social psychology* (Vol. 11). New York: Academic Press.

Triandis, H. C. (1971). *Attitude and attitude change.* New York: Wiley.

Triandis, H. C. (1977). *Interpersonal behavior.* Monterey, Calif.: Brooks/Cole.

Tversky, A. (1972). Elimination by aspects: A theory of choice. *Psychological Review, 79,* 281–299.

Tversky, A., & Kahneman, D. (1973). Availability: A heuristic for judging frequency and probability. *Cognitive Psychology, 5,* 207–232.

Webb, P. H. (1978). *Consumer information acquisition in a difficult media environment: The case of television clutter.* Unpublished doctoral dissertation, Stanford University.

Wells, W. D., Leavitt, C., & McConville, M. (1971). A reaction profile for TV commercials. *Journal of Advertising Research, 11,* 11–17.

Wright, P. (1973). The cognitive processes mediating acceptance of advertising. *Journal of Marketing Research, 10,* 53–62.

Wright, P. (1981). Cognitive responses to mass media advocacy. In R. E. Petty, T. M. Ostrom, & T. C. Brock (Eds.), *Cognitive responses in persuasion.* Hillsdale, N.J.: Lawrence Erlbaum Associates.

Wright, P., & Barbour, F. (1977). Phased decision strategies: Sequels to an initial screening. *TIMS Studies in the Management Sciences, 6,* 91–109.

Zajonc, R. B. (1968). Attitudinal effects of mere exposure. *Journal of Personality and Social Psychology Monograph 9,* (2, Part 2), 1–28.

Zajonc, R. B. (1980). Feeling and thinking: Preferences need no inferences. *American Psychologist, 35,* 151–175.

2 Affective and Cognitive Antecedents of Attitude Toward the Ad: A Conceptual Framework

Richard J. Lutz
Marketing Department
University of Florida

INTRODUCTION

The past few years have witnessed a rekindling of interest in the nature and effects of consumers' affective reactions to advertising stimuli. In contrast to earlier researchers' tendency to focus primarily on these affective reactions as criterion variables in their own right, recent researchers have investigated the construct *attitude-toward-the-ad* (*Aad*) as a mediator of advertising's effects on brand attitudes and purchase intentions (Mitchell & Olson, 1981; Shimp, 1981).

The recent research attention focused on Aad parallels current persuasion research in social cognition in its explicit recognition that affective responses, as well as cognitive responses, are important indicants of overall message effectiveness. In particular, the *elaboration likelihood model* (ELM) posited by Petty and Cacioppo (1981) serves as a useful framework for integrating Aad effects and the more commonly utilized brand attribute ratings. The ELM postulates two basic routes by which a persuasive communication may exert influence on its audience: *central processing,* wherein message content is the primary influence, and *peripheral processing,* in which the audience is affected more by the source of the message or contextual factors than by actual message content. Petty and Cacioppo explicitly consider the role of audience involvement in their analysis of which persuasion route is likely to be dominant in a particular communication setting: the higher the involvement, the greater the tendency toward central processing. Given the increasingly widely held assumption that most advertising is inherently uninvolving, the peripheral route to persuasion, as represented by Aad, has intuitive appeal as a mechanism for understanding the effects of advertising on consumers.

45

A growing number of empirical studies have documented the significant explanatory power of Aad (Cacioppo & Petty, this volume; Lutz, Mac-Kenzie, & Belch, 1983; MacKenzie & Lutz, 1983; Mitchell & Olson, 1981; Moore & Hutchinson, 1983; Moore & Hutchinson, this volume; Shimp, 1981). To date, however, little systematic attention has been devoted to the conceptual origins of Aad. In many cases, the construct has been defined loosely or only operationally; its location in a nomological network of advertising-related constructs has not been established. Previous literature dealing with the Aad construct generally has been ignored and never has been well integrated. For instance, Aad has been related to advertising repetition, mechanical and executional aspects of commercials, surrounding advertising and editorial/programming contexts, and audience attitudes toward advertising in general; however, no attempt has been made to collate these research streams and generate a systematic conceptual framework.

The purpose of this chapter is to review and integrate past literature relevant to the Aad construct, with the ultimate goal of producing a conceptual framework permitting the derivation of causal hypotheses regarding the formation and change of Aad. The paper concludes with a discussion of the role of Aad in advertising pretesting methodology.

ORIGINS OF AAD

Definition

Throughout the current discussion Aad is defined as a *predisposition to respond in a favorable or unfavorable manner to a particular advertising stimulus during a particular exposure occasion.* Under this conceptual definition Aad is comprised solely of affective response to the commercial stimulus and does not refer to cognitive or behavioral responses; this definition is consistent with Fishbein and Ajzen's (1975) definition of attitude. It is also important to note that the definition of Aad focuses on a particular exposure to a particular ad and not on consumers' attitudes toward advertising in general or even their attitudes toward the ad stimulus of interest at another point in time (say, after repeated exposure to the ad). Hence, Aad is construed as situationally bound construct, an affective reaction to the ad generated at the time of exposure and may be expected to have its maximum impact on other response variables, such as brand attitude, at or immediately following the point of exposure. Aad, in comparison with brand attitudes or attitudes toward advertising in general, is seen as being more transitory and less likely to exert strong influences over an extended period of time. However, given that Aad may exhibit fairly strong effects within the exposure setting, its *indirect* influence on subsequent consumer behavior may persist.

A Structural Perspective

Most prior research incorporating Aad has implicitly or explicitly adopted what Petty and Cacioppo (1981) would label a *central* processing perspective regarding the origins of Aad. For example, Lutz, MacKenzie, and Belch (1983) attempted to predict Aad through use of an index of cognitive responses to ad execution elements and a measure of advertiser credibility. That is, Aad was modeled as a function of antecedent perceptual responses, which is a direct analog to modeling brand attitude as a function of brand attribute perceptions. But, just as Aad has been shown to explain variance in brand attitudes over and above brand attribute perceptions (e.g., Mitchell & Olson, 1981), it is similarly expected that the determinants of Aad are not all cognitively based reactions to the advertising stimulus. In other words, it is postulated that Aad may also be formed through a more *peripheral processing* mechanism.

Figure 2.1 depicts a structural model of the cognitive and affective antecedents of Aad. This figure serves as an organizing focus for the bulk of the remainder of the present paper. It is argued that the five "first order" classes of determinants of Aad can be arrayed along a central-peripheral processing continuum, with Ad Credibility and Mood anchoring the central and peripheral processing endpoints, respectively.

The structural model is grounded in prior research and represents an attempt to integrate several previously unrelated streams of advertising research. The main goal of this analysis is to derive an adequate structural model to both guide and position future investigations. Once the structural model has been established, then research can begin to focus on the important questions pertaining to the processes underlying the structure. Ultimately, the processes must be understood in order to fully explain the Aad construct's role in advertising; positing a comprehensive structural model is an important step in assuring that the process-oriented research addresses the full range of determinants of Aad.

Cognitive and Affective Antecedents of Aad

As shown in Fig. 2.1, five major classes of variables are identified as potential direct, or first-order, determinants of Aad: Ad Credibility, Ad Perceptions, Attitude toward the Advertiser, Attitude toward Advertising, and Mood. Underlying these first-order determinants, subsystems of "second order" determinants exert indirect effects on Aad. Each of these antecedent variables and its underlying subsystem is discussed in turn below. Moving from left to right in the figure corresponds to a movement from central processing to peripheral processing, a postulate developed further in the following discussion.

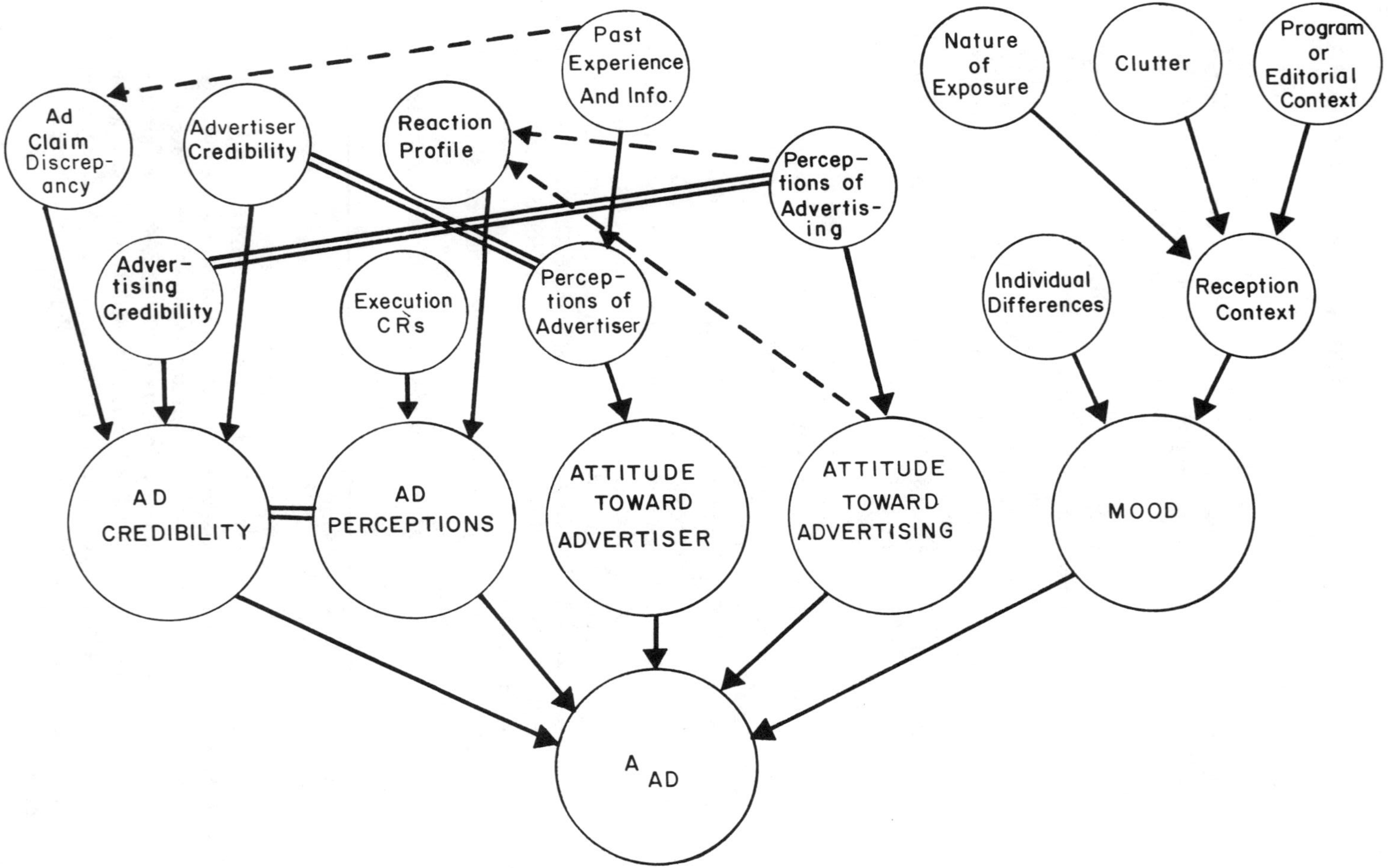

FIG. 3.1 [illegible] model of cognitive and affective antecedents of attitude toward the ad

Ad Credibility.   Ad Credibility is defined as the extent to which the audience perceives claims made about the brand in the ad to be truthful and believable. In this case, a central processing model is assumed, as the consumer is seen as forming an attitude toward the ad based on his or her perceptions of the ad's credibility. It should be noted that Ad Credibility is only one of many possible perceptual responses to a commercial stimulus, the remainder of which are treated in the second major class of determinants, Ad Perceptions. Ad Credibility is treated separately purely for heuristic reasons. There exists such a wealth of persuasion research investigating the effects of credibility, that it seemed advisable to treat it in this fashion. The solid double lines connecting Ad Perceptions and Ad Credibility in Fig. 2.1 are intended to serve as a reminder that the latter is, in fact, a special case of the former.

Ad Credibility is thought to have a direct positive influence on Aad; other things equal, the higher the credibility of the ad, the more favorably the consumer responds to it. Viewed from a central processing perspective, the mechanism through which Ad Credibility exerts its effect on Aad is identical to the *expectancy-times-value* perspective on brand attitude formation (cf., Fishbein & Ajzen, 1975). The subjective likelihood of the ad being credible, multiplied by the subjective value of credibility, would serve as a portion of the cognitive structure underlying Aad. The remaining elements of this cognitive structure would be housed in the Ad Perceptions construct.

Underlying Ad Credibility is the Ad Credibility Subsystem, which consists of three constructs: perceived Ad Claim Discrepancy, Advertiser Credibility, and Advertising Credibility. Ad Claim Discrepancy is the degree to which the message recipient perceives a discrepancy between what is being claimed about the brand in the ad and the actual characteristics or benefits of the brand. Inconsistencies beween claims and performance serve to damage Ad Credibility, a relationship postulated by Fishbein and Ajzen (1975). Fundamental to the consumer's ability to perceive a claim discrepancy is his or her prior experience and/or information with respect to the advertised brand, as depicted by the dashed arrow in Fig. 2.1.

Advertising Credibility represents consumers' perceptions of the truthfulness and believability of advertising in general, not simply the particular ad in question. As was the case with Ad Credibility, Advertising Credibility is merely one of a number of perceptual dimensions along which consumers may assess advertising as an institution, hence the solid double line connecting Advertising Credibility and Perceptions of Advertising, a more general category discussed later. Some evidence (e.g., Bauer & Greyser, 1968) suggests that consumers have a tendency to evaluate particular advertising stimuli in light of their general beliefs about advertising. A syllogistic reasoning process may underlie such an effect: "In general, advertising is not credible; this is an ad; therefore, this ad is not credible."

The final component of the Ad Credibility Subsystem is Advertiser Credibility, which refers to the perceived truthfulness or honesty of the sponsor of the ad. Again, as indicated by the double bond between Advertiser Credibility and Perception of Advertiser, the former is seen as a single dimension of the latter multidimensional construct. As was the case with Advertising Credibility, the impact of Advertiser Credibility on Ad Credibility also is seen as the outcome of a logical syllogism: "The sponsor is credible; this ad is for the sponsor's brand; therefore, the ad is credible."

As is evident from the preceding discussion, Ad Credibility relies on a reasonably high level of cognitive activity on the part of the message recipient in order to affect Aad. Indeed, the Ad Claim Discrepancy construct requires processing of at least some portion of message content; hence, this determinant of Aad represents a mixture of central and peripheral processing. In situations where Ad Credibility enters into the explanation of Aad, it should be the dominant influence among the five first order determinants. The rationale for this assertion is that the Ad Credibility Subsystem represents the highest level of involvement of the five postulated antecedents of Aad; therefore, attitudinal reactions emanating from this source would tend to carry more weight in the mind of the consumer when compared with more peripheral sources of affect.

Ad Perceptions.   While credibility undoubtedly has received the most research attention of any perceptual dimension of persuasive messages, numerous other perceptual characteristics of advertising stimuli have been investigated over the years. Ad Perceptions is defined as a multidimensional array of consumer perceptions of the advertising stimulus, including executional factors but excluding perceptions of the advertised brand. The distinction made here is that between brand cognitions (i.e., beliefs about the brand) and ad cognitions (i.e., beliefs about the ad per se) (cf., Lutz, MacKenzie & Belch, 1983).

As shown in Fig. 2.1, two distinct but related streams of research have attempted to assess Ad Perceptions: Reaction Profiles and Ad Execution Cognitive Responses. Both of these approaches have focused on perceptual reactions to ads, but from entirely different perspectives. The Reaction Profile research has been largely atheoretical and has treated Ad Perceptions primarily as a dependent variable. In contrast, Ad Execution Cognitive Responses flow from the cognitive response theory of persuasion (cf., Greenwald, 1968; Wright, 1980) and are cast in a role of mediating variables which may assist in explaining communication effects.

Relatively few studies have adopted the Ad Execution Cognitive Response approach (Batra & Ray, 1983; this volume; Belch, 1981, 1982; Lutz & MacKenzie, 1982; Lutz, MacKenzie, & Belch, 1983; MacKenzie & Lutz, 1983). The same basic measurement approach underlies all of these research

efforts: Free responses elicited immediately following exposure to an advertising message are content analyzed into a set of mutually exclusive and collectively exhaustive *cognitive response* categories. The earliest marketing applications of cognitive response theory (e.g., Wright, 1973) simply borrowed
the cognitive response categories which had been used in the social psychology literature, e.g., counterarguing, support arguing, source derogation, curiosity. These categories of response are heavily message- and source-
oriented and do not capture the essence of many consumer responses to
advertising stimuli, which led subsequent advertising researchers to develop
cognitive response coding schemes more suited to the advertising domain,
with its simpler and shorter messages. For example, the Batra and Ray (1983)
typology includes six separate Ad Execution Cognitive Response categories:
source derogations, emotional feelings (positive and negative), liking of
executional elements, and evaluation of execution (positive and negative).
The only two studies that used Ad Execution Cognitive Responses to predict
Aad (Lutz, MacKenzie, & Belch, 1983; MacKenzie & Lutz, 1983) found a reasonably strong positive relationship between the two constructs.

The cognitive response approach to assessing Ad Perceptions is somewhat
unwieldly due to its open-end response format and subsequent content analysis. The Reaction Profile approach yields more easily quantifiable data and
hence is more amenable to repeated routine use. It is not surprising, therefore, that the Reaction Profile was pioneered by advertising agency researchers (cf. Wells, 1964) and that most research utilizing this approach has been
conducted by industry. A typical Reaction Profile consists of a 20 to 30 item
adjective checklist designed to tap a variety of perceptual dimensions of ad
response.

Table 2.1 contains a listing of Reaction Profile studies that have appeared
in the literature since its inception in 1964. Presumably, one of the inherent
advantages of a close-ended response format is the ease of comparability of
findings across ads and/or studies. While it appears that this advantage has
been capitalized upon by advertising agencies in their day-to-day research activities, this advantage has not been realized in the published literature. Vir-

TABLE 2.1
Reaction Profile Research

Wells (1964)	Aaker and Bruzzone (1981)
Leavitt (1970)	Mehrotra, Van Auken, and Lonial (1981)
Plummer (1971)	Aaker and Norris (1982)
Wells, Leavitt, and McConville (1971)	Burke and Edell (1982)
Leavitt (1975)	Olson, Schlinger, and Young (1982)
McEwen and Leavitt (1976)	Schlinger (1982)
Schlinger (1979a,b)	Lastovicka (1983)
Schlinger and Green (1980)	Meyer-Hentschel (1983)

tually every stuudy has included some adjectives not present in other studies, and there has been no consensus reached with respect to the underlying dimensionality of the Reaction Profile. For instance, Wells, Leavitt, and McConville (1971) identified six stable dimensions: humor, vigor, sensuousness, uniqueness, personal relevance, and irritation. Working from the same data base, Plummer (1971) identified seven dimensions: entertainment (or stimulation), irritation, familiarity, empathy (or gratifying involvement), confusion, informativeness (or personal relevance), and brand reinforcement. Schlinger (1979b) included seven factors: brand reinforcement, alienation, relevant news, entertainment, confusion, empathy, and familiarity. Aaker and Bruzzone (1981), working from a different but overlapping set of adjectives, offered four dimensions: entertaining, personal relevance, dislike, and warm, while Burke and Edell (1982) found that a three-factor solution corresponding roughly to the Evaluation, Potency and Activity dimensions underlying the Semantic Differential predicted Aad as well as the six factors proposed by Wells, Leavitt, and McConville (1971).

At this juncture, then, there exists no universal set of perceptual dimensions that can be said to represent the Ad Perceptions construct. Both the Reaction Profile and Ad Execution Cognitive Response measurement approaches are characterized by rather fuzzy boundaries. Lastovicka (1983), in the only direct comparison of the two approaches, demonstrated adequate reliability and convergent and discriminant validity for the Personal Relevance and Entertainment dimensions, but not for the Confusion factor. His results provide at least partial support for the notion that the two approaches are tapping the same cognitive domain, i.e., Ad Perceptions.

Only one study has directly examined the ability of the Reaction Profile to predict Aad (Burke & Edell, 1982). Their six-factor solution yielded R^2 levels from .67 to .71, thus providing evidence of a strong relationship between Ad Perceptions and Aad. Although it was not explicitly modeled in this fashion, the underlying mechanism by which Ad Perceptions influence Aad can be cast in an expectancy-times-value framework, as was suggested in the disdiscussion of Ad Credibility effects. Consumers are seen as attaching some value (positive or negative) to each underlying perceptual dimension; an index of cognitive structure underlying Aad can then be constructed which should provide a good explanation, at least under conditions where consumers' involvement levels are sufficient for them to engage in central processing to a limited degree.

Thus far, the two influences on Aad that have been treated, i.e., Ad Credibility and Ad Perceptions, both entail some degree of central processing. Aad is viewed as being formed on the basis of perception and analysis of various aspects of the ad. The remaining three first order determinants of Aad rely more heavily on the peripheral processing mode, in that they are all affective rather than cognitive antecedents.

Attitude toward the Advertiser.   Consumers' affective reactions to the sponsor of the ad stimulus of interest are expected to carry some weight in the formation of Aad. Attitude toward the Advertiser is defined as a learned predisposition to respond in a consistently favorable or unfavorable manner to the sponsoring organization, consistent with Fishbein and Ajzen's (1975) definition of attitude. In contrast to Aad, Attitude toward the Advertiser is seen as less transitory and hence is representative of an accumulation of both information and experience over time. This attitudinal construct is expected to have "spillover" effects on consumers' reactions to ads emanating from the advertiser. The actual mechanism underlying this presumed spillover may be one of simple affect transfer, although congruity theory and the literature on communicator attractiveness offer somewhat different explanations (e.g., Chaiken & Eagly, 1983). It is likely that the process by which Attitude toward the Advertiser affects Aad is more or less automatic, with little active cognitive contemplation.

Figure 2.1 depicts the Advertiser Attitude Subsystem that may give rise to Attitude toward the Advertiser. Consistent with an expectancy-times-value approach to attitude formation, Perceptions of the Advertiser are seen as the immediate precursors of Attitude toward the Advertiser. As was discussed earlier, Advertiser Credibility is, no doubt, a dominant perceptual dimension which has been treated separately in this analysis. Other possible perceptual dimensions include attractiveness, reputability, and country of origin ("buy American!"). The source of these perceptions is consumers' direct and indirect knowledge of the advertister, represented by Past Experience and Information.

Attitude toward Advertising.   Attitude toward Advertising is defined as a learned predisposition to respond in a consistently favorable or unfavorable manner to advertising in general. Bauer and Greyser (1968), in their classic study *Advertising in America: The Consumer View,* were the first to examine Attitude toward Advertising in systematic fashion. Utilizing a national probability sample of nearly 2000 consumers, they found that 41% of the American public was generally favorable toward advertising, 14% was unfavorable, and 42% was either "mixed" or indifferent. Furthermore, Bauer and Greyser demonstrated a relationship between consumers' attitudes toward advertising and their subsequent ratings of specific ads as being annoying, enjoyable, informative, or offensive, categories that are utilized in the Reaction Profile studies discussed previously. Hence, Fig. 2.1 includes a dashed arrow from Attitude toward Advertising to Reaction Profile; this relationship would be consistent with an *indirect* effect of Attitude toward Advertising on Aad, working through the Ad Perceptions subsystem. However, the effect is also postulated as being *direct* from Attitude toward Advertising to Aad, through a process of affect transfer.

Attitude toward Advertising is seen as rooted in the consumer's Perceptions of Advertising (see Fig. 2.1). Bauer and Greyser (1968) identified eight underlying belief dimensions, including such items as advertising's perceived causal relationship to prices, product quality, the standard of living and unnecessary consumption. Bartos and Dunn (1974), in their follow-up to the Bauer and Greyser study, incorporated a battery of 42 perceptual statements hypothesized to underlie Attitude toward Advertising. Again, many of these items were identical to items included in various Reaction Profile studies, hence the dashed arrow from Perceptions of Advertising to Reaction Profile, representing a possible logical syllogistic process whereby general beliefs about advertising exert influence on perceptions of a particular ad. As was the case with other relationships in Fig. 2.1 where perceptual factors lead to an attitudinal construct, the hypothesized mechanism by which Perceptions of Advertising impact on Attitude toward Advertising is an expectancy-times-value process.

Mood.   Mood is defined as the consumer's affective state at the time of exposure to the ad stimulus. This construct is conceptually similar to Rokeach's (1968) notion of *attitude-toward-the-situation,* Russell and Mehrabian's (1977) *pleasure* dimension of situations, and Csikszentmihalyi and Kubey's (1981) situational *affect.* The essential character of the Mood determinant of Aad is that it is an affective state whose effects on Aad are felt entirely through a process of affect transfer; there is virtually no likelihood that this effect would be cognitively mediated, but instead would be an automatic reaction on the part of the consumer. Indirect support for the impact of Mood on Aad was provided by Srull (1983), who showed that Mood at the time of exposure affects brand attitudes. At a conceptual level, Gardner and Raj (1983) have suggested that Mood is an important mediator of advertising effects.

The two immediate precursors of Mood, as shown in Fig. 2.1, are Individual Differences and Reception Context. Individual Differences refer to the "trait" component of an individual consumer's Mood—i.e., a predispositional tendency to evaluate situations positively or negatively. This general predisposition would have an impact on the consumer's Mood "state" at the time of commercial exposure. In addition, Mood is a function of Reception Context, which in turn is made up of several dimensions: Nature of Exposure, surrounding ad Clutter, and surrounding Program/Editorial Context.

Nature of Exposure refers to the consumer's motivations at the time of exposure. For instance, the consumer may be oriented toward entertainment and thus regard advertising stimuli as unwanted intrusions in a "forced exposure" situation (Hansen, 1972); this is typical of the electronic media. On the other hand, ad exposure may be the result of a consumer-instigated search for information, wherein commercial stimuli are at the top of the consumer's goal hierarchy (Beattie & Mitchell, this volume; Gardner, Mitchell, & Russo, 1978).

Clutter is an increasingly important factor in advertising exposure, as more and more ads are inserted into a given amount of air time or a magazine issue. Webb (1979) and Webb and Ray (1979) have demonstrated the negative effects of Clutter, with the latter study documenting increased levels of negative cognitive response to target commercials as Clutter increased. Soldow and Principe (1981) measured consumers' attitudes toward commercials and found a direct negative relationship between Aad and Clutter.

Finally, the surrounding Program/Editorial Context has long been recognized by advertisers as an important input to advertising effects. This has been referred to as "qualitative media effects" (Sissors & Petray, 1976; Weilbacher, 1960) and serves primarily as a heuristic device for media buyers; such effects are generally difficult to quantify. Gensch (1970) summarized many of these qualitative media effects, and subsequent researchers have attempted to document the impact of Program/Editorial Context (e.g., Cannon, 1982; Clancy & Kweskin, 1971; Kennedy, 1971). Some researchers have focused attention on Aad as a relevant dependent variable (Crane, 1964; Soldow & Principe, 1981; Winick, 1962) and have shown Program/Editoral Context effects on Aad.

Moderator Variables.   Up to this point, the relationships depicted in Fig. 2.1 have been portrayed as main effects, with no discussion of possible moderating influences. It is clear, however, that the potential impact of any advertising stimulus on Aad and/or other measures of advertising effectiveness is conditioned by a host of moderator variables. Table 2.2 presents a list of potential moderators, some of which have been examined empirically and some of which have been discussed but not tested.

Bauer and Greyser (1968) found evidence for the moderating effects of product class interest (positive), prior brand preference (positive for the advertised brand), and medium (positive for print, negative for electronic). Wells (1980) has suggested that products can be arrayed on an "approach-avoidance" continuum, and furthermore, that a product's position on this dimension determines the degree to which Aad is a relevant measure of ad effectiveness. Messmer (1979) documented a decrement in Aad with repetition

TABLE 2.2
Potential Moderator Variables

Interest in Product Class
Prior Brand Preference
Repetition
Type of Appeal
Type of Medium

of a commercial as well as the effect of prior brand preference. Gelb and Pickett (1983) showed a positive relationship between the perceived humor of an ad and Aad, and Puto and Wells (1984) have demonstrated the differential effectiveness of *transformational* versus *informational* appeals. Thus, Fig. 2.1 must be viewed as a drastic oversimplification of the structural antecedents of Aad. The structure as portrayed is merely the skeleton; an analysis of each particular advertising exposure situation is required to complete the picture with appropriate moderating influences.

IMPLICATIONS FOR ADVERTISING PRETESTING

One of the most persistent problems in advertising and media planning is commercial *wearout* (Schultz, 1979). Axelrod (1980) has stated that one dimension of wearout is the "ability of a commercial to generate and maintain favorable attitudes toward itself [i.e., Aad]" (p. 14). Given Messmer's (1979) and Calder and Sternthal's (1980) findings of decreases in Aad with repeated exposure to an ad, the Aad construct appears to be a potentially important one for understanding, predicting, and perhaps forestalling commercial wearout.

   Throughout the present analysis, a distinction has been maintained between *central processing* and *peripheral processing* of commercial stimuli (cf., Petty & Cacioppo, 1981). In their initial analysis, Petty and Cacioppo treated central processing as pertaining to message *content* and peripheral processing as related to the *context* of the message (e.g., source characteristics). It is argued here that, in an advertising setting, Aad serves as a useful summary construct for a peripheral processing route to changes in brand attitudes and purchase intentions. It is further argued that Aad can also be seen as the culmination of central and peripheral processes, with the five first order determinants of Aad shown in Fig. 2.1 being characterized by increasing amounts of peripheral processing as one moves from Ad Credibility to Mood. In a sense, then, the present analysis takes the Petty and Cacioppo (1981) notions a step further by suggesting that the context of a message can be apprehended in both central and peripheral fashion by consumers.

   Figure 2.2 suggests a typology of advertising persuasion mechanisms. The two basic dimensions underlying the typology are Processing Mode — Central or Peripheral — and Focus of Processing — Ad Content or Ad Context. The introduction of Ad Context as an explicit focus of processing activity is an extension of Petty and Cacioppo's thinking. In their Elaboration Likelihood Model, peripheral processing of message content is implicitly assumed to result in central processing of the message context; they expect elaborated cognitive processing of source characteristics, for example, to replace message-

FOCUS OF PROCESSING

PROCESSING MODE	AD CONTENT	AD CONTEXT

FIG. 2.2.   A typology of ad-based persuasion mechanisms. Key: 1 = Classic message-based persuasion; 2 = Dual mode persuasion; 3 = Pure affect transfer; 4 = Contextual Evaluation transfer.

oriented cognitive responses. The ELM, then, is represented by the two lefthand cells in Fig. 2.2. Importantly for advertisers, Fig. 2.2 provides an analysis of ad effects when both content and context are processed only peripherally, a situation not dealt with by the ELM.

Classic Message-Based Persuasion.   This persuasion mechanism, as shown in Fig. 2.2, corresponds to a high involvement situation in which the consumer is actively processing the informational content of the ad, with only peripheral regard to contextual factors (Petty, Cacioppo, & Schumann, 1983). As shown in Fig. 2.3, Classic Message-Based Persuasion emphasizes the cognitive domain at the expense of the affective. Any cognitive reactions the consumer may have to the ad itself (Cad) are seen as being analyzed for their potential spillover effects on cognitions about the brand (C_B). An example of this process would be an ad credibility judgment that leads directly to a consumer accepting or rejecting a claim made in the ad. Aad as well as its affective antecedents (e.g., Mood) are seen as inconsequential in this situation, and, in fact, Aad may not exist in the mind of the consumer. Given Lastovicka and Bonfield's (1982) recent provocative research regarding the exist-

PERSUASION MECHANISM	CHARACTERISTICS OF EXPOSURE SITUATION

Message-Based Persuasion

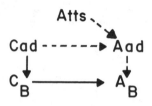

*High consumer involvement
*Information search mode
*Nondistinctive ad

Dual Mode Persuasion

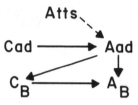

*High consumer involvement
*Information search mode
*Distinctive ad or a pretest "set"

Pure Affect Transfer

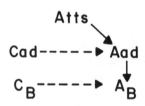

*Low consumer involvement
*Nondistinctive ad
*"Typical" ad exposure situation, especially TV

Contextual Evaluation Transfer

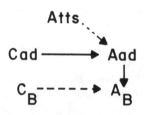

*Low consumer involvement
*Distinctive ad or a pretest "set"
*"Typical" ad pretesting situation

FIG. 2.3. Characteristics of ad exposure situations underlying ad-based persuasion mechanisms. Key: Cad = Ad cognitions; Aad = Attitude toward the ad; C_B = Brand cognitions; A_B = Brand attitude; Atts = Attitude toward Advertising (in general), Attitude toward the Advertiser, Mood. Solid arrows indicate strong positive relationships; dashed arrows indicate relationships hypothesized to be zero or near-zero.

ence of consumer brand attitudes, it is not difficult to imagine a situation in which consumers do not form attitudes toward ads. Where the consumer is actively seeking product information, and the ad is relatively nondistinctive in its creative and executional elements, then straightforward cognitive processing with little or no affective overtones can result.

Dual Mode Persuasion.   As shown in Fig. 2.2, dual mode persuasion is characterized by central processing of both the ad's content and its contextual factors. Once again, this is a highly involved consumer who is seeking information. The difference between dual mode persuasion and message-based persuasion is that the ad itself is distinctive in some aspect, leading to affective contributions to the overall persuasive effectiveness of the ad. Alternatively, the ad may not be inherently distinctive, but it becomes a focus of attention in an ad pretest setting, where consumers are instructed to evaluate the ad. Figure 2.3 depicts the hypothesized structure of dual mode persuasion. Ad cognitions are focused on in some detail by the consumer, resulting in the formation of Aad. More global attitudinal precursors of Aad are not expected to exert much influence, since the consumer is attending to the ad carefully, and is therefore unlikely to simply transfer prior attitudinal judgments over to it. Aad then exerts its influence in two ways: (1) it affects consumer acceptance/rejection of message claims (C_B), and (2) it impinges on brand attitude directly through a process of affect transfer. This pattern of results has been obtained in an ad pretest setting when close-ended measurement of both Cad and C_B was utilized (MacKenzie, Lutz, and Belch, in preparation). Since it relies on both cognitive and affective reactions as significant influences, dual mode persuasion should exhibit the more persistent persuasive effects over time. Stated another way, if an advertiser can communicate some highly relevant brand information to the consumer, and do so in an entertaining or distinctive fashion, the likelihood of long-term advertising effectiveness is enhanced.

Pure Affect Transfer.   Figure 2.2 shows that pure affect transfer occurs when the consumer processes both ad content and context only peripherally. As shown in Fig. 2.3, this situation is expected to occur when consumer involvement is low and there is nothing exceptional about the ad's execution which would attract attention to it. This scenario might be labeled the "typical" ad exposure situation, particularly for television advertising. In this situation, the consumer is seen as devoting little cognitive capacity to the ad; instead, prior attitudes toward the advertiser, advertising in general, or the situation (i.e., Mood) transfer over to Aad, which in time transfers over to brand attitude. This account partially parallels the process by which Puto and Wells 1984 have argued that "transformational" advertising appeals have their effect. Obviously, "pure" affect transfer is a knotty problem for the advertiser, particularly since it may occur frequently.

Contextual Evaluation Transfer. This persuasion mechanism corresponds to the ELM's peripheral processing mode: Consumer involvement is low, but the ad is in some way distinctive. Again, this distinctiveness may be imposed by the situation if advertising pretesting is being undertaken. In fact, one might argue that this represents a "typical" ad pretest setting. Consumers in such pretests are often instructed to give their reactions to commercial stimuli, with the goal being to disguise the intent of the pretest to assess impact on brand attitude. However, data from such pretests that have been gathered in a free response format show a heavy preponderance of ad-oriented cognitions (e.g., Lutz & MacKenzie, 1982). Thus, ad content has not been fully processed, as depicted in Fig. 2.2. As Fig. 2.3 shows, ad cognitions are focused on enough to result in the formation of Aad; furthermore, prior affective antecedents of Aad are not thought to exert much influence. Brand cognitions play little or no role in the formation of brand attitude; instead Aad transfers over to A_B.

SUMMARY

Consideration of the antecedents of Aad has some important implications for advertisers. It has been argued that the two situations that may correspond to advertising pretesting are dual mode persuasion and contextual evaluation transfer. In both cases, Aad is hypothesized as playing a major role in the formation of brand attitude. Similarly, under pure affect transfer, which was argued to be the situation most representative of a "typical" advertising exposure, Aad was postulated to be a major causal influence. However, in the latter situation, as opposed to the former (pretest) situation, Aad is seen as emanating primarily from affective antecedents; the ad context has not been processed centrally. Thus, an advertiser attempting to base potential ad effectiveness decisions on pretest data may be working with a measure of Aad that is artificially polarized due to the pretest "set." The same ad viewed in a more naturalistic setting may not be accompanied by the same attitudinal reaction because it is processed only peripherally or, worse yet, not at all. There is considerable evidence that Aad influences brand attitudes in pretest situations but no evidence that it operates in naturalistic exposure settings. The present analysis suggests that even if Aad does operate in the consumer's "real world," it may operate differently than it appears based on research to date. The research challenge is to document the exact nature and magnitude of these differences if they do exist.

REFERENCES

Aaker, D. A., & Bruzzone, D. E. (1981). Viewer perceptions of prime-time television advertising. *Journal of Advertising Research, 21*(5), 15–23.

Aaker, D. A., & Norris, D. (1982). Characteristics of TV commercials perceived as informative. *Journal of Advertising Research, 22*(2), 61–70.

Axelrod, J. N. (1980). "Advertising wearout." *Journal of Advertising Research, 20*(5), 13–16.

Bartos, R., & Dunn, T. (1976). *The consumer view of advertising 1974.* New York: American Association of Advertising Agencies.

Batra, R., & Ray, M. L. (1983). Operationalizing involvement as depth and quality of cognitive response. In R. P. Bagozzi & A. M. Tybout (Eds.), *Advances in Consumer Research, Vol. X.* Ann Arbor: Association for Consumer Research, 309–13.

Bauer, R. A., & Greyser, S. A. (1968). *Advertising in America: The consumer view.* Boston: Harvard University.

Belch, G. E. (1981). An examination of comparative and noncomparative television commercials: The effects of claim variation and repetition on cognitive response and message acceptance. *Journal of Marketing Research, 18* (August), 33–49.

Belch, G. E. (1982). The effects of television commercial repetition on cognitive response and message acceptance. *Journal of Consumer Research, 9,* 56–65.

Burke, M., & Edell, J. A. (1982). *Exploring the multi-dimensional nature of attitude toward the ad.* Unpublished working paper. Duke University.

Calder, B. J., & Sternthal, B. (1980). Television commercial wearout: An information processing view. *Journal of Marketing Research, 17,* 173–86.

Cannon, H. M. (1982). A new method for estimating the effect of media context. *Journal of Advertising Research, 22*(5), 41–8.

Chaiken, S., & Eagly, A. H. (1983). Communication modality as a determinant of persuasion: The role of the communicator salience. *Journal of Personality and Social Psychology, 45,* 241–56.

Clancy, K. J., & Kweskin, D. W. (1971). TV commercial recall correlates. *Journal of Advertising Research, 11*(2), 18–20.

Crane, L. E. (1964). How product, appeal, and program affect attitudes toward commercials. *Journal of Advertising Research, 4*(2), 15–8.

Csikszentmihalyi, M., & Kubey, R. (1981). Television and the rest of life: A systematic comparison of subjective experience. *Public Opinion Quarterly, 45,* 217–28.

Fishbein, M., & Ajzen, I. (1975). *Belief, attitude, intention and behavior: An introduction to theory and research.* Reading, Mass.: Addison-Wesley.

Gardner, M. P., Mitchell, A. A., & Russo, J. E. (1978). Chronometric analysis: An introduction and an application to low involvement perception of advertisements. In H. K. Hunt (Ed.), *Advances in consumer research, Vol. V.* Ann Arbor: Assocation for Consumer Research, 581–9.

Gardner, M. P., & Raj, S. P. (1983). Responses to commercials in laboratory versus natural settings: A conceptual framework. In R. P. Bagozzi & A. M. Tybout (Eds.), *Advances in consumer research, Vol. X.* Ann Arbor: Association for Consumer Research, 142–6.

Gelb, B. D., & Pickett, C. M. (1983). Attitude-toward-the-ad: Links to humor and to advertising effectiveness. *Journal of Advertising, 12*(2), 34–42.

Gensch, D. H. (1970). "Media factors: A review article." *Journal of Marketing Research, 7,* 216–25.

Greenwald, A. G. (1968). Cognitive learning, cognitive response to persuasion and attitude change. In A. G. Greenwald, T. C. Brock, & T. M. Ostrom (Eds.), *Psychological foundations of attitudes.* New York: Academic Press, 147–70.

Hansen, F. (1972). *Consumer choice behavior: A cognitive theory.* New York: Free Press.

Kennedy, J. R. (1971). How program environment affects TV commercials. *Journal of Advertising Research, 11*(2), 33–8.

Lastovicka, J. L. (1983). Convergent and discriminant validity of television commercial rating scales. *Journal of Advertising, 12*(2), 14–23, 52.

Lastovicka, J. L., & Bonfield, E. H. (1982). Do consumers have brand attitudes? *Journal of Economic Psychology, 2*, 57–75.

Leavitt, C. (1970). A multidimensional set of rating scales for television commercials. *Journal of Applied Psychology, 54*, 427–9.

Leavitt, C. (1975). Theory as a bridge between description and evaluation of persuasion. In M. J. Schlinger (Ed.), *Advances in consumer research, Vol. II*. Chicago: Association for Consumer Research, 607–13.

Lutz, R. J., & MacKenzie, S. B. (1982). Construction of a diagnostic cognitive response model for use in commercial pretesting. In J. Chasin (Ed.), *Straight talk about attitude research*. Chicago: American Marketing Association, 145–56.

Lutz, R. J., MacKenzie, S. B., & Belch, G. E. (1983). Attitude toward the ad as a mediator of advertising effectiveness: Determinants and consequences. In R. P. Bagozzi & A. M. Tybout (Eds.), *Advances in consumer research, Vol. X*. Ann Arbor: Association for Consumer Research, 532–9.

MacKenzie, S. B., Lutz, R. J., & Belch, G. E. (in preparation). *The role of attitude toward the ad as a mediator of advertising effectiveness: A test of competing explanations.*

MacKenzie, S. B., & Lutz, R. J. (1983). Testing competing models of advertising effectiveness via structural equation models. *Proceedings,* Winter Educators' Conference. Chicago: American Marketing Association, 70–5.

McEwen, W. J., & Leavitt, C. (1976). A way to describe TV commercials. *Journal of Advertising Research, 16*(6), 35–9.

Mehotra, S., Van Auken, S., & Lonial, S. C. (1981). Adjective profiles in television copy testing. *Journal of Advertising Research, 21*(4), 21–5.

Messmer, D. J. (1979). Repetition and attitudinal discrepancy effects on the affective response to television advertising. *Journal of Business Research, 7*, 75–93.

Meyer-Hentschel, G. (1983). *An arousal profile for print ads*. Unpublished working paper, Institute for Consumer and Behavioral Research, University of the Saarland, West Germany.

Mitchell, A. A., & Olson, J. C. (1981). Are product attribute beliefs the only mediator of advertising effects on brand attitude? *Journal of Marketing Research, 18* (August), 318–32.

Moore, D. L., & Hutchinson, J. W. (1983). The effects of ad affect on advertising effectiveness. In R. P. Bagozzi & A. M. Tybout (Eds.), *Advances in consumer research, Vol. X*. Ann Arbor: Association for Consumer Research, 526–31.

Olson, D., Schlinger, M. J., & Young, C. (1982). How consumers react to new-product ads. *Journal of Advertising Research, 22*(3), 24–30.

Petty, R. E., & Cacioppo, J. T. (1981). *Attitudes and persuasion: Classic and contemporary approaches*. Dubuque: A. C. Brown.

Petty, R. E., Cacioppo, J. T., & Schumann, D. (1983). Central and peripheral routes to advertising effectiveness: The moderating role of involvement. *Journal of Consumer Research, 10*, 135–46.

Plummer, J. T. (1971). A theoretical view of advertising communication. *Journal of Communication, 21*, 315–25.

Puto, C. P., & Wells, W. D. (1984). Informational and transformational advertising: The differential effects of time. In T. Kinnear (Ed.), *Advances in consumer research, Vol. XI*. Provo, UT: Association for Consumer Research, 638–43.

Rokeach, M. (1968). *Beliefs, attitudes, and values*. San Francisco: Jossey-Bass.

Russell, J. A., & Mehrabian, A. (1977). Evidence for a three-factor theory of emotions. *Journal of Research in Personality, 11*, 273–94.

Schlinger, M. J. (1979a). Attitudinal reactions to advertisements. In John Eighmey (Ed.), *Attitude Research under the Sun*. Chicago: American Marketing Association, 171–97.

Schlinger, M. J. (1979b). A profile of responses to commercials. *Journal of Advertising Research, 19*(2), 37–46.

Schlinger, M. J., & Green, L. (1980). Art-work storyboards versus finished commercials. *Journal of Advertising Research, 20*(6), 19–23

Schlinger, M. J. R. (1982). Respondent characteristics that affect copy-test attitude scales. *Journal of Advertising Research, 22*(1), 29–35.

Schultz, D. E. (1979). Media research users want. *Journal of Advertising Research, 19*(6), 13–17.

Shimp, T. A. (1981). Attitude toward the ad as a mediator of consumer brand choice. *Journal of Advertising 10, 2,* 9–15.

Sissors, J. Z. & Petray, E. R. (1976). *Advertising media planning*. Chicago: Crain Books, 142–7.

Soldow, G. F., & Principe, V. (1981). Response to commercials as a function of program context. *Journal of Advertising Research, 21*(2), 59–65.

Srull, T. K. (1983). Affect and memory: The impact of affective reactions in advertising on the representation of product information and memory. In R. P. Bagozzi & A. M. Tybout (Eds.), *Advances in Consumer Research, Vol. X.* Ann Arbor: Association for Consumer Research, 520–5.

Webb, P. H. (1979). Consumer initial processing in a difficult media environment. *Journal of Consumer Research, 6,* 225–36.

Webb, P. H., & Ray, M. L. (1979). Effects of TV clutter. *Journal of Advertising Research, 19*(3), 7–12.

Weilbacher, W. M. (1960). The qualitative values of advertising media. *Journal of Advertising Research, 1*(1), 12–7.

Wells, W. D. (1980). "Liking" and sales effectiveness: A hypothesis. *Topline, 2*(1), 1–2.

Wells, W. D. (1964). EQ, son of EQ, and the reaction profile. *Journal of Marketing, 28*(4), 45–52.

Wells, W. D., Leavitt, C., & McConville, M. (1971). A reaction profile for TV commercials. *Journal of Advertising Research, 11*(6), 11–7.

Winick, C. (1962). Three measures of the advertising value of media context. *Journal of Advertising Research, 2*(3), 28–33.

Wright, P. L. (1973). The cognitive processes mediating acceptance of advertising. *Journal of Marketing Research, 4,* 53–62.

Wright, P. (1980). Message-evoked thoughts: Persuasion research using thought verbalizations. *Journal of Consumer Research, 7,* 151–75.

The Influence of Affective Reactions to Advertising: Direct and Indirect Mechanisms of Attitude Change

3

Danny L. Moore
J. Wesley Hutchinson
University of Florida

INTRODUCTION

The influence of affective reactions to advertising on consumer response is a recurring topic in advertising research. Perhaps the major reason for interest in this area is the common belief that consumers' general liking for an advertisement influences their attitudes toward the advertised product, purchase intentions, and eventual brand choices. The intuitive hypothesis advanced by many researchers is that pleasant, well-liked ads elicit more favorable reactions toward the product than unpleasant or irritating ads (Shimp, 1981). Explanations of the hypothesized positive relationship between the valance of affective reactions and brand attitude range from motivational theories to conditioning hypotheses (Gorn, 1982; Mitchell & Olson, 1981; Shimp, 1981). The common thread uniting these speculations is that the affect or feeling evoked by an ad is assumed to transfer *directly* to the advertised product.

Silk and Vavra (1974), in a review of early research, discuss the potential *indirect* effects of liking for an ad. They note that data collected by Schwerin in the 1940's revealed a J-shaped function between consumer response and ad affect. Both pleasant and unpleasant ads elicited higher response rates to a request than neutral, matter-of-fact ads. This finding suggested that the relative intensity of affective reactions may be more important for predicting consumer response than the valence of the reaction. The logic underlying this "law of extremes" hypothesis seems to hinge on two assumptions. First, affectively extreme ads are assumed to capture more attention than affectively neutral ads. This, in turn, should enhance memory for the informational components of the ad. Secondly, the feelings evoked by the ad are not expected to transfer directly to the product, or at worst, they are expected to be associated with the product only momentarily. Consequently, if improved memory for the informational content of the ad increases the persuasive value of the ad, then both unpleasant and pleasant ads should be more effective than neutral ads. In short, the law of extremes suggests that affective reactions to advertising exert an indirect influence on brand attitude by improving memory for information contained in the ad.

This chapter examines both the direct and indirect effects of affective reactions to advertising on brand attitude. Following a proposal initially made by Silk and Vavra (1974), we expect affective reactions to transfer directly to the brand at short delays following ad exposure. After longer delays, however, both liked and disliked ads should produce more positive attitudes toward the brand than neutral ads because: (1) initial reactions to the ad are not spontaneously recalled as associates to the brand, and (2) the positive influence of the informational content of affectively extreme ads will be more enduring than neutral ads. The empirical and conceptual basis for these predictions are discussed in the following section.

DIRECT AND INDIRECT INFLUENCES OF AD AFFECT ON BRAND ATTITUDE

Current research on attitude toward the ad provides relatively strong support for the direct mechanism noted above. This work indicates that the more well-liked an ad is, the more positive responses to the brand are (Lutz, MacKenzie, & Belch, 1983; MacKenzie & Lutz, 1982; Mitchell & Olson, 1981). However, brand attitude measures are generally collected immediately following ad exposure. Consequently, it is possible that the communicative value of disliked ads was overshadowed by highly salient affective responses at the time of measurement. With increasing delays affective responses may become less salient, and hence, brand attitude may become more positive. In short, we are suggesting that a "sleeper" effect may occur such that attitudinal responses to brands associated with unpleasant or irritating ads become more positive over time.

The "Sleeper" Effect and Ad Affect

The most frequently cited explanation of sleeper effects is the dissociative cue hypothesis (Cook & Flay, 1978; Cook, Gruder, Hennigan, & Flay, 1979). According to the dissociative cue hypothesis, persuasion cues that either enhance or hinder acceptance of a message (e.g., source credibilty) tend to become dissociated from the message over time. When attitudes are assessed immediately following exposure to a persuasive communication, message context cues are likely to be spontaneously recalled as associates to the message. After a sufficient delay spontaneous recall of message context cues should decline, and attitude judgements should be more closely associated with responses to message content. Thus, the general prediction of the dissociative cue hypothesis is that the impact of message *context* cues should decline with delay and the relative importance of reactions to message *content* should increase with delay. Despite several critiques of the "sleeper" effect (Capon & Hulbert, 1973; Gillig & Greenwald, 1974), it now appears that the general prediction of the dissociative cue hypothesis holds under certain conditions (Gruder, Cook, Hennigan, Flay, Alessis, & Halamaj, 1978; Pratkanis & Greenwald, this volume).

Three variants of the dissociative cue hypothesis appear in the literature on affective reactions on advertising. Silk and Vavra (1974), Ray (1973, 1982) and Moore and Hutchinson (1983) propose that the influence of ad affect on brand attitude decays as the time between exposure and measurement increases. If so, then the attention attracted to affectively extreme ads may strengthen the effects of advertising information and eventually lead to positive attitudes toward brands associated with both pleasant and unpleasant ads. This general prediction is depicted in Fig. 3.1. While all three variants of the dissociative cue hypothesis share the common predictions shown in Fig. 3.1, there are substantial differences in the processes postulated to control the delayed effects of ad affect on consumer response.

The critical notion underlying Silk and Vavra's (1974) hypothesis is that advertising messages that produce a strong, favorable reaction to the brand will be less effective when paired with an unpleasant, irritating presentation format. Over time, however, the probability that the presentation format, or reactions to the format, will be spontaneously associated with the message content should decline, but memory for the message should endure. Consequently, the persuasive power of the message eventually will overcome any detrimental effects of presentation format. An extreme form of this hypothesis implies that the negative effects of presentation format and the positive effects of message content are mutually exclusive. That is, as long as the negative reactions to the presentation format are spontaneously associated with the brand, it is these reactions, and not message content, that contribute to brand evaluation. Once these reactions have become dissociated from the brand, however, then message content has an effect. If so, then any manipulation that lowers the probability that negative reactions will be recalled should increase the effectiveness of message content regardless of the delay between exposure and measurement.

Clearly, the process hypothesized by Silk and Vavra hinges upon several key assumptions. First, recipients must be motivated to attend to the informational content of the ad and be capable of correctly interpreting the infor-

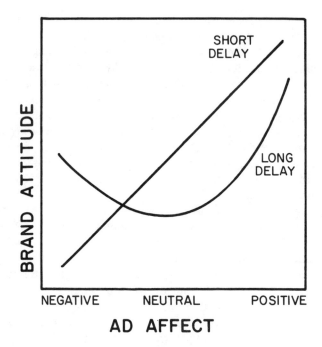

FIG. 3.1.   Hypothesized Relationship Between Ad Affect and Change in Brand Attitude for Different Amounts of Delay Between Ad Exposure and Brand Evaluation.

mation. This seems most likely to occur under high involvement conditions
(cf. Petty & Cacioppo, 1979). Secondly, affective reactions to the ad should
not alter interpretations of message content; otherwise, memory for the informational content of the message will differ for pleasant and unpleasant
ads. Finally, dissociation of affective reactions to the ad from the brand
name should be less likely as repetition of the ad increases. That is, repetition
is expected to strengthen the associative link between reactions to the ad and
the brand name.

   A learning theory interpretation of the sleeper effect is offered by Ray
(1973). Ray's central argument is that the forgetting curve for the source of a
message is steeper than the forgetting curve for the content of the message.
Presumably, this occurs because the message contains greater redundancy,
which facilitates learning. In an advertising setting, Ray's hypothesis leads to
the prediction that recall of message details should, at some point, exceed recall of message context cues because the former are more well learned.

   The primary difference between Silk and Vavra's "revised" sleeper hypothesis and Ray's learning theory interpretation concerns the role of message
context cues. Silk and Vavra argue that the probability that a context cue will
be *spontaneously* associated with the brand declines over time. Ray, on the

other hand, proposes that such cues are forgotten. However, the constraints on the sleeper effect discussed with respect to Silk and Vavra's hypothesis also apply to Ray's learning theory approach. Specifically, involvement in processing the message is implicitly assumed to be high; message context cues are not expected to interact with learning of message arguments or interpretations of the arguments; and advertising repetition is thought to weaken the sleeper effect.

The sleeper hypothesis advanced by Moore and Hutchinson (1983) is based on three assumptions. First, affective reactions, regardless of valence, should enhance brand awareness. This assumption is indirectly supported by the finding that stimuli eliciting affectively extreme reactions are recalled more frequently that stimuli eliciting little or no reaction (Dutta & Kanungo, 1975). We do not necessarily assume that brand names paired with positive or negative ads must be *recalled* more frequently than those paired with neutral ads, although this is likely. Our principal assertion is that extreme ads enhance brand awareness — that is, the feeling that one has seen or heard of a brand before (cf. Batra & Ray, 1983; Ray, 1982). Since this is a response to the brand name and requires little or no search of memory, it is perhaps the simplest type of memory effect.

The second assumption in our model is that brand awareness and brand attitude are positively correlated. Specifically, brands that achieve higher recognition scores should be given more favorable ratings than less easily recognized brands. This conjecture is supported by two types of research. First, Axelrod (1968) and Haley and Case (1979) report a positive relationship between brand recall (i.e., top-of-mind awareness) and brand attitude. Second, familiar stimuli, or stimuli that we are repeatedly exposed to, are given higher ratings on attitude scales than less familiar stimuli (Harrison, 1977; Zajonc, 1968, 1980). Thus, we expect brand attitude to increase with brand awareness.

The third assumption in our model is that changes in brand awareness are more enduring than reactions to advertising. If so, then one would eventually expect the impact of ad affect on brand attitude to decline with delay, while the weight given to brand awareness in attitudinal reactions should increase. There are at least two reasons why brand awareness should exert more enduring effects on attitudes and purchase decisions than ad-evoked feelings. The first is that brand names are usually salient retrieval cues during evaluation or purchase. Since brand awareness relies on recognition processes, one would expect the evaluation or decision situation to activate automatically a familiarity or awareness code in memory. Ad affect, however, must be retrieved as an associate to the brand name. Thus, brand awareness may have a more enduring influence on attitudes than ad affect because recognition performance decreases more slowly than recall (cf. Crowder, 1976). Brand awareness may also exert a more enduring effect on attitudes because cues in the retrieval environment favor the recall of brand-related information. During exposure to advertising or in undisguised ad test situations consumers are likely to encode both brand-related and ad-specific information (e.g., liking for the ad) either because they do not view the ad with the sole objective of evaluating the brand or because ad execution factors direct attention toward affectively valenced stimuli (e.g., an attractive model). However, in evaluation or purchase situations ad-specific information is less salient and processing objectives favor recall of brand-related information. Hence, when brands are evaluated well after ad exposure in a more natural context, ad-specific information is more difficult to recall and if it is recalled it is not likely to be weighted as heavily as it was in the exposure context. Therefore, the impact of ad affect relative to brand awareness should be lower for delayed measures.

In summary, our sleeper hypothesis is similar to previous ones in that we predict that ad affect is dissociated from the brand over time. However, we do not assume that persuasive copy points must be recalled in order to obtain a more positive appraisal of brands associated with negative ads. Instead, significant increases in brand awareness are expected to be sufficient for a sleeper effect when coupled with a decline in the accessibility of ad affect.

AD AFFECT AND BRAND AWARENESS — AN EXPERIMENT

Empirical evidence concerning the delayed impact of ad affect on brand attitude is scarce. Silk and Vavra (1974) exposed subjects to either a hard-sell or soft-sell version of a radio ad. They found that brand awareness was greater for the hard-sell commercial than the soft-sell commercial. In addition, brand preference for the advertised product was greater for the hard-sell commercial than for the soft-sell commercial when measured after a delay interval following exposure. However, other measures of attitude toward the brand revealed no differences between experimental and control groups. Finally, Silk and Vavra reported that repetition interacted with the hard-sell/ soft-sell treatment such that the advantage of the hard-sell ads on the brand preference measure disappeared with repetitions. Thus, Silk and Vavra's findings support our basic assumption to but fail to find strong effects of either brand awareness or ad affect on brand attitude.

In a previous study (Moore & Hutchinson, 1983) we found evidence supporting the hypothesized relationships among brand awareness, ad affect, and brand attitude. Subjects in the study initially related the likelihood that they would consider each of 80 brands for purchase as well as their familiarity with the brands. Brand awareness was assessed by asking subjects to choose the product category associated with the 80 brand names. Correct identification of the product category was assumed to be indicative of familiarity with the brand. Next, 40 print ads for brands contained in the initial rating set were displayed for 10 seconds. During this time, ratings of affective reactions to the ads were collected with ratings of ad familiarity. Following ad exposure, brand consideration and familiarity measures were collected immediately, and at two- and seven-day delays. The critical results in this study were: (1) Both immediately following ad exposure and at two days delay, change in brand consideration ratings (measured from the preexposure baseline) were a positive, linear function of ad affect; (2) at seven days delay, change in brand consideration was a J-shaped function of ad affect — both negative and positive ads led to higher ratings of brand consideration than neutral ads; and finally, (3) the proportion of correct brand-product associations was also a J-shaped function of ad affect at seven days delay.

Although these results were encouraging, we were reluctant to draw strong conclusions from them due to two significant weaknesses in the experimental design. First, both affective reactions to the stimuli and brand awareness were post hoc measures and were not explicitly manipulated. Second, our measures of brand awareness (i.e., product class knowledge) and brand attitude (i.e., purchase consideration), although appropriate, were not the most conceptually direct measures of their respective hypothetical constructs. This latter problem is easily corrected (see below); however, the former problem is pervasive in advertising research and affords no simple solution. At the heart of the problem is the fact that emotional reactions to stimuli selected from actual or realistic advertising vary tremendously from person to person (see Silk & Vavra, 1974); thus, it is extremely difficult to manipulate ad affect systematically and reliably across individuals. Reliable manipulations of affective reaction typically come at a cost in terms of external validity (e.g., Gorn, 1982). In light of this problem, we decided to adopt a dualistic approach. We initiated one line of research that maintained the realistic stimuli used in our first study (again measuring ad affect post hoc), focusing only on the role of brand familiarity in mediating the delayed effects of ad affect. A second line of research is currently under way that simplifies the advertising stimuli to name/picture pairs so that affect and familiarity can be independently and reliably varied across individuals. Only the first of these research streams is discussed here.

The results of Silk and Vavra's (1974) study coupled with our initial work suggest that the influence of ad affect on brand attitude may change as a function of time. This evidence is admittedly weak, however. Silk and Vavra report no significant impact of ad affect on brand attitude, but a significant effect for brand awareness. In our initial study we found the predicted delayed effects of ad affect on brand attitude and brand awareness. However, this study did not examine whether brand awareness mediated the delayed relationship. Therefore, we felt that it was necessary to replicate the initial study and experimentally manipulate brand awareness in order to determine the plausibility of an indirect mechanism.

Overview and Hypotheses of the Experiment

The purpose of this experiment was to replicate and extend the findings of our initial work. Therefore, the procedures involved in this experiment closely resemble those of our first study. However, unlike the first study we manipulated initial awareness of brand names by exposing one group of subjects repeatedly to the names of products depicted in the ads, and another group to unrelated brand names. We expected the experimental manipulation to create equal levels of awareness for all brand names and thus, to attenuate the indirect effects of affectively extreme ads on brand awareness. The specific hypotheses tested in the experiment were:

1. Brand awareness and ratings of emotional reactions to the ad are curvilinearly related such that both negative and positive ads produce greater increments in brand awareness than neutral ads;
2. Attitude toward the brand and rated purchase likelihood are linearly related to ratings of emotional reactions to the ad immediately following exposure, but curvilinearly related for delayed measures;
3. Prior familiarity or awareness of a brand attentuates the indirect effect of ad affect on brand attitude by creating equal levels of brand awareness for positive, neutral, and negative ads. This hypothesis predicts a main effect for prior exposure to brand names and an interaction between exposure and ad affect for brand awareness measures (see below);
4. The amount of variance in brand attitude ratings accounted for by brand awareness increases with delay while the variance accounted for by emotional reactions to the ad decreases with delays. Variants of this hypothesis are examined to test specific memory models of how the direct and indirect effects of affective reactions change over time.

Procedures

A sample of 169 introductory marketing students participated in two evening experimental sessions. The first session lasted about 90 minutes. After an initial briefing, participants completed a two-part questionnaire, which we will refer to as Brand Test 1, the first part of which assessed self-reported brand familiarity (Brand Familiarity) and knowledge of the product class associated with the brand (Brand Knowledge) for each of 40 brands, listed in a random order.[1] The response scale for Brand Familiarity was unusual in its emphasis on mere brand name familiarity since this aspect of brand familiarity was experimentally manipulated. It was structured as a seven point scale of familiarity with each level defined explicitly, as follows.

1. No familiarity;
2. Brand name only;
3. Brand name and vague impression of product class;
4. Brand name and product class only;
5. Brand name, product class, and low specific knowledge;
6. Brand name, product class, and moderate specific knowledge;
7. Brand name, product class, and high specific knowledge.

Following the Brand Familiarity scale, there was a blank provided for recording the name of the product class associated with the brand, if the respondent had any idea what it was.

Part 2 assessed Brand Liking and Purchase Likelihood for each of the same 40 brands, again listed in a random order. Both measures were seven point scales. The midpoint of the Brand Liking scale was defined as neutrality, with lower points indicating negative attitudes and higher points indicating positive attitudes. The midpoint of the Purchase Likelihood scale was defined as "neither more nor less likely than other brands in the class," with higher and lower points indicating higher and lower likelihoods. Respondents were instructed that they could refer back to previous judgements while they were completing Part 1 if they so desired, but once they had begun Part 2, they were not to refer back to Part 1. This procedure was included to minimize method covariance between the familiarity and attitude measures.

Following Brand Test 1, participants were trained for free recall of twenty brand names. The training consisted of studying a randomized list of the brand names for two minutes, followed by a three minute free recall period. This procedure was repeated twice. Recall on the third trial was generally very good (overall mean recall was 83%). This list of brand names to be memorized was one of three types: (1) 20 of the 40 rated brands which were to appear subsequently in ad exposures, (2) 20 of the 40 rated brands which would be omitted from ad exposure, and (3) 20 brands that had not been rated and would not occur in subsequent ad exposures. This treatment is referred to as Training and the three list types are called Same, Different and Other, respectively. As noted earlier, the intent of the training was to bring mere brand

---

[1]The 40 brands consisted of brands that were associated with the twenty most positively and twenty most negatively rated ads. The 80 ads in the first study were chosen to minimize initial brand familiarity and to span the range of affective reactions.

name familiarity to a maximum for some brands. If brand name familiarity is a valid operationalization of brand awareness, and if, as hypothesized earlier, brand awareness is mediating the effects of extreme affective reactions to ads, then this pretreatment should nullify the effect in the Same condition by making the brand names equally familiar, regardless of the affective reaction to the ad. Figure 3.2 illustrates the intended effect of Training. The actual effects of this manipulation were somewhat different from this and are discussed in more detail below.

After the training, participants were shown slides of actual print advertisements for 20 of the 40 rated brands. The 40 brands had been randomly split in half, and two randomized orders of presentation of each half were used across participants. Each ad was displayed for 20 seconds. During this time, participants rated their familiarity with the ad (Ad Familiarity) and their emotional reactions to the ad (Ad Affect) on seven point scales. The Ad familiarity scale ranged from "definitely not seen before" to "definitely have seen before." The Ad Affect scale ranged from "very negative" to "very positive" and the midpoint was defined to be neutral. Examples of negative reactions (e.g., offensive, irritating, etc.) and positive reactions (e.g., humorous, heart-warming, etc.) were given in the instructions. No brand names were included on the response forms.

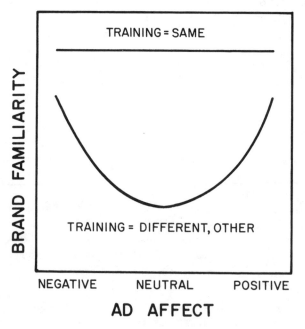

FIG. 3.2.   Hypothesized Relationship Between Ad Affect and Change in Brand Familiarity for the Three Types of Brand Name Training.

Following exposure to the ads participants were given a distractor task of memorizing 20 extraneous brand names in order to remove recency effects from the subsequent ad recall. Then approximately 5 minutes were given for free (unaided) recall of the brand names of the products in the ads. Finally, cued (aided) recall of the ads was measured. Participants were given a list of 80 brand names (i.e., names from all three Training conditions as well as the 20 extraneous names used in the distractor task) and were instructed to circle the names associated with the advertisements they had just seen.

Participants were randomly assigned to an intersession delay of either two or seven days. The first task of the second session was Brand Test 2. This questionnaire was identical to Brand Test 1 except that the ordering of the brands in each part was newly randomized. Following the Brand Test, free recall and cued recall of the ads were assessed just as they were in the first session. The second session typically lasted 30 minutes or less.

Summary of the Design.   The overall design of the study included two between-subjects factors, Training (same, other and different) and Delay (two- or seven-days), and Ad Affect as a within-subjects factor. Ad affect was measured rather than manipulated due to the considerations noted above. In addition to the major experimental factor, several list orders were used to randomize stimulus presentation. Since there were no effect of the randomization procedures on any of the dependent variables, only the effects of the experimental factors are reported here.

Results

The data were pretreated in three ways prior to analysis. First, different scores for brand familiarity, brand knowledge, brand liking, and purchase likelihood were computed by subtracting Brand Test 1 values from Brand Test 2. The purpose of this procedure was to control for the likely prior experience that respondents had with the product categories. Secondly, means for each difference variable were obtained for each level of Ad Affect on a within subject basis. Thus, each subject could potentially contribute seven data points to the analysis on each measure. However, many subjects did not use each level of the ad affect scale at least once, and consequently, some non-orthogonality was present in the data. Finally, preliminary analyses of the data revealed that the critical hypothesized effects were more evident when initial familiarity with the brand was low. This finding is consistent with our hypothesis that indirect effects are mediated by changes in brand name familiarity. Therefore, in all of the analyses that follow, data were included for a given respondent only for brands for which no product category was given in the Brand Knowledge question of Brand Test 1.

Brand Attitude. Overall, the results of this study were similar to those of the first study (Moore & Hutchinson, 1983). We expected Ad Affect to interact with Delay such that the attitudes associated with negative ads became more positive with time; attitudes associated with positive ads became less positive with time; and attitude associated with neutral ads exhibited no effect of delay (Hypothesis 2). Thus, a sleeper effect was expected, and the nature of the effect of Ad Affect on Brand Liking over time was expected to shift from a relatively linear pattern to a curvilinear pattern. Figure 3.3 displays attitude change (i.e., inter-session differences in Brand Liking and Purchase Likelihood) as a function of Ad Affect for the two Delay conditions. The pattern of these means, although consistent with Hypotheses 2, is nevertheless somewhat peculiar. The expected interaction is limited to the two extreme values of Ad Affect (i.e., ads rated 1 or 7). Overall, this interaction is not statistically significant; however, the contrast testing the interaction specifically at the extreme points is significant for both Brand Liking and Purchase Likelihood $F(1,425) = 7.32$, $p < .01$, and $F(1,420) = 10.20$, $p < .01$, respectively). The main effect of Ad Affect was also statistically significant for the two dependent measures ($F(6,425) = 5.84$, $p < .01$ and $F(6,420) = 2.35$, $p < .05$, respectively).

We believe that there are at least two potential reasons why the expected linear/curvilinear interaction was not more robust. First, even though we preselected the ads to be affectively extreme, there seem to have been too few genuinely extreme affective reactions. This may be a result of the medium (print is generally regarded as less emotionally involving than broadcast media) or the fact that actual ads were used (ads that generate significant negative affect seldom get beyond the copy test phase of production). Second, Training did not have precisely the effect that was intended. Participants in a pilot study for this experiment had told us that because of the intensive training on brand names, they were very sensitive to brand names in the ads. In fact, they were specifically looking for them. Initially, our assessment of this was that it would probably heighten the effects of brand name familiarity and thus make our manipulations stronger.

Brand Familiarity and Brand Knowledge. The obtained effects of Training on Brand Familiarity and Brand Knowledge are shown in Fig. 3.4. The main effects of Training were as expected and statistically significant ($F(2,129) = 4.27$, $p < .03$, for Brand Familiarity, and $F(2,130) = 7.22$, $p < .01$, for Brand Knowledge). That is, rated Brand familiarity and Brand knowledge were greater for the Same condition than for Different and Other. The expected main effect of Ad Affect and the expected interaction of Ad Affect and Training, however, were not obtained (compare Figs. 3.2 and 3.4). In fact, there was no significant effect of Ad Affect on the two familiarity variables, which is inconsistent with Hypothesis 1. Apparently, Training sen-

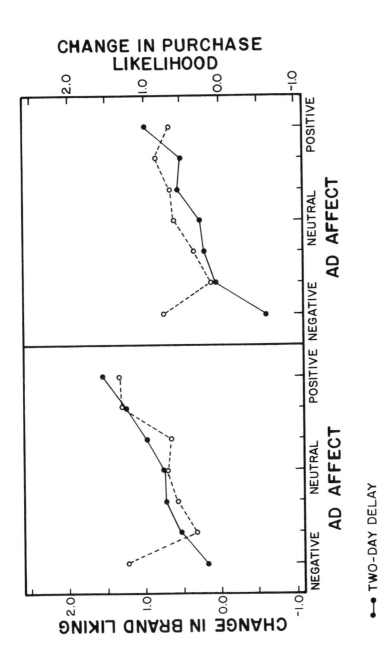

FIG. 3.3. Obtained Relationship Between Ad Affect and Change in Brand Attitude for Different Amounts of Delay Between Ad Exposure and Brand Evaluation.

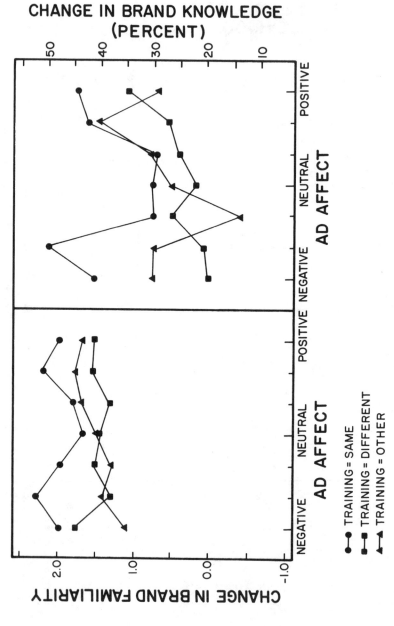

FIG. 3.4.   Obtained Relationship Between Ad Affect and Change in Brand Familiarity for the Three Types of Brand Name Training.

sitized participants to brand names in general as well as those they were specifically trained on, and therefore, the effects of Ad Affect on brand name familiarity were not selectively maximized. If anything, the curves are flattest when the Training condition was Different or Other. This is exactly the opposite of the intended effect (see Hypothesis 3). Perhaps this is due to proactive interference of Training brands on memory for ad exposure brands when they are not the same. In any case, this general sensitization to brand names would obviously disrupt the hypothesized indirect mechanism (i.e., brand awareness) in all conditions.

Further Tests of the Direct and Indirect Mechanisms (Hypothesis 4). Fortunately, although the first link in the indirect mechanism (i.e., the relationship between affective reactions to advertising and brand awareness) was disrupted, the second link (i.e., the relationship between brand awareness and brand attitude) was still open to investigation with these data. Theorizing about sleeper effects has emphasized the importance of forgetting certain aspects of the message context. In the present situation, one plausible hypothesis is that as long as the ad can be retrieved during brand evaluation, there is a direct transfer of ad affect to the brand. Only when retrieval fails does the increment in brand familiarity have a positive effect on brand attitude. Under this hypothesis, the two mechanisms are *mutually exclusive* for any particular brand evaluation. That is, various associations in memory involving the brand result from exposure to the ad. During brand evaluation, if these associations are traced to the ad they will transfer affective reactions from the ad to the brand, but the increased brand awareness will not have an effect on brand evaluation. Conversely, if they are not traced to the ad, then the increased brand awareness will have a positive effect. This hypothesis results in at least three testable predictions. There should be no effect of Delay if the retrievability of the ad is held constant (Prediction ME.1). An effect of Ad Affect should occur only when retrieval succeeds (Prediction ME.2), while an effect of Brand Familiarity should occur only when retrieval fails (Prediction ME.3).

A second plausible hypothesis is that both mechanisms are always operative, but they have differential "decay" curves. The direct mechanism has a stronger immediate effect followed by fast decay. The indirect mechanism has only moderate initial effects, but these effects are more persistent (see Hutchinson & Moore, in press). The implications of this hypothesis are dependent on precisely what is hypothesized to decay with time. If it is assumed that *affective components* of evaluation including and affect, once formed, persist independently of their antecedents (cf. Lichtenstein & Srull, this volume), then the retrievability of ad information should not affect attitude change for either the direct or the indirect mechanisms. The hypothesis in this case is essentially that at exposure the emotional/evaluative reaction to the ad produces an affective component for brand evaluation that is relatively stronger, but less persistent than the concomitant increment in brand awareness. This predicts that the effects of Ad Affect and Brand Familiarity will decrease differentially with Delay (Prediction AC.1), but not retrievability (Prediction AC.2).

A third related hypothesis assumes, as does the Mutual Exclusion Hypothesis, that *ad specific information* must be retrieved in order for there to be an effect of the direct mechanism. The indirect mechanism, however, is independent of ad retrieval. Again differential decay rates are assumed. In this case, the effect of Ad Affect would occur only when retrieval succeeds, regardless of Delay (Prediction AI.1), and Delay would diminish the effect of Brand Familiarity regardless of retrievability (Prediction AI.2). Schematic diagrams of the three hypotheses are given in Fig. 3.5.

In order to test these hypotheses with the present data some measure of the retrievability of ad specific information is necessary. The most appropriate of the various ad memory measures used in the study is Cued Ad Recall (Session 2). The cue used in this measure is simply the brand name, as is presumably the case in brand evaluation. There are some limitations, however. Subjects were not instructed to retrieve ad information in the Brand Tests and recalling that there was an ad for a particular brand is no guarantee that either the affective reaction to the ad or sufficient affect-generating information from the ad was also recalled. Thus, for a variety of reasons, it is possible that the direct mechanism was inoperative during Brand Test 2 even though subsequent Cued Ad Recall was successful. The converse, however, is much less likely. That is, if there was successful retrieval of any significant ad information during the Brand Test, it is highly unlikely that subsequent Cued Ad Recall would fail. Thus, Cued Ad Recall is a reasonable post hoc measure of the retrievability of ad specific information during brand evaluation; however, it is likely to be a better measure of the failure to retrieve ad information.

Bearing the above discussion in mind, a nine-term regression model was fit separately to the Brand Liking and Purchase Likelihood measures for data from the two Delay Groups. The purpose of the analysis was to test the predictions of the three hypotheses, concentrating on the effects of Delay and retrievability (i.e., Cued Ad Recall). The regression equation contained four first-order variables, four second-order variables, and an additive constant. The four first-order variables were dummy variables for Stimulus Set (i.e., which of the two 20 ad subsets served as the exposure set), Training (i.e., two dummy variables for the three levels of Brand Name Training), and Cued Ad Recall (i.e., Successful vs. Unsuccessful). These variables were not critical for testing the hypotheses; they were used to remove systematic variance from the error term. The four second-order variables were Ad Affect (Successful Cued Ad Recall), Ad Affect (Unsuccessful Cued Ad Recall), Brand

Familiarity (Successful Cued Ad Recall), and Brand Familiarity (Unsuccessful Cued Ad Recall). Values for the successful Cued Ad Recall variables were derived by subtracting the appropriate experimental cell mean from the observed value of Ad Affect and Brand Familiarity when the ad was successfully recalled on the cued recall test; if the ad was not recalled, the value of the Successful Cued Ad Recall variables were set to zero. A similar procedure was followed in deriving values for the Unsuccessful Cued Ad Recall variables, except, zero values were assigned to successfully recalled ads. This procedure produced three desirable properties in the critical second-order varia-

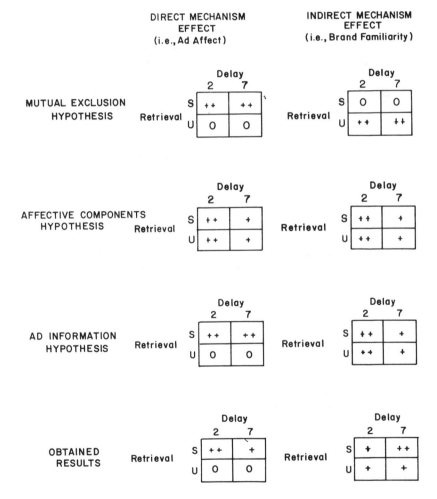

FIG. 3.5.   Predictions of Three Alternative Hypotheses about Direct and Indirect Mechanism Effects, and the Obtained Results.

bles: (1) the variables were uncorrelated with experimental treatment effects, (2) the variables were uncorrelated with one another, and finally, (3) the regression coefficients for the variables reflect whether or not Ad Affect and Brand Familiarity are related to Liking and Purchase Likelihood when ads are successfully or unsuccessfully recalled.

Since the hypotheses being tested pertain to changes in the regression coefficients of each second-order variable over time, unstandardized regression coefficients are reported (see Table 3.1).[2] Also since the correlations between the four second-order variables wee either equal to zero by definition, or were close to zero empirically, the unstandardized coefficients for the same variable can be interpreted as an index of the contributions of that variable over time. The unstandardized regression coefficients for both first- and second-order variables are given in Table 3.1. Our discussion of these results pertains only to the second-order variables because these are the only variables critical for testing the indirect and direct mechanism hypothesis.

The pattern of regression coefficients for Ad Affect and Brand Familiarity are consistent for both dependent measures, so they are not discussed separately. There are three aspects of the obtained coefficients that are relevant to our hypotheses. First, there is no effect of Ad Affect unless Cued Ad Recall succeeded. This contradicts prediction AC.1 of the Affective Component Decay Hypothesis since it predicts no effect of retrievability. This is, however, predicted by the other two hypotheses (i.e., ME.2 and AI.1). Second, the effect of Ad Affect diminishes with time for brands with successful Cued Ad Recall. This argues against the Mutual Exclusion Hypothesis (ME.1) and the Ad Information Decay Hypothesis (AI.1). It is not strong disconfirmation since, as was discussed earlier, successful Cued Ad Recall does not necessarily require retrieval of the information that would be required in the direct mechanism. In fact, since any memory trace from the ad leads to successful Cued Ad Recall, retrieval failure for relevant ad information typically occurs *earlier* than cued recall failure. Therefore, the decrease in the effectiveness of Ad Affect is consistent with those models once the measure of retrievability is taken into account. A more problematic result for the Mutual Exclusion Hypothesis is that Brand Familiarity has a significant, and non-

---

[2] When the inter-correlations between the independent variables in a regression equation are close to zero, as they are here, the unstandardized regression coefficient is a particularly robust index of the absolute contribution of each variable. It is not affected by changes in error variance, changes in the variances of the other variables or changes in the correlations between the other independent variables and the dependent variable. The standardized regression coefficient and the correlation coefficient, on the other hand, can be strongly affected by such extraneous changes. The reason for this is analogous to the reason for the robustness of the unstandardized regression coefficient when the range of variation is restricted (see Cohen & Cohen, 1975, pp. 64–66). Essentially, all extraneous changes in the variances of the dependent and independent variables will be exactly compensated by reciprocal changes in the correlation coefficient, leaving the unstandardized regression coefficient unaffected.

TABLE 3.1
Unstandardized Coefficients from a Regression Analysis of Brand Attitude Change

	Dependent Variables			
	2-Day Delay		7-Day Delay	
	Liking	*Purchase*	*Liking*	*Purchase*
First-order Variables				
Stimulus Set	.012[a]	.323	− .451	− .425
	(.144)	(.148)	(.147)	(.149)
Cued Recall	.734	.338	.665	.554
	(.145)	(.150)	(.148)	(.150)
Training (Same)	.178	.047	− 1.86	− .382
	(.186)	(.189)	(.181)	(.184)
Training (Other)	.297	.489	.197	.554
	(.176)	(.181)	(.171)	(.173)
Second-order Variables				
"Direct Mechanism" Effects:				
Ad Affect (Successful Cued Recall)	.308	.233	.142	.108
	(.062)	(.064)	(.061)	(.062)
Ad Affect (Unsuccessful Cued Recall)	.031	.024	.049	.024
	(.070)	(.074)	(.068)	(.069)
"Indirect Mechanism" Effects:				
Brand Familiarity (Successful Cued Recall)	.322	.186	.478	.371
	(.057)	(.059)	(.058)	(.058)
Brand Familiarity (Unsuccessful Cued Recall)	.285	.141	.312	.016
	(.110)	(.114)	(.101)	(.103)
Intercept	.210	− .507	1.21	.940
	(.267)	(.279)	(.268)	(.272)
Model Statistics:				
F	11.56	5.69	14.99	11.10
Variance Accounted For	18.2%	10.0%	21.2%	16.6%
df	424	416	453	453

[a]Coefficients that differ significantly from zero ($p < .05$) are underlined and standard errors are given in parentheses below each coefficient.

decreasing, effect regardless of the amount of delay or the success of cued re-call. Under the mutual exclusion hypothesis, an effect should be found only when Cued Ad Recall fails (ME.3). Taking the imperfections of Cued Ad Re-call into account does not help since a greater effect of Brand Familiarity when Cued Ad Recall fails would still be predicted. On the other hand, the ef-fect of Brand Familiarity actually increases with time for brands associated with successful Cued Ad Recall. Both decay hypotheses have difficulty ex-plaining this (see AC.2 and AI.2), patricularly since this is exactly the condi-tion in which the effect of Ad Affect decreases, suggesting mutual exclusion.[3]

Since none of the three hypotheses is entirely consistent with the results, some synthetic view must be sought. The most striking aspects of the ob-tained regression coefficients are that (1) Ad Affect had an effect only when Cued Ad Recall was successful, while Brand Familiarity had a significant ef-fect regardless of Cued Ad Recall, (2) the effectiveness of Brand Familiarity increased over time when Cued Ad Recall was successful, while the effective-ness of Ad Affect declined over time in this situation. Given this, some ver-sion of the Mutual Exclusion Hypothesis seemed most appropriate. In fact, the Mutual Exclusion Hypothesis can be retained if the following two as-sumptions are made: (1) a constant increment in brand familiarity resulted from the experimental session regardless of ad exposure, and (2) failures in Cued Ad Recall for the two-Day Delay were due mainly to encoding failures. The first assumption does not seem problematic since the Brand Test and Cued Ad Recall in Session 1 exposed each person to each brand name three times. The second assumption is much stronger than the first, but it too is plausible. It is possible that some proportion of the ads simply were not ef-fectively encoded at exposure. That is, strong elaborative brand associations in memory were not made at the time of exposure. This could have resulted from a variety of factors, including lack of attention to the ad, poor brand name salience and visual distraction from other ad elements. In any case, such ads are not likely to have any appreciable effect on brand attitude either directly or indirectly. If significant retrieval failures do not occur until after two days, but before seven, then the effect of Brand Familiarity should be in-sensitive to Cued Ad Recall after a two-Day Delay. After a seven-Day Delay, however, the effect of Brand Familiarity should reflect the substantial incre-ments in familiarity for brands where Cued Ad Recall succeeded, but re-trieval of the relevant ad specific information failed. We suggest that, al-though complicated, this explanation is plausible, and it is more consistent with these data than any of the others we have discussed.

---

[3]A constant effect of Brand Familiarity or Ad Affect is potentially attributable to method covariance, since these measures as well as Brand Liking and Purchase Likelihood were obtained from seven-point rating scales. The differential changes in the coefficients shown in Table 3.1 are not easily explained this way, however.

CONCLUSIONS

The results of the study reported above provide mixed support for our model. Consistent with our general hypothesis, the regression results indicated that the effects of ad effect decrease more rapidly with delay than the effects of brand awareness, which actually increased over time. Also, responses to brands associated with negative ads were more favorable after a seven-day delay. However, the results pertaining to the connection between ad affect and brand awareness were equivocal. Consequently, we cannot draw strong conclusions about the indirect mechanism in our model from this data.

The correlational nature of the design, combined with the failure of the familiarity manipulation, present additional constraints on our conclusions. Experiments that we are currently conducting should remedy these problems and provide a more rigorous test of our formulations. Despite the design problems we encountered in the present study, our results underscore the importance of memory in predicting the delayed affects of advertising. At the most general level, our work is based on the assumption that brand attitude is a function of information stored in memory. The more available a given item of information is, the more likely it is that the information will be used in formulating an opinion or attitude about the brand. If various types of information decay at different rates, then brand attitude should change with time, assuming that a differential amount of positive or negative information decays at a faster rate. The influence of memory on brand attitude seems to be a particularly fruitful area for future research since most purchase decisions do not occur immediately following exposure to an end.

Beyond the methodological difficulties inherent in research on the effects of ad affect, there are serious conceptual problems confronting future work in this area. Ad affect currently is somewhat poorly conceptualized. Part of the problem is that the concept has an unfortunate intuitive appeal. It seems easy to generate examples of consumers' feelings about an ad influencing their opinions and attitudes toward the advertised product. However, the causal significance of these feelings is unclear. Ads may be liked or disliked because the product itself evokes strongly held opinions. Moreover, there is little evidence concerning the construct validity of ad affect. This evidence can be obtained only in research where the affective qualities of the ad are experimentally manipulated. In short, future work on ad affect must necessarily turn to carefully controlled experiments rather than informative, but inferentially weak designs. This is precisely the problem we are addressing in our current research. Batra and Ray (this volume) also note that the concept of ad affect will benefit from careful consideration of its dimensionality. Many of the ideas they present concerning brand familiarity and conditioning effects of attitude toward the ad are consistent with our conceptualization. Finally, the source of attitude toward the ad is likey to have important effects on the causal links with brand attitude. Lutz (this volume) presents several ideas concerning what aspects of advertising are likely to generate attitudinal reactions. The next step in this line of thought is to determine how the source of attitude toward the ad influences brand attitude. It is quite possible that different sources of affective reactions are linked to brand attitude through different routes. If so, then it would seem fruitless to pursue research on the global effects of attitude toward the ad.

In sum, we suggest that both the valence and intensity of feeling evoked by an ad exert an influence on brand attitude. While we do not believe that ads are especially strong affective stimuli, we do believe that within the range of reactions to advertising, those ads on the poles of an affective continuum have a greater impact on brand familiarity than neutral, matter-of-fact advertising. It may be that extreme ads receive more attention at exposure or that associations resulting from those ads are stronger. In either case, the benefits of increased brand familiarity would seem to be particularly important for low involvement situations and for new, unfamiliar brands.

ACKNOWLEDGMENTS

Support for this research was provided by a summer research grant from the College of Business Administration and the Center for Econometric Decision Sciences at the University of Florida. The authors wish to express appreciation to Linda Alwitt, Joel Cohen, Richard J. Lutz and Andy Mitchell for comments on an earlier draft of the chapter.

REFERENCES

Axelrod, J. N. (1968). Advertising measures that predict purchase. *Journal of Advertising Research, 8,* 3–17.

Batra, R., & Ray, M. L. (1983) "Advertising situations: The implications of differential involvement and accompanying affect responses." In R. Harris (Ed.), *Information Processing Research in Advertising.* Hillsdale, N.J.: Lawrence Erlbaum Associates, 127–158.

Capon, N., & Hulbert, J. (1973). The sleeper effect — an awakening. *Public Opinion Quarterly, 37,* 333–358.

Cohen, J., & Cohen, P. (1975). *Applied multiple regression/correlation analysis for the behavioral sciences.* Hillsdale, N.J.: Lawrence Erlbaum Associates.

Cook, T. D., & Flay, B. R. (1978). The persistence of experimentally induced attitude change. In L. Berkowitz (Ed.), *Advances in experimental social psychology: Volume 11.* New York, NY: Academic Press, 1–57.

Cook, T. D., Gruder, C. L., Hennigan, K. M., & Flay, B. R. (1979). History of the sleeper effect: Some logical pitfalls in accepting the null hypothesis. *Psychological Bulletin, 86,* 662–679.

Crowder, R. G. (1976). *Principles of learning and memory.* Hillsdale, NJ: Lawrence Erlbaum Associates.

Dutta, S., & Kanungo, R. N. (1975). *Affect and memory: A reformulation.* Oxford: Pergamon Press.

Gillig, P., & Greenwald, A. G. (1974). Is it time to lay the sleeper effect to rest? *Journal of Personality and Social Psychology, 29,* 132–139.

Gorn, G. J. (1982). The effects of music in advertising on choice behavior: A classical conditioning approach. *Journal of Marketing, 46,* 94–101.

Gruder, C. L., Cook, T. D., Hennigan, K. M., Flay, B. R., Alessis, C., & Halamaj, J. (1978). Empirical tests of the absolute sleeper effect predicted from the discounting cue hypothesis. *Journal of Personality and Social Psychology, 36,* 1061–1074.

Haley, R. I., & Case, P. B. (1979). Testing thirteen attitude scales for agreement and brand discrimination. *Journal of Marketing, 43,* 20–32.

Harrison, A. A. (1977). Mere exposure. In L. Berkowitz (Ed.), *Advances in experimental social psychology: Volume 10.* New York: Academic Press, 39–83.

Hutchinson, J. W. and Moore, D. L. (in press) Issues surrounding the examination of delay effects in advertising. In T. Kinnear (Ed.), *Advances in consumer research,* Vol. II, Ann Abor: Association for Consumer Research.

Lutz, R. J., MacKenzie, S. B., & Belch, G. E. (1983). Attitude toward the ad as a mediator of advertising effectiveness: Determinants and consequences. In R. P. Bagozzi & A. M. Tybout (Eds.), *Advances in consumer research: Volume X.* Ann Arbor: Association for Consumer Research, 532–539.

MacKenzie, S. B., & Lutz, R. J. (1982). *Monitoring advertising effectiveness: A structural equation analysis of the mediating role of attitude toward the ad.* Working Paper No. 117, Center for Marketing Studies, University of California, Los Angeles.

Mitchell, A. A., & Olson, J. C. (1981). Are product attribute beliefs the only mediator of advertising effects on brand attitude? *Journal of Marketing Research, 18,* 318–332.

Moore, D. L., & Hutchinson, J. W. (1983). The effects of ad affect on advertising effectiveness. In R. P. Bagozzi & A. M. Tybout (Eds.), *Advances in consumer research: Volume X.* Ann Arbor: Association for Consumer Research, 526–531.

Petty, R. E., & Cacioppo, J. T. (1979). Issue involvement can increase or decrease persuasion by enhancing message-relevant thoughts. *Journal of Personality and Social Psychology, 37,* 1915–1926.

Ray, M. L. (1973). Psychological theories and interpretations of learning. In S. Ward & T. S. Robertson, *Consumer behavior: Theoretical sources* (pp. 45–117). Englewood Cliffs, NJ: Prentice-Hall, Inc.

Ray, M. L. (1982). *Advertising & communication management.* Englewood Cliffs, NJ: Prentice-Hall, Inc.

Shimp, T. A. (1981). Attitude toward the ad as a mediator of consumer choice behavior. *Journal of Advertising, 10,* 9–15.

Silk, A. J., & Vavra, T. G. (1974). The influence of advertising's affective qualities on consumer response. In D. Hughes & M. L. Ray (Eds.), *Buyer/consumer information processing.* Chapel Hill, NC: University of North Carolina Press, 157–186.

Zajonc, R. B. (1986). Additional effects of mere exposure. *Journal of Personality and Social Psychology Monograph Supplement, 9,* 1–27.

Zajonc, R. B. (1980). Feeling and thinking: Preference need no inferences. *American Psychologist, 35,* 151–175.

11 PERSUASION

4 Central and Peripheral Routes to Persuasion: The Role of Message Repetition

John T. Cacioppo
University of Iowa

Richard E. Petty
University of Missouri-Columbia

INTRODUCTION

People are subjected to a nearly constant barrage of persuasive appeals. Prior to fully awakening, individuals are exposed to radio announcers proclaiming the merits of various wares, television newsprograms that are all too frequently interrupted by flashy exhibitions of products, packages adorned with appeals regarding their contents, newspapers replete with announcements of seemingly never-ending sales, and billboards designed to change how you feel toward items ranging from toothpaste to political candidates. Apparently, people's exposure to persuasive appeals does not lessen as the day continues, either. Recent estimates place the average American as the target of over 1500 persuasive appeals per day from national advertisers alone (Will, 1982).

Given the costs involved in designing, testing, and producing effective communications, and the fact that the vast majority of the target audience is not exposed to any single presentation of an appeal, *repeated* presentations of persuasive communications are commonplace. In this chapter, we consider the cognitive and attitudinal effects of repeatedly presenting either the same or similar persuasive communications to individuals over a short period of time. There are several suppositions underlying our analysis that should be stated at the outset. First, given people's limited capacity for processing information and the deluge of persuasive communications to which people are exposed daily, we have assumed that people have neither the capability nor the motivation to attend to and deliberate upon all of the appeals to which they are exposed. In this regard, we are in agreement with Miller, Maruyama, Beaber, and Valone (1976), who noted almost a decade ago that:

> it may be irrational to rationally scrutinize the plethora of counterattitudinal messages received daily. To the extent that one possesses only a limited amount of information-processing time and capacity, such scrutiny would disengage the thought processes from the exigencies of daily life (p. 623).

We have also assumed, however, that individuals have neither the luxury of being able to, nor apparently the inclination to, ignore all these appeals. Anecdotal support for this assumption can be found in social phenomena such as a thriving multi-billion dollar advertising industry, the continued popularity and impact of religious orations, and the increasingly effective use of social surveys to tailor the appeals and appearances of political candidates to the electorate. Experimental support for this assumption is abundant in social psychology, where people have been found to express more agreement to appeals, even when the appeal has little personal relevance, when the communicator speaks quickly (Miller et al., 1976), the appeal emanates from an expert (Petty, Cacioppo, & Goldman, 1981) or attractive communicator (Chaiken, 1979; Norman, 1976), celebrities endorse the product (Petty, Cacioppo, & Schumann, 1983), and so forth (for a recent review, see Petty & Cacioppo, 1981).

THE ELABORATION LIKELIHOOD MODEL
OF PERSUASION

Several years ago, we outlined a framework with which to organize social psychological research on persuasion (Petty & Cacioppo, 1980, 1981). In this model, which is presented in Fig. 4.1, recipients are viewed as being neither invariantly cogitative nor universally mindless when dealing with persuasive appeals, but rather various factors, and combinations of factors, are viewed as determining people's motivation and ability to think carefully about the merits of the arguments for a recommendation. When conditions foster people's motivation *and* ability to engage in issue-relevant thinking, the *elaboration-likelihood* is said to be high. This means that people are likely to: (a) attend to the appeal; (b) attempt to access relevant associations, images, and experiences from memory; (c) scrutinize and elaborate upon the externally provided message arguments in light of the associations available from memory; (d) draw inferences about the merits of the arguments for a recommendation based upon their analysis of the data extracted from the appeal and ac-

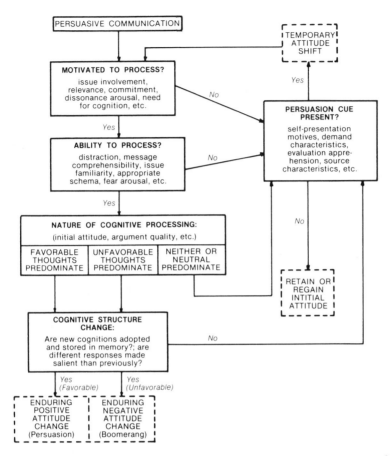

FIG. 4.1. The elaboration-likelihood model of attitude change. (Adapted from Petty & Cacioppo, 1981.)

cessed from memory; and (e) consequently derive an overall evaluation of, or attitude toward, the recommendation. This conceptualization suggests that, when the elaboration likelihood is high, there should be evidence for the allocation of cognitive resources to the persuasive appeal. Moreover, the resultant attitude is expected to be relatively enduring since the thoughts and associations from which it is derived are central to the attitude object and, as a result of the issue-relevant thinking, this attitude is an integrated part of the schema for the attitude object. Finally, the attitude is expected to be relatively predictive of subsequent behavior because: (a) the recipients are more likely to have related the incoming information to their previous experiences with and knowledge about the attitude object instilling more confidence in and willingness to act upon their attitudes; (b) achieved a temporally stable and accessible evaluation of the object, making it more likely that the measured attitude will be accessible at the point of behavior; and (c) considered appropriate actions regarding the attitude object across a wide range of personally relevant settings, minimizing the need for individuals to reconsider their attitude when faced with the costs of a relevant behavior.

As factors in the persuasive setting reduce the recipients' motivation or ability to think about an issue—as for example occurs when recipients view the appeal as being personally inconsequential (Petty & Cacioppo, 1979a, b), are engaged in a distracting task during their exposure to the appeal (Petty, Wells, & Brock, 1976), or possess little prior knowledge on the issue (Cacioppo & Petty, 1980b; Wood, 1982)—there is a reduction in the likelihood that the recipients will relate the incoming information to their prior knowledge about and experiences with the attitude object in an effort to evaluate the merits of the arguments for the recommendation. The notion is that when elaboration likelihood is low, recipients will either conserve their cognitive resources (e.g., napping during personally inconsequential television advertisements) or expend cognitive resources on another task (e.g., searching for a snack during the advertisement). If elaboration likelihood is near zero, then little or no attitude change will be forthcoming. If the elaboration likelihood is low (but not near zero), recipients adopt a strategy wherein they are more likely to attempt to derive a "reasonable" attitude based upon a superficial analysis of the recommendation. That is, when elaboration likelihood is low, the acceptance or rejection of the appeal is not based on the careful consideration of issue-relevant information, but rather it is based upon (a) the issue or object being associated with positive or negative cues, which have no intrinsic link to the attitude stimulus (e.g., although an attractive model can serve as an argument for the merits of a beauty production, it would more likely be a peripheral cue for a refrigerator); or (b) the recipients draw a single inference based upon various cues in the persuasion context (e.g., the more arguments for a recommendation, the better it must be).

We have suggested that there are central and peripheral routes to persuasion, with the "central route" representing the processes involved when elaboration likelihood is high and the "peripheral route" typifying the processes operative when elaboration likelihood is low. It should be apparent that these "routes" represent positions on a continuous dimension ranging from high to low elaboration likelihood rather than two mutually exclusive and exhaustive "types" of message processing. When elaboration likelihood is high, issue-relevant thinking tends to be the most direct determinant of the recipient's reactions to the recommendation, whereas when elaboration likelihood is low, the more important determinant of persuasion tends to be cues that, although perhaps peripheral to the personal merits of the appeal, allow the recipient to attain a reasonable position without diligently considering the merits of the specific recommendation.

An analogy may help to clarify the distinction we wish to draw between the processes involved when travelling the central versus peripheral route to persuasion. Consider first the case of a student who has studied diligently for an exam. The student knows the material over which he is being tested, reads each test question and set of answers, relates this incoming information to what he remembers about the material, attempts to integrate these various data, and selects the option that is judged to be the most veridical. This manner of processing the question posed to the student corresponds to the message processing we have suggested is invoked when elaboration likelihood is high in a persuasion context. There is no guarantee that the student's response will be correct or that his attempts to relate the material from the test question to the prior knowledge he has about the topic will necessarily be logical. However, the student's responses are more likely to be reliable (enduring) and correct than if his answers were based upon a simpler, peripheral analysis of the question. Note, too, that the student's comprehension of the question and prior knowledge of material relevant to the topic are viewed as being distal rather than proximal mediators of his response to the question; these factors affect how the student interprets, elaborates upon, and evaluates the incoming information, but it is the nature of the topic-relevant thinking that is viewed as being the most immediate determinant of the student's response to the question.

The responses of this student, who went through the effortful process of culling through data to evaluate the merits of the various options, can be *contrasted* with the reactions of a student who, either because he doesn't care (i.e., low motivation) or didn't study (i.e., low ability), reads each question and set of answers but fails to retrieve information from memory that is related specifically to the topic in question. The responses of this latter student generally are not random, but rather they are more likely to reflect the operation of simple and often times specious decisional rules evoked by peripheral cues, such as the position of the answer within the set of answers (e.g., "a" is seldom the correct answer) or previous responses (e.g., "b" was marked twice previously, so I'll try "c"). Note that the incoming information may still be related to prior knowledge, but this body of knowledge is largely irrelevant to the true merits of the person's various options. Thus, as the student's elaboration likelihood decreases, obvious features in the testing (persuasion) setting that signal which option (position) is likely to be acceptable or correct are more likely to be the target of information (attitudinal) processing — even though all of the externally provided information (message arguments) may well be comprehended, and these features are more likely to be related to associations that have no intrinsic link to the specific question (issue) under consideration.

Evidence in social psychology supports the view that different processes are involved under high and low elaboration likelihood conditions. For example, the quality of the arguments contained in a message has a greater impact on persuasion under conditions of high than low issue involvement (Petty & Cacioppo, 1979a, b; Petty, Cacioppo, & Heesacker, 1981) and for individuals high than low in need for cognition (Cacioppo, Petty, & Morris, 1983). Conversely, peripheral cues such as the expertise or attractiveness of the communicator have a greater impact on persuasion under conditions of low than high involvement (Chaiken, 1980; Petty, Cacioppo, & Goldman, 1981; Petty, Cacioppo, & Schumann, 1983). There is also evidence in consumer psychology that is consistent with this analysis. Wright (1974), for example, exposed people to an ad for a soybean product under high and low involvement conditions and measured the number of source comments (derogations) and message comments (counterarguments) generated after exposure. Wright (1974) predicted that involvement would increase both kinds of comments, but consistent with the present analysis he found that more message comments were made under high than low involvement, while more source comments were made under low than high involvement conditions. Finally, we have recently found that when the conditions in a persuasion setting suppress the elaboration likelihood, then the number of arguments for a recommendation can serve as a simple cue (e.g., "the more reasons, the better the recommendation"), but when the existing conditions in the persuasion setting foster a high elaboration likelihood, the number of arguments serves as fuel for careful, effortful deliberations regarding the merits of the recommendation (Petty & Cacioppo, 1984). In our study, subjects were exposed to either three or nine arguments for a counterattitudinal appeal that was personally consequential (high involvement) or inconsequential (low involvement). In addition, half of the subjects read strong arguments for the recommendation, and the remaining subjects read weak arguments for the recommendation. We found that the attitudes of subjects who believed the appeal was unimportant and, hence, unworthy of extensive issue-relevant thought were influenced by the simple number of arguments. The attitudes of subjects who believed the appeal was important, however, were influenced by the quality of the message arguments; indeed, the provision of nine arguments, if anything, tended to fuel subjects' discrimination between the strong and weak versions of the persuasive communication.

In the remainder of this chapter, we consider the role within this model played by one of the most pervasive and ecologically valid message factors: message repetition.

MESSAGE REPETITION

The most common empirical finding in the area of message repetition is that persuasion first increases then wears out as the number of repetitions increases (e.g., Appel, 1971; Cacioppo & Petty, 1979, 1980a; Gorn & Goldberg, 1980; Grass & Wallace, 1969; Miller, 1976). Miller (1976), for example, investigated the impact of exposure frequency on attitude toward the recommendation to "REDUCE FOREIGN AID." This sentiment was stated in a headline and in smaller print as "Help Stop the Outflow of U.S. Dollars— Equalize Our Balance of Payments" (Miller, 1976, p. 230). Subjects were 115 undergraduate students who lived in a 9–story dormitory building. The posters were placed on the walls of the commons area of the dormitory at a spacing of 50 linear feet (moderate exposure condition) or 8.5 linear feet (high exposure condition). Subsequently, students' attitudes were assessed using a 10-item questionnaire that dealt with a variety of political and social issues. Miller (1976) found that moderate exposure led to significantly more positive attitudes toward the recommendation than held previously and than did high exposure. He speculated that psychological reactance was aroused in the high exposure condition by presenting the same appeal repeatedly within a small segment of time and area and that this accounted for the absence of immediate attitude change in this condition.

Although Miller's (1976) study is interesting, particularly given the naturalistic setting in which it was conducted, no direct evidence was provided regarding the processes underlying this effect. Several years ago, we attempted to capture this phenomemon in a laboratory to examine more closely the possible reasons for message repetition initially increasing but ultimately decreasing the effectiveness of a persuasive appeal. In our first study (Cacioppo & Petty, 1979), college undergraduates were led to believe that they were assisting researchers by providing subjective reactions to the sound quality of audiotapes. Subjects were told that the tapes were made during a public meeting of a university faculty committee, and that they would have several occasions to examine the tape-recording. In fact, we presented a tape-recorded set of cogent arguments supporting the recommendation to increase university expenditures. In half of the conditions, it was noted in the opening comments of the taped message that the increase in university expenditures would be funded by instituting a visitor's luxury tax, and in the remaining conditions subjects were informed in opening comments that an increase in student tuition would be used to cover these expenditures. The recommendations when funded by luxury taxes was viewed as proattitudinal, while the same recommendation when funded by higher student tuition was viewed as counterattitudinal by students. Finally, subjects were randomly assigned either to hear one of these two versions of the message one, three, or five times in succession, or simply to rate how they felt about the appeal under one of these two funding conditions (no-message control groups).

The results, which are depicted in Fig. 4.2, provided a conceptual replication of Miller's (1976) findings in a laboratory context: Subjects agreed most with the recommendation when it was supported by strong arguments and

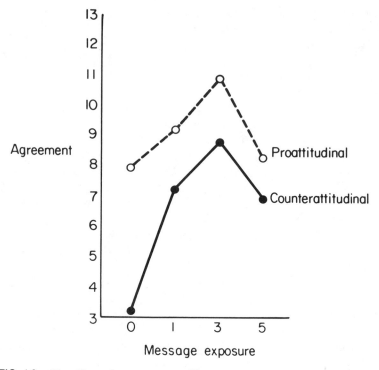

FIG. 4.2.   The effects of preexposure position and message repetition on agreement. (From Cacioppo & Petty, 1979.)

presented a moderate (three) number of times. Analyses also indicated that recall increased with message repetition, suggesting that the recipients extracted more information from the message with each additional exposure even though the simple ability to recall these arguments made them no more or less likely to agree with the recommendation.

A second experiment was conducted to investigate other possible mediators of the repetition effect (Cacioppo & Petty, 1979). Of particular interest in the follow-up experiment was the possibility that a recipient's *issue-relevant* thinking would be influenced by message repetition and would predict the person's susceptibility or resistance to persuasion more accurately than would their recollection of the message arguments. Subjects heard the previously tested pro- or counterattitudinal advocacy either one, three, or five times in succession. Afterwards, subjects were instructed to list everything about which they had thought during the preceding minutes, rated their attitude toward increasing university expenditures, completed ancillary measures, and responded to a measure of their incidental learning of message arguments (for a detailed discussion of these procedures and their validity and reliability, see Cacioppo & Petty, 1981).

The results are depicted in Fig. 4.3. All of the major findings from Miller (1976) and our initial study were replicated. Moderate repetition of a persuasive communication proved most effective, regardless of the position advocated, suggesting that repetition not only provided more opportunities for an individual to process message arguments but repetition also aroused feelings of tedium or psychological reactance that ultimately proved detrimental to persuasion. Recall of the message arguments increased across repetition lev-

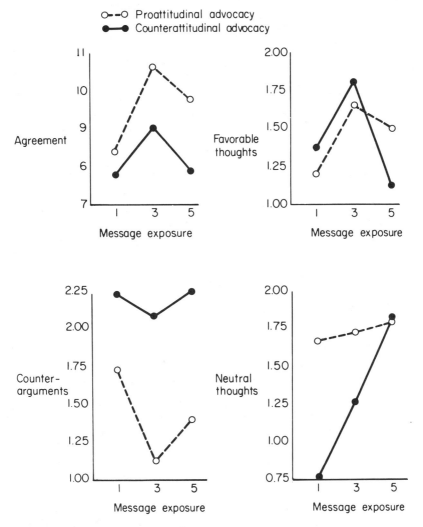

FIG. 4.3.   The effects of preexposure position and message repetition on agreement and cognitive response. (From Cacioppo & Petty, 1979.)

els, suggesting that subjects were continuing to extract some information from the communication across levels of repetition. However, the within-cell correlations between recall and agreement in the experiment were near zero and nonsignificant, again indicating that the simple act of learning the message arguments was not sufficient for achieving agreement (cf. Cacioppo, Petty, & Morris, 1983; Greenwald, 1968; Insko, Lind, & LaTour, 1976; Petty, Cacioppo, & Schumann, 1983; Wood, 1982). Importantly, analyses of the thought-listing data indicated that the pattern of cognitive responses elicited by the repeatedly presented message paralleled that observed for attitudes toward the recommendation: The production of unfavorable thoughts decreased then increased, whereas the production of favorable thoughts tended to increase then decrease. The pattern observed for issue-irrelevant thinking (e.g., complaints of boredom), on the other hand, increased across repetitions, as would be expected if the repeated presentation of the same message was arousing feelings of tedium.

We might note that these results are unlikely to be limited to the laboratory, for Gorn and Goldberg (1980) recently reported that children who viewed commercials in the context of a Flintstone television program preferred a product (*Danish Hill* ice cream) more when they saw a commercial for the product a moderate (three) than a low (one) or high (five) number of times during the program. Gorn and Goldberg also recorded the spontaneous verbalizations produced by the children during the commercials. Like us, they found that high exposure frequencies were accompanied by clear expressions of displeasure and annoyance. Remarks such as "Oh, not again" and "Not another one" apparently were common in the high exposure frequency condition.

THEORETICAL ANALYSIS

These data led us to propose that message repetition guides a sequence of psychological reactions to a persuasive communication best conceptualized as a two-stage attitude-modification process (Cacioppo & Petty, 1979, 1980a; Petty & Cacioppo, 1981). The first component revolves around the fact that repeated presentations provide recipients with a greater opportunity to consider the content and implications of the content of a persuasive communication. That is, limitations in people's information-processing can be partially overcome by presenting a (persuasive) communication repeatedly, with the cumulative elaboration likelihood increasing monotonically as repetition increases.

The second component of our model of message repetition concerns the biased nature of the recipients' information processing activity. We reasoned that moderate repetitions of a persuasive message facilitated the relatively objective consideration of the merits of a recommendation, but that as tedium and reactance were aroused, the information processing turned agonistic and was increasingly directed toward the context of the appeal (e.g., thoughts were more likely to be directed toward the setting or the advertisement per se). One reaction available to recipients when they are exposed excessively to a persuasive communication is to take steps to avoid the appeal or to remove themselves from the persuasion setting (e.g., by turning the page in a magazine or selecting another station on the radio or television). Changes in attitude toward the recommendation would be unlikely in these instances.

In instances where the costs of avoiding the appeal are higher—such as when listening to a radio someone else controls, in a research setting, or in the midst of an interesting television program—the reactance or tedium elicited by overexposure to a persuasive communication may begin to *bias* the recipients' cognitive responses (e.g., issue-relevant thinking, source-relevant thinking, ad-relevant thinking) such that the appeal is viewed through increasingly jaundiced eyes. Recent work in cognitive psychology on mood and information processing has outlined a mechanism capable of biasing cognitive responding at excessive exposure frequencies in the manner we have suggested. Specifically, it has been argued that some information in memory is stored with a mood feature, which can serve as a retrieval cue (e.g., Bower, 1981; Clark & Isen, 1982; Harvey, Enzle, & Ko, 1982; Isen, Shalker, & Karp, 1978). This means that a positive mood increases access to information for which positive mood is a feature, and a negative mood increases access to information for which negative mood is a feature. If excessive exposures arouse a negative mood and activate negative memory bases, the negatively biased cognitive responses to the message can be directed toward the setting or advertisement, features that have no intrinsic link to the true merits of the recommendation, or they can be directed toward determining the merits of the arguments for the recommendation. To the extent that the former process predominates, overexposure should lead to negative attitudes toward both the advertisement and the attitude-object, but the negative attitudes toward the advertisement should be more enduring than the attitudes toward the recommendation since the cognitive responses, though perhaps central to the merits of the ad, are peripheral to the merits of the recommendation. This implies that attitudes toward the advertisement would manifest as an inverted-U function across exposure frequencies, whereas attitudes toward the recommendation would share this pattern initially but would unfold as a satiation effect over time. Indeed, relatively enduring negative attitudes toward the recommendation would be expected only to the extent that overexposure to an appeal led recipients to generate arguments against the merits of the recommendation (central route).

THE ROLE OF MESSAGE REPETITION:
EMPIRICAL TESTS

We and our colleagues have recently completed several studies designed to examine various implications of the model of message repetition outlined above. The first two experiments were designed to address the notion that moderate levels of repetition can enable recipients to extract more from and think more about the arguments for a recommendation, whereas the next two experiments were designed to extend this work and to examine the effects of high levels of message repetition.

Recall that we suggested that moderate levels of message repetition provide people with additional opportunities to think about the merits of the appeal. Moderate repetition of a message is neither necessary nor sufficient for recipients being likely to think about the merits of a recommendation, but rather it is viewed as being a contributory cause. If, for instance, the message is sufficiently complex that recipients cannot complete their scrutiny of the implications and merits of the arguments in a single exposure, even if they were motivated to do so, then a moderate number of re-exposures to the message should enhance both the amount of information extracted from the message and their realization of the personal benefits or costs of the recommendation being accepted. In a test bearing upon this hypothesis, undergraduate students enrolled in introductory psychology participated in a study, which they believed concerned subjective judgments of the sound quality of audio-tapes. We constructed a set of strong and a set of weak arguments supporting the recommendation that all seniors be required to pass a comprehensive exam in their major area of study prior to their being allowed to graduate. (Strong arguments are defined operationally as those that elicit primarily favorable issue-relevant thinking, whereas weak arguments are defined as message arguments that elicit primarily unfavorable thoughts when people are instructed to think about them.) Half of the subjects were exposed to the strong set of arguments, and half were exposed to the weak arguments. In addition, some heard the message once, others heard it repeated three times. Immediately following the last presentation (either the first or third, depending upon condition), subjects were told that since their attitudes toward the recommendation might affect how they rated the sound quality of the audiotape, we wanted to know how they felt about the recommendation to institute senior comprehensive exams. Subjects' expressed their attitudes toward the exams using four semantic-differential scales.

The strong version of the message elicited more favorable thoughts, $F(1,101) = 8.19$, $p < .01$, fewer unfavorable thoughts, $F(1,101) = 11.33$, $p < .001$, and more positive attitudes toward the recommendation, $F(1,101) = 21.21$, $p < .001$, than the weak version of the message. The important question in the present study, of course, concerned whether moderate repetitions of the strong message increased the likelihood that subjects would elaborate upon the message arguments, realizing the cogency of the strong arguments and the specious nature of the weak arguments. As depicted in Fig. 4.4, a significant Message Repetition × Argument Quality interaction on the attitude measure, $F(1,101) = 4.80$, $p < .05$, indicated subjects *were* more likely to realize the merits of the recommendation supported by strong arguments and the faults of the recommendation supported by the weak arguments after hearing these message arguments three times rather than once. Analyses of recall, on the other hand, indicated only that more arguments were recalled after three presentations ($M = 5.33$) than after one presentation ($M = 3.90$).

The data from this study are consistent with the notion that moderate repetition of a persuasive message increases the ability of recipients to extract information from and scrutinize the message arguments and, therefore, to respond in a more discriminating manner to strong and weak arguments for a recommendation. In the present research, we have operationalized "moderate repetitions" as three presentations. Although the model we have outlined does not predict the number of repetitions that represents moderate repetition in an absolute sense, it does yield predictions about factors that increase or decrease the value representing "moderate repetition." For instance, to the extent that a persuasive message is: (a) sufficiently complex that scrutiny

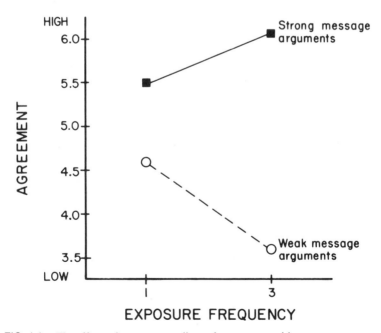

FIG. 4.4.   The effects of argument quality and message repetition on agreement.

of the message arguments cannot be completed in a single presentation, (b) presented in a distributed rather than massed fashion, or (c) embedded among a heterogeneous rather than homogeneous set of messages, the number of repetitions that will maximize the relatively objective processing of the message arguments should increase. Thus, if the arguments for a recommendation are *strong,* the preceding factors (e.g., distributed presentations) should extend the point of "wearout" for the advertisement.

Corlett (1984) recently completed a conceptual replication of this study using mock television advertisements rather than audiotaped editorials. The advertisement concerned a little-known beer and was embedded among other advertisements in a 60-minute television show. The advertisement provided information about the ingredients and manufacturing process used in the production of the beer. Throughout the monologue, a bottle of beer was depicted in the center of the screen. At the onset of the ad, the label of the beer was facing away from the camera. As the ad began, the bottle began to rotate slowly, completing a 180-degree rotation shortly before completion of the advertisement.

Pilot testing was undertaken to develop descriptions (i.e., verbal arguments for the product) that elicited primarily favorable thoughts (i.e., strong arguments) or unfavorable thoughts (i.e., weak arguments) for the recommendation to try the beer. For example, the water used in producing the beer was described as coming from clear springs in the strong version of the message, but was described as coming from the city water supplies in the weak version of the message. Following pilot testing, strong and weak versions of the advertisements were produced. The strong and weak versions of the advertisement were each designed to be 40 seconds in length and had identical visual components. A parallel set of advertisements were created except that the speed of speech and rotation of the bottle was increased to complete the advertisement in 30 rather than 40 seconds, yielding a more rapid presentation of the same strong or weak message arguments. This was done to examine whether slightly faster presentations disrupted viewers' message processing.

After preparation of the stimulus materials, students were recruited for a study in communication. Subjects viewed a color videotape of the Phil Donahue Show. The show contained five commercial breaks and began and ended with commercial breaks. Subjects were randomly assigned to the experimental conditions of a 2 (Argument quality: strong vs. weak) × 2 (Speed of Speech: normal vs. rapid) × 5 (Message Repetition: 0, 1, 3, 5, or 7) between-subjects factorial. No more than one beer advertisement appeared during any given commercial break, and all subjects who were exposed to the advertisement (i.e., all except the 0-exposure conditions) saw the beer advertisement during the final commercial break. Additional presentations of the advertisement were distributed randomly throughout the remaining six commercial breaks. Subjects in the 7-repetition condition, of course, were exposed to the beer advertisement once during each commercial break. At the conclusion of the videotape, subjects tried to recall message arguments and expressed their attitudes toward various objects, including the advertised beer.

Corlett (1984) found that the exposure of subjects to the target advertisement during every commercial break (i.e., the 7-exposure condition) actually had a detrimental effect on subjects' recall of the material in the advertisement: recall increased with repetition until the 7-exposure condition, which produced poorer recall than did five exposures and approximately the same level of recall as did three exposures. This suggests that subjects turned their attention away from the television advertisement when it appeared predictably and often. Results also showed that the manipulation of speed of speech had no effect, perhaps because the manipulation of speed of speech was modest and the message itself was neither long nor complex.

More interestingly, subjects' attitudes did not parallel their level of recall of the advertisement, but rather Corlett found evidence for a higher-order interaction. Specifically, repetition led men to develop more positive attitudes toward the product when strong arguments were used and it led to more negative attitudes toward the product when weak arguments were used. This interaction replicates the results reported above in which subjects listened to either strong or weak arguments a single time or three times in succession. Repetition led women, on the other hand, to develop slightly more negative attitudes toward the beer regardless of the quality of the message arguments. As Corlett (1984) noted, these results are interesting in light of the observations that: (a) males are estimated to consume 80% to 83% of all beer sold, (b) the primary target audience for beer advertisements is men aged 18 to 49, (c) men comprise the majority of the actors in beer commercials, and (d) beer advertisements are more commonly placed in magazines and time-slots that appeal generally to men. These results suggest that men may have been more interested in and thoughtful about the simple beer advertisement than women.

A factor to consider is that in all of our previous work on message repetition, people have received exactly the same message at each exposure frequency. If the messages were varied somewhat, it is reasonable to propose that tedium or boredom could be forestalled. In fact, in previous repetition research in which the ads were varied rather than held constant, tedium effects have been rare (e.g., McCullough & Ostrom, 1974; but see Calder & Sternthal, 1980). Thus, it might be hypothesized that tedium should occur at higher levels of repetition when the repeated ads differ than when they are the same.

In order to provide an initial exploration of the effects of involvement, variation, and repetition on extent of thinking and attitudes, Schumann

(1983) conducted a study in which all three variables were manipulated. In this study, 360 undergraduates were exposed to 1, 4, or 8 advertisements for a fictitious new pen, the Omega 3, in the context of a simulated television program. The ads for the pen were either always identical or different and were viewed under conditions of either high or low involvement. All of the undergraduates were led to believe that they would be evaluating the format of a new television talk show that might appear on a local cable television station. The show was presented to subjects as a slide presentation with an accompanying audio portion. The slide show included a number of interview and information segments (e.g., interview with a punk rock group, information about college student cheaters, etc.), combined with brief commercial segments. After viewing the 45-minute simulated TV show, all subjects completed a questionnaire booklet which asked about the extent to which they thought about the key product (pens) during the presentation, and measured recall of and attitude toward the ad and product.

In the high involvement conditions, subjects were led to believe that after exposure to the simulated show and completing the questionnaire they would be allowed to select a ballpoint pen from several available brands. They were also told that one of the brands available was to be advertised in the simulated program. In the low involvement conditions, subjects were also led to believe that they would be allowed to select a free gift from among several available brands, one of which was to be advertised in the simulated program. However, the gift choice concerned an irrelevant product (mouthwash). In previous research, this manipulation has been shown to enhance thinking about the product-relevant information provided (Petty, Cacioppo, & Schumann, 1983).

Each of the ads for the Omega 3 pen contained six product-relevant arguments for the pen. In order to create the variation conditions, eight different versions of the pen ad were created. Several features of the ads were manipulated to create the different versions. Although the substantive content of the arguments remained the same in each, the ads presented the arguments in a different order, with slightly different wording, in a different print type, and with a different featured user of the pen (e.g., homemaker, artist, educator). In addition to presenting the ad visually, an audiotape was constructed for each ad that introduced the product and described a few of the product-relevant attributes that were also contained in the ad. In the *same* exposure repetition conditions, subjects saw and heard one of the eight versions of the ad either four or eight times. In the *variation* conditions, subjects saw and heard a different version of the ad either four or eight times.

In order to check on the extent to which repetition, variation, and involvement affected thinking, subjects were asked to indicate on a 10-point scale the extent to which they thought about pens during the slide presentation. A main effect for repetition, $F (2,344) = 34.38$, $p < .001$, revealed that subjects reported thinking more about pens as repetition increased. In addition, a main effect for variation, $F(1,344) = 3.69$, $p < .05$, revealed that subjects thought more about the ads when they were varied than when they were the same. A marginal Repetition × Variation interaction ($p < .09$) revealed that the variation effect was only apparent under the four and eight repetition conditions. Finally, an Involvement × Repetition interaction was also obtained on this measure, $F(2,344) = 3.60$, $p < .05$. This interaction resulted from the fact that increasing involvement enhanced reported thinking about pens in the one-exposure conditions, but not in the multiple-exposure conditions. Thus, as expected, all three variables had an impact on the reported amount of product-relevant thinking in which subjects engaged. Perhaps of most interest is that high involvement subjects began thinking about the advertised product earlier in the exposure sequence than low involvement subjects.

Subjects were given a free recall test in which they were asked to list all of the products for which they saw ads, and all of the brand names they encountered. The repetition manipulation was the only one to affect the recall measures. As repetition increased, so did the likelihood of recall of the product category, $F(2,348) = 9.07$, $p < .0001$, and the Omega 3 brand name, $F(2,348) = 20.75$, $p < .0001$.

Of most interest, however, were the measures of attitude toward the ad and the Omega 3 pen. Because the high and low involvement subjects showed quite different patterns on the attitude measures, separate Repetition × Variation analyses were conducted for each group. As a measure of attitude toward the ad, subjects were asked to rate how much they liked the ad on a 10-point scale. Under high involvement, no significant effects were obtained (see bottom panel of Fig. 4.5). Under low involvement, however, a significant Repetition × Variation interaction was obtained, $F(2,175) = 6.73$, $p < .005$. This interaction resulted from the fact that subjects had similar attitudes toward the same and different ads under the one- and four-exposure conditions, but significantly different attitudes toward the ads under eight-exposure conditions ($p < .05$). When the ads were different, attitudes toward the ad increased from four to eight exposures, but when the ads were the same, attitudes decreased from four to eight exposures (see top panel of Fig. 4.5). An analysis of attitude toward the product showed a similar pattern (see Fig. 4.6). Under high involvement, a curvilinear pattern was observed. Under low involvement, a marginal Repetition × Variation interaction ($p < .10$) revealed that attitudes toward the product increased from one to eight exposures when the ads were varied, but showed a curvilinear pattern when the ads were the same. Similar to the effect observed on the ad attitude measure, the variation manipulation affected product attitudes only when the ad was repeated eight times ($p < .10$).

In sum, these data provide some support for the view that tedium can be forestalled by varying the content of ads, but that it is only under low involvement conditions that this forestalling takes place. Under high involvement,

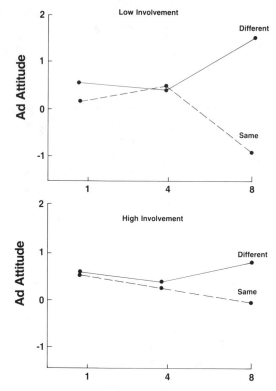

FIG. 4.5. The effects of involvement, ad variation, and repetition on attitudes toward the ad. (Adapted from Schumann, 1983.)

people are motivated to process the ad at relatively low repetition levels so that by high repetition levels, they tend to show a tedium effect whether the ads are the same or different. On the other hand, under low involvement, subjects show a tedium effect only if the ads are exactly the same in content, but not if they are varied.

The fact that the variation manipulation has no effect on high involvement subjects is consistent with our view that under high involvement people are motivated to think about the product-relevant information provided and the form of information presentation is not particularly important in determining their attitudes. The form of presentation was important in determining both ad and product attitudes for low involvement subjects, however. There are two possible reasons for this. One explanation makes the assumption that variation affects the attitudes of low involvement subjects via the peripheral route. The other makes the assumption that variation affects attitudes via the central route.

The peripheral route notion makes the assumption that low involvement subjects, being unmotivated to think about the product-relevant arguments, formed their attitudes simply on the basis of the pleasantness of the ads or the

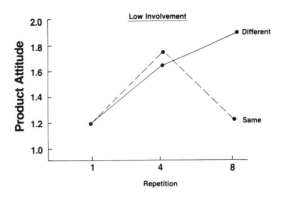

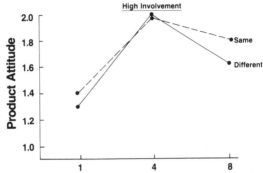

FIG. 4.6.   The effects of involvement, ad variation, and repetition on attitudes toward the advertised product. (Adapted from Schumann, 1983.)

cue value of the ads. Repeating the same ads is likely to lead to boredom whereas presenting different ads is probably more interesting even if the ads are not scrutinized. These mood states may directly affect attitude ratings. Alternatively, when low involvement subjects saw different people associated with the product (in the different versions of ads), they may have assumed that the product was more popular. This "popularity cue" may have affected the attitudes of low involvement subjects without their engaging in any extensive product relevant thinking. Thus, variation may have affected the attitudes of low involvement subjects via the peripheral route.

On the other hand, the different versions of the ad may have motivated more product-relevant thinking on the part of the low involvement subjects and induced attitude change via the central route. Although low involvement subjects were generally unmotivated to think about the pen product, when they saw so many different ads, this may have piqued their curiosity and may have led them to scrutinize the product-relevant information provided. Since they were relatively unmotivated to think, it would take a relatively large number of exposures before this thinking could be completed. If the variations in the ad motivated increased thinking about the cogent arguments provided, favorable attitudes would result. In work currently in progress we are attempting to pin down these various possibilities. An important implication of this research is that if variation works via the peripheral route, the attitudes formed should be less enduring and less predictive of purchase intentions than if variation works via the central route.

ACKNOWLEDGMENTS

We thank William Cleve Corlett, David Schumann, and Joseph Sidera for their assistance in this research. Address correspondence to John T. Cacioppo, Department of Psychology, University of Iowa, Iowa City, IA 52242, or to Richard E. Petty, Department of Psychology, University of Missouri, Columbia, MO 65211.

REFERENCES

Appel, V. (1971). On advertising wearout. *Journal of Advertising Research, 11,* 11–13.

Bower, G. H. (1981). Mood and memory. *American Psychologist, 36,* 129–148.

Cacioppo, J. T., & Petty, R. E. (1979). The effects of message repetition and position on cognitive response, recall, and persuasion. *Journal of Personality and Social Psychology, 37,* 97–109.

Cacioppo, J. T., & Petty, R. E. (1980a). Persuasiveness of communications is affected by exposure frequency and message quality: A theoretical and empirical analysis of persisting attitude change. In J. F. Leigh & C. R. Martin (Eds.), *Current issues and research in advertising.* Ann Arbor, MI: University of Michigan Press. Pp. 97–122.

Cacioppo, J. T., & Petty, R. E. (1980b). Sex differences in influenceability: Toward specifying the underlying processes. *Personality and Social Psychology Bulletin, 6,* 651–656.

Cacioppo, J. T., & Petty, R. E. (1981). Social psychological procedures for cognitive response assessment: The thought-listing technique. In T. V. Merluzzi, C. R. Glass, & M. Genest (Eds.), *Cognitive assessment.* New York: Guilford Press.

Cacioppo, J. T., Petty, R. E., & Morris, K. J. (1983). Effects of need for cognition on message evaluation, recall, and persuasion. *Journal of Personality and Social Psychology, 45,* 805–818.

Calder, B. J., & Sternthal, B. (1980). Television commercial wearout: An information processing analysis. *Journal of Marketing Research, 17,* 173–186.

Chaiken, S. (1979). Communicator physical attractiveness and persuasion. *Journal of Personality and Social Psychology, 38,* 1387–1397.

Chaiken, S. (1980). Heuristic versus systematic information processing and the use of source versus message cues in persuasion. *Journal of Personality and Social Psychology, 39,* 752–766.

Clark, M. S., & Isen, A. M. (1982). Toward understanding the relationship between feeling states and social behavior. In A. Hastorf & A. M. Isen (Eds.), *Cognitive social psychology.* New York: Elsevier North Holland.

Corlett, W. C. (1984). *Central or peripheral routes to attitude change: The role of repetition in television commercial wearout.* Unpublished doctoral dissertation, The University of Iowa.

Gorn, G. J., & Goldberg, M. E. (1980). Children's responses to repetitive TV commercials. *Journal of Consumer Research, 6,* 421–425.

Grass, R., & Wallace, W. H. (1969). Satiation effects of television commercials. *Journal of Advertising Research, 9,* 3–8.

Greenwald, A. G. (1968). Cognitive learning, cognitive response to persuasion, and attitude change. In A. G. Greenwald, T. C. Brock, & T. M. Ostrom (Eds.), *Psychological foundation of attitudes.* New York: Academic Press.

Harvey, M. D., Enzle, M. E., & Ko, Y. (1982, June). *Perceiver mood, outcome valence, and causal attribution: Rose-coloured glasses and jaundiced eyes.* Paper presented at the annual meeting of the Canadian Psychological Association, Montreal.

Insko, C. A., Lind, E. A., & LaTour, S. (1976). Persuasion, recall, and thoughts. *Representative Research in Social Psychology, 7,* 66–78.

Isen, A. M., Shalker, T., Clark, M., & Karp, L. (1978). Affect, accessibility of material in memory and behavior: A cognitive loop? *Journal of Personality and Social Psychology, 36,* 1–12.

McCullough, J. L., & Ostrom, T. M. (1974). Repetition of highly similar mssages and attitude change. *Journal of Applied Psychology, 59,* 395–397.

Miller, N., Maruyama, G., Beaber, R., & Valone, K. (1976). Speed of speech and persuasion. *Journal of Personality and Social Psychology, 34,* 615–625.

Miller, R. L. (1976). Mere exposure, psychological reactance and attitude change. *Public Opinion Quarterly, 40,* 229–233.

Norman, R. (1976). When what is said is important: A comparison of expert and attractive sources. *Journal of Experimental Social Psychology, 12,* 294–300.

Petty, R. E., & Cacioppo, J. T. (1979a). Effects of forewarning of persuasive intent and involvement on cognitive responses and persuasion. *Personality and Social Psychology Bulletin, 5,* 173–176.

Petty, R. E., & Cacioppo, J. T. (1979b). Issue involvement can increase or decrease persuasion by enhancing message relevant cognitive responses. *Journal of Personality and Social Psychology, 37,* 1915–1926.

Petty, R. E., & Cacioppo, J. T. (1980). Effects of issue involvement on attitude in an advertising context. *Proceedings of the Division 23 Program, 88th Annual American Psychological Association Meeting,* 75–79.

Petty, R. E., & Cacioppo, J. T. (1981). *Attitudes and persuasion: Classic and contemporary approaches.* Dubuque, IA: William C. Brown.

Petty, R. E., & Cacioppo, J. T. (1984). The effects of involvement on responses to argument quantity and quality: Central and peripheral routes to persuasion. *Journal of Personality and Social Psychology, 46,* 69–81.

Petty, R. E., Cacioppo, J. T., & Goldman, R. (1981). Personal involvement as a determinant of argument-based persuasion. *Journal of Personality and Social Psychology, 41,* 847–855.

Petty, R. E., Cacioppo, J. T., & Heesacker, M. (1981). The use of rhetorical questions in persuasion: A cognitive response analysis. *Journal of Personality and Social Psychology, 40,* 432–440.

Petty, R. E., Cacioppo, J. T., & Schumann, D. (1983). Central and peripheral routes to advertising effectiveness: The moderating role of involvement. *Journal of Consumer Research, 10,* 135–146.

Petty, R. E., Wells, G. L,, & Brock, T. C. (1976). Distraction can enhance or reduce yielding to propaganda: Thought disruption versus effort justification. *Journal of Personality and Social Psychology, 34,* 874–884.

Schumann, D. (1983). Effects of repetition, involvement, and advertisement variation on persuasion. Unpublished manuscript, University of Missouri.

Will, G. F. (1982, May 10). But first, a message from . . . . *Newsweek,* 98.

Wood, W. (1982). Retrieval of attitude-relevant information from memory: Affects on susceptibility to persuasion and on intrinsic motivation. *Journal of Personality and Social Psychology, 42,* 798–810.

Wright, P. L. (1974). Analyzing media affects on advertising responses. *Public Opinion Quarterly, 38,* 192–205.

5
Conceptual and Methodological Issues in Examining the Relationship Between Consumer Memory and Judgment

Meryl Lichtenstein
Thomas K. Srull
University of Illinois at Urbana-Champaign

INTRODUCTION

This chapter is concerned with the relationship between memory and evaluative judgment, a topic that has long been of concern to researchers in both psychology and consumer behavior. Despite this interest, however, the literature in both areas is confusing and, in many cases, it at least gives the appearance of being contradictory. We attempt to address the major theoretical and methodological issues involved in investigating the relationship between memory and judgment in the present paper. A model related to the psychological processes involved in memory and judgment is outlined, and several empirical tests of the model are then reported.

From a historical perspective, there has been more work related to the relationship between memory and judgment in the area of attitudes and attitude change than in any other. It has long been assumed, for example, that the ultimate effect of a persuasive message, such as an advertisement, on both attitudes and behavior is a function of the information conveyed *and* the degree to which it is learned and remembered by the recipient. This assumption has been made by a number of leading theorists in the field (see e.g., Hovland, Janis, & Kelley, 1953; McGuire, 1968; Miller & Campbell, 1959; Watts & Mcguire, 1964).

Researchers interested in various aspects of social judgment have also been concerned with the relationship between memory and judgment. The bulk of this work has been related to impression formation and various types of attributions. In both cases, the person is assumed to recall specific episodic events involving the target, and then determine the implications of these events for the judgment to be made. Theorists differ on how elaborate the intervening combinatorial process is hypothesized to be but there is almost universal agreement that there should be a strong relationship between the evaluative implications of whatever events are recalled and the extremity of any evaluative judgment that is made. The extent of this agreement is so strong that Carlston (1980a) has simply referred to this as the "traditional model."

It is not terribly surprising that similar assumptions have been made in the area of consumer judgment as well. Bettman (1979) has reviewed several specific areas in which a strong correspondence between memory and judgment is assumed in specific theories. In addition, however, similar assumptions are often implicitly made in areas of research that are much more atheoretical in nature. For example, advertisers often use memory tests to determine the "effectiveness" of a particular ad. Similarly, the Federal Trade Commission often relies on memory tests to determine how information obtained at an earlier time might influence a point of purchase decision.

THE NATURE OF THE PROBLEM

It is "sad but true" that there is little empirical evidence in any of these domains to support the assumptions that are implicitly or explicitly made. In the attitude domain, for example, there is a long line of studies that have found only weak relationships between memory for information in a persuasive communication and attitude formation and attitude change (Greenwald, 1968; Insko, 1964; Miller & Campbell, 1959; Watts & McGuire, 1974). In fact, it was precisely this type of "problem" that led to the "cognitive response" approach to the study of persuasion that is so dominant today (see Greenwald, 1968, for an early demonstration of the importance of examining cognitive responses and Petty, Ostrom, & Brock, 1981, for a recent review of the existing literature).

The same type of weak relationships between memory and judgment have been found in the other two domains as well. For example, in a classic impression formation study, Anderson and Hubert (1963) provided subjects with trait adjectives. Their essential finding was that there are strong primacy effects in impression formation (cf. Asch, 1946) but reasonably large *recency* effects in recall. They conluded from this that the impression judgments and memory for the trait adjectives are independently stored and accessed in memory. Dreben, Fiske, and Hastie (1979) recently reported a conceptually similar study in which they replicated these effects. These investigators also found that temporal delays had a large effect on recall but very modest changes in impression ratings. They also concluded from this that there is some independence between episodic memory and abstract evaluative impressions (see also Riskey, 1979).

Many other examples of this also exist. Fiske and her colleagues (Fiske, 1981, 1982: Fiske, Kenny, & Taylor, 1982; Fiske, Taylor, Etcoff, & Laufer, 1979; Taylor & Fiske, 1975, 1978, 1981) have discussed relevant findings in the area of attribution and Bettman (1979) has discussed several examples in the area of consumer judgment.

Even from such a cursory glance at the literature one can see that many psychological theories assume, either implicitly or explicitly, that there should generally be a strong correspondence between the evaluative implications of information that is accessible in memory at the time of judgment and the extremity of the judgments that are made. The evidence discussed above obviously poses a great theoretical problem.

There are also applied aspects of the problem, however, that are directly relevant to those interested in the effects of advertising. For example, many researchers interested in the effects of advertising attempt to use direct cognitive measures in order to assess the effectiveness of any given ad. These would include things like free and cued recall, various types of recognition measures, and so forth, and they are used to assess the impact of both content or "informational" variables and format or "noninformational" variables. Such attempts also rest on the implicit assumption that there is a strong correspondence between memory and impression judgments. As noted above, however, the bulk of the empirical evidence that exists suggests that recall is only very weakly related to evaluative judgments. On the one hand, advertisers need to know what type of information from their ads is extracted and retained over long periods of time. On the other hand, since recall is only weakly related to judgment or other types of attitudinal types of variables, some have recently suggested that it is a poor and misleading empirical strategy to rely on any type of memory measure to assess the effectiveness of any given ad campaign.

In the following sections of the paper, we attempt to explicate the conditions under which a strong correspondence between memory and judgment should and should not be expected on conceptual grounds. In the process of doing so, we outline a general model that can be used to conceptualize the judgment process. Finally, we report the results of several empirical investigations that test aspects of the model.

A PROPOSED SOLUTION

One of the most important conceptual distinctions in contemporary cognitive psychology is that between "retrieval" and "computational" processes (see e.g., Lachman, Lachman, & Butterfield, 1979; Shoben, 1980). Imagine you are asked "Is the Buick Regal a luxury automobile?" A retrieval model would suggest that, at least for most people, the answer to such a question has already been determined and stored in memory. Thus, one simply needs to "retrieve" it from memory in order to answer such a question.

In contrast, a computational model would suggest, at least for most of us, that the answer to such a question has *not* already been determined. Rather, in order to answer such a question, we need to retrieve whatever information we can about the Buick Regal, compare it to our referents for "luxury automobile," and then "compute" or figure out an answer on the spot. Of course, if we were asked the same question again, we would not need to re-compute an answer but simply retrieve our previous judgment.

Although the distinction between retrieval and computational processes is not often discussed, it has been applied to a number of areas related to consumer information processing (see i.e., Bettman, 1979; Burke, 1980; Brucks & Mitchell, 1981; Mitchell & Smith, 1982; Smith, Mitchell, & Meyer, 1982). We would like to suggest that the distinction is also crucial to an understanding of the recall-judgment "problem" described earlier. In particular, the model we would like to propose suggests that the subject's information processing objectives or "goals" are a critical mediation variable that determines the nature of the relationship between recall and judgment. The reason for this is that such processing objectives often determine whether such judgments have been pre-stored or need to be computed on the spot.

The model postulates that when a person acquires product-related information with the (explicit or implicit) objective of making an evaluation of that product, the global evaluation will be made at the time of information acquisition and stored in memory separately and independently from the specific information presented in the ad. If the person is later asked to make a specific judgment, the evaluation will have already been "computed" and will simply be accessed at that time. This is consistent with a large body of psychological evidence that suggests that such self-generated evaluations are much more accessible in memory than externally presented information (Carlston, 1980a, 1980b; Hertel, 1982, 1983; Johnson & Raye, 1981; Ostrom, Lingle, Pryor, & Geva, 1980; Slamecka & Graf, 1978). Thus, under these conditions, there is no reason to expect any strong relationship between the specific facts that are recalled and the global evaluation that is made. One can see that this is a very straightforward retrieval model in which the previous judgment and the specific episodic facts on which it is based are independently stored and accessed. It is a process that is consistent with the conceptualizations outlined by Anderson and Hubert (1963) and Dreben et al. (1979).

There is at least one alternative process that might also occur. For example, when a person acquires product-related information with no specific objective in mind, or only a very general objective such as to comprehend the information being presented, a global evaluation of the product will not be made at the time of information acquisition. If later asked to make a specific evaluation of the product, the person will be forced to retrieve the previously acquired information, or some subset of it, and use it as a basis for his/her evaluation of the product. In other words, a judgment will have to be computed on the spot. Under these conditions, a strong relationship between the global evaluation and the evaluative implications of the information that is recalled would therefore be expected. However, as Hastie, Park, and Weber (1984) have concluded after an extensive review of the literature, these conditions are almost directly opposite to those that have been previously investigated.

Several experiments designed to investigate implications of this model are reported below. It is important to note, however, that the two processes described are not mutually exclusive. As McGuire (1980) has noted, one can find support for almost any reasonable hypothesis under some conditions. The task is therefore to outline, as closely as possible, the boundary conditions under which each process is likely to dominate. Here concentrate on the role of information processing objectives as a determinant of precisely when various retrieval and computational processes will be activated. There are doubtlessly other determinants as well, but no type of advertising situation can be reasonably understood without considering the processing objectives of the message recipient.

Experiment 1

The first experiment was designed to be a direct test of the model proposed. Since both applied and theoretical issues are of concern, three separate types of stimulus materials were examined. Initially, American and European magazines were searched for print ads that: (a) were as complex as possible in the sense that they contained a large amount of attribute information, and (b) pertained to products with which subjects were likely to have little prior familiarity. For example, one ad was five paragraphs long and described a computer-based instrument that could translate English prose into five separate languages with correct syntactic structure.

The ads were then modified to produce three separate stimulus sets. Each set contained ten distinct attribute statements. One of the resulting ads was primarily positive in tone, one was primarily negative in tone, and one was generally neutral.

To collect normative ratings, these ads were given to 67 college students who were asked, "Assuming you wanted to purchase a product similar to the _____, how desirable do you think this particular brand would be?" Subjects made one rating for each product on a scale ranging from 0 ("very undesirable") to 20 ("very desirable"). The Positive Ad received a mean rating of

14.03, the Negative Ad received a mean rating of 7.67, and the Neutral Ad received a mean rating of 10.87.

Each of the three stimulus replications included a 2 × 2 × 2 completely balanced factorial design with 30 subjects randomly assigned to each of the resulting eight data cells. The first variable concerned the processing objectives of the subjects. Subjects in the *on-line* condition were told to read the ad with the purpose of forming an evaluation of the product so that they would later be able to judge how desirable it would be relative to other competing brands. Subjects in the *impression-after* condition were told that the ad was written by an undergraduate advertising major. Their task was to read the ad in order to judge how grammatical, coherent, and interesting it was.

The second variable of interest was temporal delay. Some subjects completed the dependent measures after a *5-minute* delay, while others completed them after *48 hours*. Finally, subjects in the *recall-judgment* condition were asked to recall the ad in as much detail as possible and then asked to make the judgment (along the same scale described above). Subjects in the *judgment-recall* condition were given the two tasks in the opposite order.

The mean levels of recall and judgment, and the within-cell correlations between recall and judgment are presented in Table 5.1 for Neutral Ad condition, in Table 5.2 for the Positive Ad condition, and in Table 5.3 for the Negative Ad condition.

TABLE 5.1
Mean Levels of Recall and Judgment, and the Correlations Between Recall and Judgment for the Neutral Ad Condition of Experiment 1

	5 Minute		48 Hour	
	Recall-Judgment	Judgment-Recall	Recall-Judgment	Judgment-Recall
Recall				
On-line	5.3	5.1	2.3	2.4
Impression-after	6.7	4.8	4.3	2.6
Judgment				
On-line	11.2	10.7	10.5	11.3
Impression-after	10.8	11.3	11.0	10.6
Correlations				
On-line	.32	.24	.28	.11
Impression-after	.56	.67	.72	.63

TABLE 5.2

Mean Levels of Recall and Judgment, and the Correlations Between Recall and
Judgment for the Positive Ad Condition of Experiment 1

	5 Minute		48 Hour	
	Recall-Judgment	Judgment-Recall	Recall-Judgment	Judgment-Recall
Recall				
On-line	4.8	4.6	2.5	2.1
Impression-after	5.8	4.3	3.8	2.4
Judgment				
On-line	14.6	14.2	15.0	13.8
Impression-after	13.9	13.9	15.6	13.6
Correlations				
On-line	.24	.18	.21	.16
Impression-after	.67	.58	.71	.62

TABLE 5.3

Mean Levels of Recall and Judgment, and the Correlations Between Recall and
Judgment for the Negative Ad Condition of Experiment 1

	5 Minute		48 Hour	
	Recall-Judgment	Judgment-Recall	Recall-Judgment	Judgment-Recall
Recall				
On-line	5.7	5.3	2.7	2.3
Impression-after	5.4	4.6	3.6	1.6
Judgment				
On-line	7.3	7.2	7.8	6.9
Impression-after	8.2	7.9	6.8	7.3
Correlations				
On-line	.26	.17	.32	.15
Impression-after	.59	.68	.54	.71

Although there are some subtle nuances in both the recall and judgment data (which cannot be discussed here due to space limitations), one can see that there is virtually no difference between the on-line and impression-after subjects in terms of overall levels of recall or mean levels of evaluative judgment. Due to the large number of subjects in each cell, these means can be considered quite stable. However, there are consistently large differences in the correlations between recall and judgment for the two groups, and this is true in all three stimulus replication conditions. In fact, the correlation is higher in the impression-after than on-line condition in *every one* of the twelve conditions observed. Thus, it is clear that the processing objectives of the subject is a critical mediating variable in determining the nature of this relationship. These data are at least consistent with the hypothesis that the impression-after subjects are engaging in some type of computational activity at the time of judgment, while on-line subjects are simply retrieving a prior evaluation.

It should be noted that these differences in the size of the correlations are not due to a "restriction of range" associated with levels of recall in the on-line condition. An examination of the data indicates that the only systematic difference in variability is associated with the length of the delay, with more variability in levels of recall being associated with the longer delay. It is noteworthy in this regard that the same difference in the size of the correlations occurs in both the short and long delay conditions. In both cases, the correspondence between recall and judgment is much greater in the impression-after than in the on-line condition.

Experiment 2

The second experiment represents a much more subtle test of the process model proposed. It is based on the fact that prior retrieval attempts typically aid subsequent recall. That is, consider a group of subjects who attempt to recall information at $Time_1$ and then again at $Time_2$. Their performance at $Time_2$ will generally be better than that of a control group who only recalls at $Time_2$. This is a very robust phenomena (Allen, Mahler, & Estes, 1969; Belmore, 1981; Erdelyi & Kleinbard, 1978: Gotz & Jacoby, 1974; Izawa, 1971; Lachman & Laughery, 1968; Modigliani, 1976), and it is usually interpreted to mean that prior attempts to recall strengthen the traces of the retrieved items.

Experiment 2 also investigated the role of "on-line" and "impression-after" processing strategies. The procedure was similar to that used in the first experiment with several important exceptions. First, each subject received information pertaining to two separate ads. This was necessary because pilot testing indicated that we were very close to obtaining floor effects on our dependent measure when only a single ad was used. To maximize the likelihood that the two ads would be processed independently, they were also chosen from two separate and distinct product classes.

In order to examine the effects of intervening cognitive activity, three separate experimental groups were created. One hour after receiving the information, one third of the subjects attempted to recall as much of the information in as much detail as possible. Then, after a 48 hour delay, they tried to recall the information again in as much detail as possible. A second group made evaluative judgments (along the same scale described previously) for each of the products after one hour. Then, after a 48 hour delay, they also tried to recall the information in as much detail as possible. Finally, as a control condition, one third of the subjects were not asked to complete any task after one hour but were asked to recall as much of the original information, in as much detail as possible, after 48 hours.

Thus, the design was a 2 × 3 completely balanced factorial with the following factors: processing objectives (on-line vs. impression-after) and nature of the intervening activity (none vs. recall vs. judgment). There were fifteen subjects randomly assigned to each of the resulting six data cells. The dependent variable of prime theoretical interest is the number of attribute units recalled by subjects after 48 hours.

For purposes of analysis, the number of attribute units recalled was summed across the two ad conditions to provide a composite index. The mean number of attribute units recalled by on-line and impression-after subjects is presented in Table 5.4 as a function of the type of intervening activity required.

One can consider the group that had no intervening task as a baseline control condition. One can see that levels of recall did not differ appreciably as a function of processing conditions in this condition. However, subjects who recalled after one hour showed much higher levels of recall after 48 hours than did the control subjects. This replicates earlier findings reported in the literature (Allen et al., 1969; Belmore, 1981; Erdelyi & Kleinbard, 1978; Gotz & Jacoby, 1974; Izawa, 1971; Lachman & Laughery, 1968; Modigliani, 1976). Note that this is true for both the on-line and impression-after subjects and, as before, there is very little difference between the on-line and impression-after subjects in this condition in terms of overall levels of recall.

TABLE 5.4
Mean Levels of Recall in Experiment 2 as a Function of Processing
Objectives and Type of Intervening Activity

	Intervening Activity		
Processing Objectives	Nothing	Recall	Judgment
On-Line	4.7	6.3	4.5
Impression-After	4.4	6.9	6.6

The most important condition in terms of the underlying theory is that where intervening judgments were made after a one hour delay. The model suggests that impression-after subjects will need to retrieve the original information in order to make such a judgment. If this is true, the same type of recall advantage after 48 hours as is seen with the "recall" group should be observed. In other words, the model suggests that the ultimate recall of impression-after subjects in the "intervening judgment" condition should be: (a) greater than that in the "no intervening activity" condition, and (b) not significantly different than that in the "intervening recall" condition. As can be seen in Table 5.4, both hypotheses received strong support.

The model also makes specific predictions about the on-line subjects in the "intervening judgment" condition. The model suggests that the on-line subjects will have already formed the evaluation at the time of information acquisition. Thus, after one hour, they will need not review the original information in order to make the judgment, but simply retrieve their original evaluation from memory. If this processs does occur, however, the ultimate memory performance of such subjects should not be as great as that of subjects in the "intervening recall" condition. In fact, this is exactly what occurred.

Discussion

The two experiments reported here represent considerable progress in our understanding of the relationship between memory and judgment. The first experiment demonstrated that the relationship between memory and judgment is mediated by the processing strategy one adopts at the time of information acquisition. In particular, correlations reported between the evaluative implications of the attribute items recalled and the global evaluative judgment were consistently higher in the impression-after than on-line conditions. It is worth noting that this was true despite the *overall* levels of recall *and* judgment being approximately equal in the two groups. This basic effect was obtained in 12 out of 12 independent comparisons and it generalized across predominantly negative, neutral, and predominately positive information sets.

It is also worth noting that the correlations for the on-line subjects in Experiment 1 were consistently greater in the recall-judgment than the judgment-recall conditions. This was true after both a five minute and 48 hour delay. This finding suggests that forcing on-line subjects to recall the original information influences judgments that immediately follow. This is just one indication that such judgments are quite "overdetermined." It is equally clear, however, that the previous evaluation continues to have a predominate influence. This can be seen in Tables 5.1–5.3 In no case do the correlations even begin to approximate those obtained from the impression-after subjects.

Although the results of Experiment 1 clearly show that the role of processing objectives needs to be considered in evaluating the relationship between recall and judgment, Experiment 2 is much more diagnostic from a conceptual point of view.

The theory presented in this chapter suggests that consumers who have an objective of forming an evaluation of a product at the time of information acquisition will form an evaluation that is stored and accessed independently of the original information. If the person is required to make an explicit evaluation at some later time (e.g., to mark a scale in an experiment, or specifically required to make a purchase decision), the consumer will simply retrieve from memory the previously formed evaluation that has been stored. Because of the independent storage mechanism that is used, there is no reason to expect a strong relationship between the evaluative implications of the attributes recalled and the global evaluative judgment. The data indicate the obtained correlations are universally positive, but several of them are near zero, and none of them are very high. This is a very simple and straightforward retrieval model that is consistent with the work of both Anderson and Hubert (1963) and Dreben et al. (1979).

The theory also suggests that people will not form a global evaluation of the product at the time of information acquisition unless this is part of their processing objective. This was examined in the present experiments by having some subjects rate the ads for how grammatical and coherent they were written. According to the theory, if such "impression-after" subjects are asked to evaluate the product at some later time, they will have to retrieve the original information, or some subset of it, and use this information as a basis for "computing" an overall evaluation of the product at the time of judgment. The data indicate that the relationships between recall and judgment under such conditions are invariably quite high. It is important to note that such a computational model is quite different from a simple retrieval model in terms of the underlying psychological processes that are hypothesized.

The results of Experiment 2 provide strong converging evidence in support of the theory proposed. The fact that intervening evaluative judgments increase levels of recall (compared to a no-intervening-task control group) for impression-after subjects but *not* for on-line subjects is difficult to explain without postulating differential retrieval mechanisms.

SOME METHODOLOGICAL CAUTIONS

We have been confronted with several methodological issues in the process of conducting this research that have not been raised previously. However, they seem well worth presenting as cautionary notes for future investigators.

First, we conducted several experiments with multiple ads pertaining to various brands within the same product class. To make a long story short, it is very difficult to detect differences as a function of processing set using these types of materials. This is particularly true when the "impression-after" variable is operationalized in terms of a memory set. It happens that subjects given information about competing brands from the same product class spontaneously form global evaluations of each brand as a mnemonic device in organizing the information presented. As a consequence, a prior evaluation is formed in each case and no differences as a function of processing set can be detected.

This problem is somewhat alleviated by using a more sterile "impression-after" condition (e.g., proofreading) *or* by using a smaller number of ads. However, the ideal situation is to use a reasonably sterile impression-after condition and, if not a single ad, a small number, each of which pertains to a different product class.

The second methodological issue to consider is how to determine the relationship between recall and judgment in quantitative terms. The data reported here are based on the correlation between the (normatively determined) evaluative implications of each attribute recalled and the extremity of the evaluative judgment made.

In a very influential article, Reyes, Thompson, and Bower (1980) have recently suggested that a preferential recall model might be more appropriate. In its simple form, attributes would be divided into positive (P) and negative (N) and a ratio of the number of positive attributes recalled to all attributes recalled can be considered. Thus, the simple preferential recall model can be represented as: $P/(P + N)$.

A more sensitive index in relating recall to judgment is given by Luce's (1959) preferential choice model, as in Eq. (1):

$$\text{Evaluation} = \frac{\Sigma R_p S_p}{\Sigma R_p S_p + R_n S_n} \qquad (1)$$

where $R_p S_p$ is any positive attribute recalled weighted by its perceived significance for the final evaluation, and $R_N S_N$ is any negative attribute recalled weighted by its perceived significance for the final evaluation.

TABLE 5.5
Hypothetical Data Demonstrating the Relationship Between Mean
Scale Values and the Luce Preferential Choice Model

Subject	Scale Values of Items Recalled	Mean Scale Value	Luce Index
1	6, 8, 3, 3	5.0	14/20 = .70
2	7, 8, 2, 3	5.0	15/20 = .75
3	6, 8, 1	5.0	14/15 = .93

The index suggested by Reyes et al., (1980) is similar but not identical to the correlational procedure used in the present investigation. For example, Table 5.5 shows hypothetical recall protocols from three subjects, where the scale values of the individual items recalled can range from 1–9. One can see that as the mean scale value of the items recalled remains constant, the Luce index can change rather dramatically.

In fact, the Luce index was computed in each of the conditions reported here and no appreciable differences in the results were obtained. This is due to the fact that the two resulting indices were very highly correlated themselves. In the studies reported in this paper, the average correlation between the two composite indices was .84.

It should also be noted that the weights used in this investigation were based on group norms. Using individually determined weights will certainly increase the size of the correlations. However, the size of this increase will need to be determined by subsequent research. More generally, the conditions under which one index proves to be more sensitive than the other will need to be addressed by future investigators. As Hastie et al. (1984) note, however, it will also be important to postulate specific psychological models of the judgment process that correspond to such equations.

A FEW REMAINING ISSUES

The experiments reported in this chapter are obviously just an initial step in understanding a very important and complicated problem. There are a large number of remaining issues to be investigated, but two would seem to be most important. First, advertisers are often interested in recognition and cued recall, as opposed to free recall situations. We have not investigated either recognition or cued recall performance within the present paradigm and this represents a ripe area for future research. In particular, researchers should look for both similarities and differences between free recall and other types of memory measures, and attempt to construct theoretical models that can account for them (see Lynch & Srull, 1982, for some suggestions as to how this might be accomplished).

Second, an important limitation of the present research is that it was confined to ads pertaining to previously unfamiliar targets. This was done intentionally to avoid the problem of addressing the way in which prior knowledge about a product affects the processing of new information. However, advertisers are obviously often interested in the effects of advertising pertaining to products with which consumers already have some degree of prior familiarity. This introduces a substantial level of complexity, but it is a problem that will need to be addressed in future work.

In summary, we believe that the theory and research presented here can be used to address the paradoxical nature of much of the existing literature pertaining to the relationship between memory and judgment. The conceptual distinction between retrieval and computational processes has already proved to be extremely useful in understanding the nature of this relationship, and we believe that it will continue to be useful in future work. It is hoped that the theory presented gives advertisers some insight into the conditions under which they can expect to find a strong correspondence between memory and judgment. It is equally important for them to also be able to identify, based upon theoretical considerations, those conditions under which such a strong correspondence should *not* be expected.

REFERENCES

Allen, G. A., Mahler, W. A., & Estes, W. K. (1969). Effects of recall tests on long term retention of paired associates. *Journal of Verbal Learning and Verbal Behavior, 8,* 463–470.

Anderson, N. H., & Hubert, S. (1963). Effects of concomitant verbal recall on order effects in personality impression formation. *Journal of Verbal Learning and Verbal Behavior, 2,* 379–391.

Asch, S. E. (1946). Forming impressions of personality. *Journal of Abnormal and Social Psychology, 41,* 258–290.

Belmore, S. M. (1981). Imagery and semantic elaboration in hypermnesia for words. *Journal of Experimental Psychology: Human Learning and Memory, 7,* 191–203.

Bettman, J. R. (1979). *An information processing theory of consumer choice.* Reading, MA: Addison-Wesley.

Brucks, M., & Mitchell, A. (1981). Knowledge structures, production systems, and decision strategies. Advances in Consumer Research, 8, 750–757.

Burke, R. (1980). *A preliminary model of consumer cognition.* Unpublished manuscript, University of Florida, Center for Consumer Research, Gainesville.

Carlston, D. E. (1980a). Events, inferences, and impression formation. In R. Hastie, T. M. Ostrom, E. B. Ebbesen, R. S. Wyer, D. L. Hamilton, & D. E. Carlston (Eds.), *Person memory: The cognitive basis of social perception.* Hillsdale, NJ: Lawrence Erlbaum Associates, 89–119.

Carlston, D. E. (1980b). The recall and use of observed behavioral episodes and inferred traits in social inference processes. *Journal of Experimental Social Psychology, 16,* 779–804.

Dreben, E. K., Fiske, S. T., & Hastie, R. (1979). The independence of item and evaluative information: Impression and recall order effects in behavior-based impression formation. *Journal of Personality and Social Psychology, 37,* 1758–1768.

Erdelyi, M., & Kleinbard, J. (1978). Has Ebbinghaus decayed with time? The growth of recall (hypermnesia) over days. *Journal of Experimental Psychology: Human Learning and Memory, 4,* 275–289.

Fiske, S. T. (1981). Social cognition and affect. In J. H. Harvey (Ed.), *Cognition, social behavior, and the environment.* Hillsdale, NJ: Lawrence Erlbaum Associates.

Fiske, S. T. (1982). Schema-triggered affect: Applications to social perception. In M. S. Clark & S. T. Fiske (Eds.), *Affect and cognition.* Hillsdale, NJ: Lawrence Erlbaum Associates, 55–78.

Fiske, S. T., Kenny, D. A., & Taylor, S. E. (1982). Structural models for the mediation of salience effects on attribution. *Journal of Experimental Social Psychology, 18,* 105–127.

Fiske, S. T., Taylor, S. E., Etcoff, N. L., & Laufer, J. K. (1979). Imaging, empathy, and causal attribution. *Journal of Experimental Social Psychology, 15,* 356–377.

Gotz, A., & Jacoby, L. L. (1974). Encoding and retrieval processes in long-term retention. *Journal of Experimental Psychology, 102,* 291–297.

Greenwald, A. G. (1968). Cognitive learning, cognitive response to persuasion, and attitude change. In A. G. Greenwald, T. C. Brock, & T. M. Ostrom (Eds.), *Psychological foundations of attitudes.* New York: Academic Press, 147–170.

Hastie, R., Park, B., & Weber, R. (1984). Social memory. In R. S. Wyer & T. K. Srull (Eds.), *Handbook of social cognition: Vol. II.* Hillsdale, NJ: Lawrence Erlbaum Associates.

Hertel, P. T. (1982). Memory for reactions and facts: The influence of subsequent information. *Journal of Experimental Psychology: Learning, Memory, and Cognition, 8,* 513–529.

Hertel, P. T. (1983). *Remembering reactions and facts: The source of bias generation.* Unpublished manuscript, Trinity University.

Hovland, C. I., Janis, I. L., & Kelley, H. H. (1953). *Communication and persuasion.* New Haven: Yale University Press.

Insko, C. A. (1964). Primacy versus recency in persuasion as a function of the timing of arguments and measures. *Journal of Abnormal and Social Psychology, 69,* 381–391.

Izawa, C. (1971). Massed and spaced practice in paired-associate learning: List versus item distribution. *Journal of Experimental Psychology, 89,* 10–21.

Johnson, M. K., & Raye, C. (1981). Reality monitoring. *Psychological Review, 88,* 67–85.

Lachman, R., Lachman, J. L., & Butterfield, E. C. (1979). *Cognitive psychology and information processing: An introduction.* Hillsdale, NJ: Lawrence Erlbaum Associates.

Lachman, R., & Laughery, K. R. (1968). Is a test trial a training trial in free recall learning? *Journal of Experimental Psychology, 76,* 40–50.

Luce, R. D. (1959). *Individual choice behavior.* New York: Wiley.

Lynch, J. G., & Srull, T. K. (1982). Memory and attentional factors in consumer choice and decision making: Concepts and research methods. *Journal of Consumer Research, 9,* 18–37.

McGuire, W. J. (1968). Nature of attitudes and attitude change. In G. Lindzey & E. Aronson (Eds.), *Handbook of social psychology: Vol. III,* 2nd ed. Reading, MA: Addison-Wesley, 136–314.

McGuire, W. J. (1980). The development of theory in social psychology. In R. Gilmour & S. Duck (Eds.), *The development of social psychology.* New York: Academic Press, 53–80.

Miller, N., & Campbell, D. T. (1959). Recency and primacy in persuasion as a function of the timing of speeches and measurements. *Journal of Abnormal and Social Psychology, 59,* 1–9.

Mitchell, A. A., & Smith, T. R. (1982). The applicability of computational process models for representing consumer behavior. *Advances in Consumer Research, 9,* 125–131.

Modigliani, V. (1976). Effects on a later recall by delaying initial recall. *Journal of Experimental Psychology: Human Learning and Memory, 2,* 609–622.

Ostrom, T. M., Lingle, J. H., Pryor, J. B., & Geva, N. (1980). Cognitive organization of person impressions. In R. Hastie, T. M. Ostrom, E. B. Ebbesen, R. S. Wyer, D. L. Hamilton, & D. E. Carlston (Eds.), *Person memory: The cognitive basis of social perception.* Hillsdale, NJ: Lawrence Erlbaum Associates, 55–88.

Petty, R. E., Ostrom, T. M., & Brock, T. C. (Eds.). (1981). *Cognitive responses in persuasion.* Hillsdale, NJ: Lawrence Erlbaum Associates.

Reyes, R. M., Thompson, W. C., & Bower, G. H. (1980). Judgmental biases resulting from differing availabilities of arguments. *Journal of Personality and Social Psychology, 39,* 2–12.

Riskey, D. R. (1979). Verbal memory processes in impression formation. *Journal of Experimental Psychology: Human Learning and Memory, 5,* 271–281.

Shoben, E. J. (1980). Theories of semantic memory: Approaches to knowledge and sentence comprehension. In R. J. Spiro, B. C. Bruce, & W. F. Brewer, (Eds.), *Theoretical issues in reading comprehension: Perspectives from cognitive psychology, linguistics, artificial intelligence, and education.* Hillsdale, NJ: Lawrence Erlbaum Associates, 309–330.

Slamecka, N. J., & Graf, P. (1978). The generation effect: Delineation of a phenomenon. *Journal of Experimental Psychology: Human Learning and Memory, 4,* 592–604.

Smith, T. R., Mitchell, A. A., & Meyer, R. (1982). A computational process model of evaluation based on the cognitive structuring of episodic knowledge. *Advances in Consumer Research, 9,* 136–143.

Taylor, S. E., & Fiske, S. T. (1975). Point-of-view and perceptions of causality. *Journal of Personality and Social Psychology, 32,* 439–445.

Taylor, S. E., & Fiske, S. T. (1978). Salience, attention, and attribution. Top of the head phenomena. In L. Berkowitz (Ed.), *Advances in experimental social psychology, Vol. II.* New York: Academic Press, 249–288.

Taylor, S. E., & Fiske, S. T. (1981). Getting inside the head: Methodologies for process analysis in attribution and social cognition. In J. H. Harvey, W. Ickes, & R. F. Kidd (Eds.), *New directions in attribution research, Vol. III.* Hillsdale, NJ: Lawrence Erlbaum Associates, 459–524.

Watts, W. A., & McGuire, W. J. (1964). Persistency of induced opinion change and retention of the inducing message contents. *Journal of Abnormal and Social Psychology, 68,* 233–241.

6

The Relationship Between Advertising Recall and Persuasion: An Experimental Investigation

Ann E. Beattie
Columbia University

Andrew A. Mitchell
University of Toronto

INTRODUCTION

One of the most prevalent methods for measuring advertising effectiveness is the use of advertising recall measures. In television advertising, for instance, the "day after" recall test is frequently used to determine the effectiveness of a particular commercial. With this method, a test commercial is run in a particular market and twenty-four hours later a random sample of consumers are called on the telephone. First, it is determined whether or not the respondent was watching the appropriate channel when the test commercial was on the air. After this has been verified, unaided and aided probes are used to determine whether the respondent remembered seeing the test commercial and what, if anything, he or she remembers about the commercial. The resulting recall score is then used as a measure of advertising effectiveness and what is recalled from the commercial is frequently used for diagnostic purposes. Many firms have a specific percentage recall base score that a commercial must exceed to be judged effective.

The use of recall as a measure of advertising effectiveness raises the critical issue of what recall actually measures. In one sense, we would like to be able to demonstrate, either theoretically or empirically, a direct link between recall and persuasion. However, published industry and academic research (reviewed in this chapter) indicates that, in general, such a link does not appear to exist. Alternatively, recall may measure one link in a causal chain between the opportunity to view an advertisement in a medium and being persuaded. One frequently mentioned hypothesis is that recall measures attention to and possibly comprehension of a commercial in traditional models of the persuasion process (Fig. 6.1). According to this hypothesis, attention to an advertisement doesn't guarantee persuasion, although all persuasive advertisements require attention. The correlation between attention and recall, how-

FIG. 6.1.   Traditional model of the persuasion process.

ever, is also inconclusive. Research in cognitive psychology indicates that while attention to a stimulus is a necessary condition for recall of that stimulus, it is not always sufficient (Norman, 1976).

Simply viewing recall as a measure of attention, then, does not appear to be entirely valid. This becomes critical if recall is used to measure advertising effectiveness, since it overlooks two important instances: (1) when factors in addition to attention affect recall and persuasion, and (2) when advertisements that are not recalled still persuade consumers. Our focus of concern in this paper is with the first instance. What level of persuasion can be expected when advertisements are recalled? Are there any specific factors or situations that may increase the validity of recall as a measure of persuasion? What factors may enhance memory for advertisements and possibly persuasion?

In this paper, we first review the published industry research examining the relationship between recall and persuasion. Second, we discuss social psychological research examining this relationship. A review of factors affecting recall and a model of the information acquisition process are then presented to set the stage for our research on recall and persuasion. Finally, a theoretical model of recall and persuasion in advertising is discussed as the basis of an initial study examining these issues.

Advertising Industry Research

Previous industry research indicates a weak relationship, at best, between recall and persuasion. Ross (1982), for instance, reported the results of a series of television commercial tests of 142 different commercials for products in 55 different categories. The advertisements were effective in changing 10% of the sampled viewers' preferences to the advertised brands as determined by the Mapes and Ross system, which measures both day after recall and brand preference change. Two weeks later, respondents were asked over the telephone about brand purchases in the relevant product categories during the elapsed time. Considering only those consumers who both changed preference to the advertised brands and purchased that brand, those who recalled the brand advertisement held a 45.8% share of product class purchases. Respondents that did not recall the advertisement for a test brand had a 40.7% share among purchases.

In sum, of all the respondents that changed preferences to the test brand, those that remembered the test commercial allocated a slightly larger percentage of their product category purchases to the test brand than did those who did not remember the test commercial. No test was made, however, to determine whether this difference was statistically significant.

Gibson (1983) reviewed eight studies that examined the relationship between recall and persuasion. All eight studies found a weak or an insignificant relationship. Young (1972), for instance, reported a correlation of .05 between recall and persuasion and Stout (1981) reported virtually no relationship for 52 different commercials that were tested.

The results of these studies indicate a weak or non-existent relationship between advertising recall and persuasion. None of these studies, however, made a micro-level examination of these issues by using psychological theory to examine factors that may affect advertising recall and mediate the relationship between advertising recall and persuasion. Consequently, they could not examine specific conditions where such a relationship might exist.

Social Psychological Research

Research in two areas of social psychology has examined the relationship between recall of presented information and persuasion. The first area where this relationship has been examined is in the persuasion literature. Here numerous studies have found either a weak or no relationship between recall of message arguments and persuasion using either correlational methods (e.g., Insko, 1969; Wilson & Miller, 1968) or comparisons of attitude and retention of information time trends (e.g., Papageorgis, 1963; Watts & McGuire, 1964). After a thorough review of the research in this area, Greenwald (1968) concluded that there appears to be little relationship between persuasion and recall of message arguments.

The results of numerous studies in impression formation, the second area, also indicate little relationship between recall of information presented in a message and persuasion. Dreben, Fiske, and Hastie (1979), for instance, presented subjects with information about hypothetical individuals and asked them to evaluate each individual. Later subjects were asked to recall as much of the presented information as possible. An information integration model (Anderson, 1971) was used to determine which information carried the most weight in forming an evaluation. An examination of the relationship between the weight placed on a particular piece of information and the probability of recalling it indicated that the correlation was near zero. In general, the size of the weight placed on a piece of information was largest for information presented first while information presented last was more likely to be recalled. Similar results were reported by Anderson and Hubert (1963).

In sum, evidence from social psychological research indicates that recalled information does not provide a clear indication of evaluation or persuasion. However, these studies only examined the relationship between recall of specific information about a single stimulus and evaluation. With advertising, concern lies with whether an advertisement is recalled at all, what affects that recall, and how memory for advertising is related to persuasion. In order to examine these issues, and the conditions when recall might accurately reflect persuasion, the cognitive underpinnings of recall should be examined. The next section reviews factors that affect recall of information and discusses how information is processed and retrieved. These models of information processing will help illustrate our own model of the recall-persuasion relationship in advertising.

Factors Affecting Recall

There has been considerable research directed at understanding the factors that affect recall of a stimulus. Three of these factors are especially relevant for the examination of the relationship between recall and persuasion. The first is the serial position of the stimulus relative to the other stimuli to be learned. It has been found, for instance, that when individuals are asked to learn a number of different words presented sequentially, they are more likely to recall the words that were presented first and those that were presented last (e.g., Murdock, 1962). This is known as the primacy and recency effect, respectively.

Another factor involves characteristics of the stimulus. A number of studies using both verbal and visual stimuli have found that distinctive stimuli are better remembered (e.g., Hunt & Mitchell, 1978; Light, Kayra-Stuart, & Hollander, 1979). Distinctiveness in these studies is defined relative to the other presented stimuli or to a previously defined set of stimuli. Theoretically, distinctive stimuli are thought to create unique memory traces, which makes them easier to locate in memory.

The processing strategy that is used during exposure to the stimuli can also affect recall. Considerable research within the depth of processing paradigm, for instance, has indicated that stimuli processed at a semantic level are recalled better than stimuli processed at a structural level (Craik & Tulving, 1975; Hyde & Jenkins, 1968). With semantic processing the focus is on the meaning of the stimulus while with structural processing the individual focuses on the appearance of the stimulus. A number of different theoretical explanations have been proposed to explain these results. Anderson and Reder (1979), for instance, have suggested that semantic processing causes more linkages to be formed in memory between the test word and other concepts in memory. The formation of these additional linkages facilitates recall. An alternative explanation, provided by Jacoby and Craik (1979), is that semantic processing causes the formation of a more distinctive memory trace which, in turn, makes it easier to locate in memory.

As mentioned previously these factors are of direct interest in any investigation of the relationship between recall and persuasion. First, in any such investigation, primacy and recency effects of information retrieval must be controlled. Second, the finding that distinctive stimuli (stimuli that are different from other members of a set) are better recalled provides a means of controlling which advertisements are recalled. Finally, the finding that type of processing (e.g., structural or semantic) affects both the amount and type of information recalled suggest that this may be an important variable affecting recall of advertisements. Since recall figures so prominently in our investigation of advertising persuasiveness, these last two points deserve elaboration. In the next section "distinctive" advertisements and their implications for recall are discussed. Cognitive models of information processing are then presented as a prelude to examining specific conditions under which recall might be tied to persuasion.

Distinctiveness

The memorability of distinctive stimuli has been researched under a variety of conditions, and has been given several labels. A brief review of this phenomena will define what it is about distinctive stimuli that makes them so memorable, and will clarify why we are interested in using distinctiveness to manipulate recall of advertisements.

The von Restorff phenomenon (see Wallace, 1965) demonstrated the superiority of learning items that are isolated in a list. Most of the research concerning the von Restorff phenomenon has limited generalizability in an advertising context, since the experimental procedure involves learning paired-associate lists. However, the operationalization of "isolation" is analogous to our conceptualization of distinctiveness. Typically, isolated items in a list are presented in color while other list items are shown in black-and-white, or the isolated item was of a different stimuli class than the rest of the list (e.g., numerals versus words). The increased learning for isolated items has been attributed to their "attention-getting value" and the increased rehearsal of those items in memory (e.g., Jenkins & Postman, 1948). A final caveat of the von Restorff phenomenon is necessary, though. While isolation of the type described above has been shown to facilitate learning, there are mixed results on the long-term memorability of isolated items in a list (see Wallace, 1965).

More recent investigations on the effects of vivid stimuli have shown that while such material is more likely to be remembered than more pallid material, there is no consistent evidence that vivid stimuli lead to more persuasion (Taylor & Thompson, 1982). Work along these lines is relevant to our discussion of advertising, since in most of the studies the vivid stimuli were embedded in a semantically rich context. Research on the vividness effect has operationalized vividness through material that is colorful, concrete, and imagery-provoking compared to more pallid and dull information. In a review of more than 50 studies on the vividness effect, Taylor and Thompson found that most show superior recall of vivid material compared to less vivid material. In discussing the vividness effect as it relates specifically to advertising, Taylor and Wood (1983) suggest that vivid information may have an impact on persuasion only when differential attention to information is allowed. In other words, when individuals are presented with numerous stimuli at the same time, they tend to focus on the vivid stimuli and evaluate these stimuli more extremely (Taylor & Fiske, 1978).

Both sets of research described here explain the effects of distinctive or vivid stimuli on recall by invoking the gestalt tradition. A distinctive "figure" receives greater attention (and perhaps more processing) than does the "ground" that it stands against. For the purpose of exploring the recall/persuasion link in advertising, the concern here lies with: (1) the greater memorability of a distinctive "figure" against "ground," and (2) the notion that such distinctive stimuli are better recalled than non-distinctive stimuli because of the greater rehearsing or processing it receives. In essence, we are concerned with manipulating overall recall via advertising distinctiveness. Any advertisement that is perceived as distinctive compared to other advertisements should be better recalled. For a more specific analysis of how information might be stored in memory, facilitating recall, we turn to a discussion of encoding in information processing.

Information Processing and Memory

In briefly discussing information processing as a factor affecting recall, semantic and structural processing were mentioned as affecting whether the meaning or "appearance" of stimuli is stored in memory. Several related findings in cognitive psychology support this effect, and suggest that semantic information is better remembered than surface or structural information. A review of these findings is important in describing how various processing strategies can affect recall of advertising information.

One standard finding in cognitive psychology is that information generated by an individual is recalled better than presented information. For instance, if someone is shown a string of numbers and asked to add them, keeping a running total, the probability of remembering a number from the running total is significantly greater than remembering one of the original string of numbers (Dosher & Russo, 1976). This phenomenon has been termed the generation effect (Slamecka & Graf, 1978).

A related finding is that an individual's memory for the meaning of sentences they have read is better than their memory for the actual wording of the sentence (Bransford, Barclay, & Franks, 1971; Sachs, 1967, 1974). For instance, if presented with the sentence, "Kleenex was purchased by the maid," subjects will remember the meaning of the sentence, but after a short period of time they will be able to recognize the sentence they saw originally only at chance levels if sentences that have similar meanings are used as foils (e.g., "The maid bought tissues").

These findings have lead to a model of memory in which the presented information is stored in episodic form and the interpreted information is integrated with previously stored semantic information (e.g., Schank, 1972; Norman & Rumelhart, 1975). According to these models, the presented information stored in episodic form decays rather quickly, however, the processed information that is integrated into the semantic network remains in retrievable form over extended periods of time.

During exposure to an advertisement, individuals may generate verbal thoughts about the advertisement. These thoughts may be counterarguments or support arguments, thoughts about the advertisement, thoughts about the usefulness of the advertised product, or even irrelevant thoughts. Some of those thoughts will be integrated into the individual's current knowledge structure about the advertised product. A memory trace of the advertisement will also be stored in memory, however, this memory trace will decay rather quickly.

An example of this process is presented in Fig. 6.2. Here an individual is exposed to an advertisement for TRIM Toothpaste. A memory trace of the original message is stored in memory (arrow 1), however, this memory trace will decay rather quickly. While exposed to the advertisement, the individual also verbally responds to the message by agreeing that TRIM Toothpaste will be effective in preventing tooth decay and makes the inference that it probably doesn't taste very good (arrow 2). Based on these verbal responses, the association "best toothpaste for preventing decay" and "doesn't taste good" are

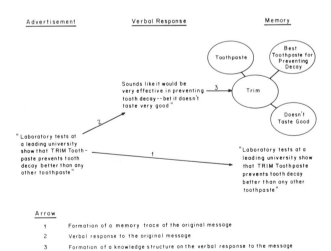

FIG. 6.2.   Model of information encoding process.

linked to the brand name in memory. These form the individual's belief system for TRIM Toothpaste and remain accessible to the individual over time.

Theoretical Framework

In previous papers, we have differentiated between brand and nonbrand processing strategies (Mitchell, Gardner, & Russo, 1981; Mitchell, 1983a). With a brand processing strategy, individuals actively process the product related information in the advertisement to form an evaluation of the advertised brand. This is similar to what Lichtenstein and Srull (this volume) refer to as on-line processing and generally reflects high consumer involvement. A nonbrand processing strategy refers to all other processing strategies where no evaluation of the advertised brand is made during exposure to the persuasive communication. This may include looking at the models used in the advertisement or trying to identify where the commercial was filmed. With a nonbrand processing strategy, the consumer will acquire some information about the advertised brand, however, it will not be organized in a coherent manner and the consumer will not form an evaluation of the advertised brand. A nonbrand processing strategy generally reflects low consumer involvement.

These two processing strategies are analogous to the semantic and structural processing strategies in the depth of processing paradigm — only here the stimuli are advertisements instead of words. With a brand processing strategy, the individual attaches meaning to the advertised product so they can decide whether or not they would be interested in purchasing it. With a nonbrand processing strategy they are only interested in the appearance of the advertisement. They may attach meaning to various aspects of the advertisement, but they do not attach meaning to the information being communicated about the advertised product.

These two processing strategies are depicted in Fig. 6.3. With brand processing, the individual generates counterarguments and support arguments during exposure to the advertisement which, in turn, results in attitude formation or change. This verbal processing also results in information about the brand being stored in memory. At the same time, a memory trace of the advertisement is also stored in memory.

With nonbrand processing, there is little, if any, verbal processing of information about the advertised product. Some verbal information, however, is acquired and a memory trace of the advertisement is stored in memory. At some later point in time, if an individual tries to form an evaluation of the brand, he or she must retrieve from memory whatever information is available about the brand. This would include whatever verbal information can be retrieved and the memory trace of the advertisement, if it can be retrieved.

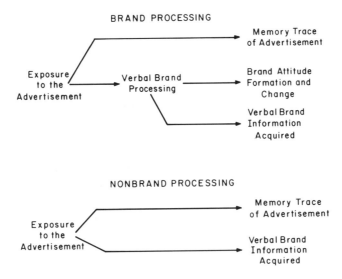

FIG. 6.3.   Alternative information acquisition processes.

These models suggest that recall of advertisements should have its greatest effect on persuasion when the individual executes a nonbrand processing strategy. With a brand processing strategy, the individual has already formed an evaluation of the advertised brand and when asked for an evaluation of the brand, the prior evaluation can simply be retrieved. With nonbrand processing though, the individual must retrieve information about the product from the memory trace of the advertisement to form an evaluation. Consequently, with nonbrand processing there should be a closer link between recall and persuasion than with brand processing.

RESEARCH GOALS

Our major research goal in designing this study was to examine factors affecting the relationship between recall and persuasion. As a preliminary test of our hypotheses, we wanted to create conditions that would be most conducive to finding a relationship between recall and persuasion, while controlling other factors that might interfere. To examine this relationship we exposed subjects to a large number of advertisements so they would not be able to remember all of them. Within our set of advertisements, though, we wanted to create advertisements that would vary in the probability of being recalled. Therefore, we also manipulated the distinctiveness of the advertisements. To avoid an attentional explanation of differential recall, subjects saw each advertisement under conditions of full attention (forced exposure). This restriction should reduce the effects of distinctiveness on persuasion (see Taylor & Wood, 1983), but rehearsal and fuller processing may still allow for better recall of distinctive advertisements.

Finally, we induced our subjects to view advertisements while engaged in a brand processing strategy or a nonbrand processing strategy. This was expected to encourage more semantic processing for those using a brand strategy, and more structural processing for those using a nonbrand strategy. In sum, then, we created a message-dense environment (e.g., Ronis, Baumgardner, Leippe, Cacioppo, & Greenwald, 1977) where our subjects saw many different advertisements, some of which were more distinctive than others, promoting better recall. Through a manipulation of processing strategy, some subjects were encouraged to focus on the advertised product, some to focus on the advertisement itself.

Three specific hypotheses were explored:

1. Distinctive advertisements are more likely to be recalled than less distinctive advertisements.
2. There will be *no* relationship between recall of an advertisement and persuasion under brand processing conditions.
3. There will be a relationship between recall of the advertisement and persuasion under nonbrand processing conditions.

METHOD

Subjects

Subjects were 31 undergraduates of both sexes from Carnegie-Mellon University who were each paid $8.00 for their participation in this study. They were recruited from business and psychology classes and through signs placed on campus.

Design

Overview. This study tested the effects of the relative distinctiveness of advertisements (Adtype) and how the advertisement information was processed (Processing strategy) on the evaluation and recall of the advertisements. The overall design was a mixed factor design with three levels of Adtype (black-and-white, color, color with product attribute emphasized) and two levels of Processing strategy (brand, nonbrand) with repeated measures on the first factor.

Each subject viewed 12 test advertisements and 20 fillers, a total of 32 advertisements. The use of filler advertisements served two purposes. First, the inclusion of those advertisements reduced the likelihood that the subjects would remember all of the 12 test advertisements. The intention here was to avoid a ceiling effect on recall for test advertisements.

The distinctiveness of the advertisements was manipulated through the relative distinctiveness of the visual element in each advertisement. The 20 filler advertisements had black-and-white pictures to provide a "baseline" or context for the test advertisements.

Stimuli.   Three criteria were used in selecting products. First, they had to be products that college students had purchased and used. Second, each product had to have a relatively small number of salient attributes. Finally, one of the salient attributes had to be depicted visually. Based on these criteria, the following product classes were selected for the test advertisements: detergent, facial tissues, light bulbs, aspirin, gum, toothpaste, ball point pens, car wax, paper towels, soft drinks, shampoo, and cellophane tape. Different products were selected for the filler advertisements.

Each advertisement contained a picture of the product, the ficticious brand name in bold print, and approximately 30 words of copy about the product. Brand names were pretested as having no discernible prior connotations. The copy mentioned the two most important attributes for each product, as determined from pretests, and the copy for each product was pretested as eliciting slightly positive reactions from undergraduates. The pictures used in the advertisements featured an artist's drawing of each product. Pretesting indicated that undergraduates perceived the advertised products as slightly positive after being exposed to the advertisements.

Distinctiveness Manipulation.   The distinctiveness of each advertisement (Adtype) was manipulated across products so that visually each product was portrayed in: black-and-white, color, or color with the most important product attribute emphasized. So, for example, the following copy for "Hadel" light bulbs would be the same under each level of Adtype mentioned above:

> Hadel light bulbs burn longer than any other light bulbs. They shine on and on and on . . . and come in all sizes and wattages. Hadel light bulbs — to brighten your life.

Under the black-and-white Adtype condition, this copy was paired with a black-and-white drawing of a glowing light bulb. Under the color Adtype condition, the copy appeared with the same drawing of a light bulb, but the drawing was in color. Under the attribute Adtype condition, the picture appearing with the copy was the same color drawing of a light bulb, but behind the light bulb were two calendars, dated 5 years apart. This drawing visually portrayed the passage of time, reinforcing the copy claim that Hadel light bulbs "shine on and on and on . . . . "

Subjects saw 12 test advertisements for different products; four of these showed the product in black-and-white, four showed the product in color, and four showed a color picture with an attribute emphasized. The pairing of the 12 test advertisements with Adtype levels was counterbalanced across subjects so approximately one-third of the subjects saw a given product advertised in black-and-white, another third saw it advertised in color, and another third saw it advertised in color with a product attribute emphasized. This allowed a within-subjects manipulation of Adtype, and counterbalancing precluded biased data due to subjects' reaction to any given product. Products were also counterbalanced across Adtype conditions, so that the same four products never appeared together under more than one Adtype condition. This precluded product order by Adtype condition effects on dependent measures.

Processing Manipulation.   While subjects viewed the 32 advertisements (12 test ads and 20 filler ads), they were asked to fill out a series of scales for each advertisement. In the brand processing condition, the scales were designed to focus subjects' attention on purchasing the advertised product. For example, one scale asked subjects to rate how interested they would be in purchasing the product. This manipulation attempted to mimic "high consumer involvement" conditions, where consumers focus attention on information concerning the product itself, rather than elements of the advertisement or other distracting stimuli. In the nonbrand processing strategy condition, subjects were asked to fill out scales for each advertisement that focused their attention on the advertisement itself. For example, one scale asked subjects to rate the "attention-getting" quality of the advertisement. This manipulation was designed to induce "low consumer involvement" in subjects, in the sense that they would focus attention on the advertisement rather than the advertised product.

Dependent Measures

The effects of advertisement distinctiveness and processing condition were tested using the following dependent measures: unaided recall, product evaluation, aided recall, perceived distinctiveness of the advertisement, confidence in the accuracy of recall, elicited brand beliefs, product interest and familiarity, and advertisement evaluations. The results presented in the next section are based only on unaided recall, aided recall, perceived distinctiveness of the advertisement, and product evaluations. These four measures are described here.

The unaided recall measure simply asked subjects to list the products featured in the advertisements that they remembered. The aided recall measure prompted subjects with the product name, and asked them to list everything they could remember about the advertisement. In order to be counted as an aided recall, the subject had to recall something unique about the advertisement. The product evaluation measure listed each test product name, and asked subjects to indicate how they felt about the product on seven point scales anchored by the adjectives "good-bad," "pleasant-unpleasant" and "like-dislike." Finally, a measure of the subjects' perceived distinctiveness of each advertisement relative to all the other advertisements was obtained by having them respond to a seven point scale anchored by the phases "about the same" and "very distinctive."

Procedure and Summary

Subjects (in groups of about 5) were exposed to 32 advertisements (on slides) in the following order: 5 filler ads (to avoid primacy effects in recall), the 12 test ads interspersed with 7 filler ads, and 8 filler ads (to avoid recency effects in recall). All of the 20 filler advertisements had the same form as the black-and-white test advertisements, to provide a baseline for advertisement distinctiveness within the context of this study. As mentioned previously, the 12 test advertisements each subject saw included 4 in black-and-white, 4 in color, and 4 in color with a product attribute emphasized. This describes the within-subjects manipulation of advertisement distinctiveness (Adtype).

While viewing the advertisements, one-half of the subjects were asked to fill out a series of scales that focused attention on the product (brand processing strategy). The other half of the subjects were asked to fill out a series of scales that focused attention on the advertisement (nonbrand processing strategy). This describes the between-subjects manipulation of Processing strategy.

After viewing all 32 advertisements, subjects were given a filler task to clear short-term memory. They were then asked for their unaided recall of the advertisements. A product evaluation measure followed, asking subjects to rate their feelings about each test product. After another filler task (again, to clear short-term memory), subjects were asked to list everything they could remember about the test advertisements in an aided recall measure. Several other dependent measures were then taken, none of which are directly relevant to the results reported here. Finally, the subjects were shown the test advertisements again and asked to rate how distinctive each advertisement was relative to the other advertisements they had just seen.

RESULTS

The results are presented in three sections. The first presents the results of the manipulation checks on the distinctiveness of test advertisements (Adtype) and the Processing strategy manipulation. The second provides the results for the dependent measures of interest: brand evaluations, unaided recall, and aided recall. The final results section discusses the relationship between brand evaluations and recall of the advertisements.

A standard Analysis of Variance (ANOVA) for the manipulation checks and dependent measures took the form: 3(Adtype: black-and-white, color, attribute emphasized) × 2(Processing strategy: brand, nonbrand) with repeated measures on the first factor. In reporting the results from this study, only effects (or lack thereof) that are relevant to hypotheses are presented.

Distinctiveness Manipulation Check

The perceived distinctiveness of each Adtype was measured by asking subjects to rate each test advertisement for distinctiveness in comparison to the other advertisements in the set. Ratings could range from one (about the same) to seven (very distinctive). A main effect for Adtype $[F (2,58) = 20.57, p < .001]$[1] indicated that subjects did perceive differences in the distinctiveness of advertisements. In fact, testing mean differences between levels of Adtype (Newman-Kuels) indicated that the black-and-white test advertisements ($M = 3.3$) were seen as less distinctive than both color advertisements ($M = 4.3$; $p < 0.05$) and attribute-emphasized advertisements ($M = 4.7$; $p < 0.05$). The difference in perceived distinctiveness between color and attribute-emphasized advertisements was in the correct direction, but was not statistically significant ($p > 0.1$). The manipulation of Adtype, then, was successful at least between black-and-white advertisements and color and attribute-emphasized advertisements.

Processing Strategy Manipulation Check

A test on the effectiveness of the Processing Strategy manipulation would involve a measure of subjects' verbal responses concerning the advertised product (brand strategy), and the advertisement itself (nonbrand strategy) during exposure to each advertisement. Since this type of measure was impractical within the confines of this study, an indirect test involved a measure

---

[1]To control for possible deviations from the homogeneity assumption, the Greenhouse and Geiser (1959) procedure was used to adjust the degrees of freedom on the F test for the within subject factors and the interactions. Since the results were similar using both the actual and adjusted degrees of freedom, only the actual degrees of freedom and probability levels are reported in this paper.

of the type of recall (concerning the product or advertisement) that subjects evidenced during aided recall. This indirect way of testing the effectiveness of the Processing strategy manipulation is justified by previous studies which indicate a close relationship between processing strategy and type of recall (e.g., Mitchell, 1984).

The subjects' statements about the test advertisements on the aided recall measure were coded by two coders (one was one of the authors) as a product statement, an advertisement statement, or a product and advertisement statement using the criteria given in Appendix A at the end of this chapter. The coders agreed on 87% of the statements. Disagreements were resolved through discussion.

An interaction between Processing Strategy and Type of Recall (product, advertisement) where subjects executing a brand strategy recall more about the product and subjects executing a nonbrand strategy recall more about the advertisement, would indicate a successful manipulation of Processing Strategy. This interaction was significant, $F(2,58) = 25.67$, $p < .001$. Pairwise tests (Newman-Kuels) indicated that subjects engaged in nonbrand processing did recall more about the advertisement than about the product, ($p < .01$) (see Fig. 6.4). Subjects engaged in brand processing, however, showed no significant difference in the amount of recall between the product and advertisement. Information about the product, then, was better recalled with a brand processing strategy than with a nonbrand strategy ($p < .05$). Subjects also recalled more about advertisements with a nonbrand strategy than with a brand strategy, however, this difference was only marginally significant ($p < 0.10$). This suggests that the Processing Strategy manipulation was successful.

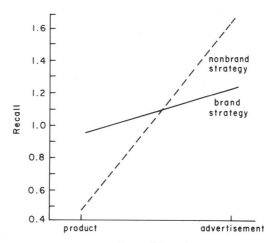

FIG. 6.4. Recall by type of recall and processing strategy.

TABLE 6.1
Brand Attitudes by Adtype and Processing Strategy

| | Processing Strategy | | |
Type of Advertisement	Brand Processing	Non Brand Processing	Overall Mean
Black and White	4.36	3.45	3.94
Color	4.10	3.81	3.96
Attribute Emphasized	4.40	4.13	4.27
Overall Mean	4.28	3.80	

Note: Brand attributes are measured on a 1 to 7 scale where higher numbers indicate more favorable brand attitudes.

Brand Attitudes

Brand attitudes for test products were averaged across three scales to increase reliability. Ratings of test products on the dimensions "bad-good," "unpleasant-pleasant" and "dislike-like" could range from one (negative evaluation) to seven (positive evaluation).

A significant main effect for Adtype was observed $[F (2,58) = 4.14,$ $p < .01]$. Pairwise tests (Newman-Kuels) indicated that products advertised with pictures where a product attribute was emphasized were evaluated more positively than products advertised with black-and-white or color Adtypes (Table 6.1).

An interaction between Adtype and Processing Strategy was also significant $[F (2,58) = 4.07, p < .01]$. A comparison of means (Newman-Kuels) indicated that when subjects engaged in a brand processing strategy, there were no differences in brand attitudes for the different Adtypes. However, when subjects were using a nonbrand strategy, products advertised with the attribute emphasized Adtypes received more positive evaluations than products advertised with black-and-white pictures $(p < .01$, respectively). Considering differences in product evaluations between Processing strategies, the only significant difference occurred when products were advertised with black-and-white pictures; a brand strategy led to higher evaluations, $(p < .01)$.[2] In sum, Adtype seemed to affect product evaluations only under conditions of non-brand processing, where products advertised with attribute emphasized ads received higher evaluations.

---

[2]This reflects a trend towards a main effect where products were evaluated more positively under conditions of brand strategy processing ($M = 4.29$) than under nonbrand strategy processing ($M = 3.73$), $F (1,30) = 2.91, p < .10$.

Recall Measures

Unaided Recall. For the unaided recall measure, subjects listed all the products featured in the advertisements they remembered without being cued in any way. This measure, then, reflects the percentage of advertisements recalled.[3] A significant main effect for Adtype indicated that subjects did show differential recall for products advertised with the different types of advertisements [F (2,58) = 4.26, $p < .01$].[4] A comparison of means (Newman-Kuels) indicates that subjects recalled more advertisements that were advertised with an attribute emphasized (58%) than products advertised in black-and-white (47% $p < .05$) or products advertised in color (42% $p < .01$). This pattern of means for unaided recall, while not precisely the same as for brand attitudes, was in the same direction: Products advertised with an attribute emphasized were both evaluated more positively and better recalled than products advertised in black-and-white. In addition, products were also evaluated more positively and recalled better in the brand processing condition, however, these differences were only marginally significant.

Aided Recall. For this recall measure, subjects were prompted with the product name, and asked to list everything they could remember about the advertisement. The subjects' recall was coded by two coders (one was one of the authors) as "definitely recalled," "maybe recalled," or "definitely not recalled." Aided recall scores could take on values of 0 (not recalled), 1 (maybe recalled), or 2 (recalled). If the subject could not remember the advertisement or confused it with another advertisement, it was judged as a "definitely not recalled." If the subject mentioned something about the advertisement that was not unique to that advertisement (e.g., it had a picture of the product) it was judged as a "maybe recalled." In order to be judged as a "definitely recalled" the subject had to mention something that was unique to that advertisement. The coders agreed on 95% of the test advertisements. Disagreements were resolved through discussion.

A significant main effect for Processing Strategy [(F (1,30) = 7.25, $p < .01$)] mimicked a trend for unaided recall (see footnote 4): Subjects engaged in brand processing recalled the advertisements better than subjects engaged in non-brand processing (see Table 6.2). There was also a significant main effect for Adtype, [F (2,58) = 12.55, $p < .001$]. A test of mean differ-

---

[3]For this analysis, the data were aggregated by Adtype to avoid use of a dichtomous dependent variable.

[4]There was also a trend toward a Processing strategy main effect, F (1,30) = 3.10, $p < .10$, where subjects engaged in a brand stragegy tended to recall more advertisements (M = 55%) than subjects engaged in a nonbrand strategy (M = 44%).

TABLE 6.2
Aided Recall by Adtype and Processing Strategy

Type of Advertisement	Processing Strategy		
	Brand Processing	Non Brand Processing	Overall Mean
Black and White	1.56	1.22	1.40
Color	1.78	1.40	1.60
Attribute Emphasized	1.76	1.64	1.71
Overall Mean	1.70	1.42	

Note: Aided recall is measured on a 0 to 2 scale where a 0 is definitely not recalled. 1 is maybe recalled and 2 is definitely recalled.

ences (Newman-Kuels) indicated that all subjects evidence better recall when products were advertised with an attribute emphasized than when products were advertised in color ($p < .05$), or in black-and-white, ($p < .001$). Color advertisements, in turn, were recalled better than black-and-white advertisements, ($p < .05$) (see Table 6.2).[5] In the next section, the relationship between the distinctiveness of the advertisements and recall is examined.

Effect of Distinctiveness on Recall

To examine whether the subjects' perception of the distinctiveness of the advertisements was related to aided and unaided recall, an analysis of covariance was performed. Here the dependent variable was the recall measure and the covariate was perceived distinctiveness. If perceived distinctiveness mediates the recall of advertisements, then the use of distinctiveness as a covariate should cause a large reduction in the size of the F ratio for the Adtype factor. This turned out to be true. In addition, the use of perceived distinctiveness as a covariate had little effect on the F ratio for the Processing Strategy factor. For instance, for aided recall, the F ratio for the Adtype factor was reduced from 12.55 to 3.90, while the F ratio for Processing strategy went from 7.25

---

[5]There was also a marginally significant interaction between Processing strategy and Adtype, $F(2,58) = 2.58, p < .10$. Pairwise tests (Newman-Kuels) indicate that subjects engaged in brand processing had better recall for color advertisements and advertisements with a product attribute emphasized than black-and-white advertisements ($p < .05$ and $p < .001$, respectively). Subjects engaged in nonbrand processing, though, showed better recall when products were advertised with an attribute emphasized than when products were advertised in color or black-and-white ($p < .05$ and $p < .001$, respectively). Of particular interest to advertisers is a comparison between the two Processing strategies at different levels of Adtype. Brand processors recalled advertisements better than nonbrand processors when products were advertised both in black-and-white ($p < .01$), and color ($p < .01$). However, there was no difference in recall between the two processing strategies when products were advertised with an attribute emphasized.

to 6.10. Consequently, although the subjects' perception of the distinctiveness of the advertisement did not eliminate the entire impact of Adtype on recall, it clearly had a major effect.

Recall and Brand Attitudes

The previous analyses demonstrated a similar pattern of means by Adtype and Processing strategy for the aided and unaided recall measures and brand attitudes. This section explores these relationships directly.

In order to examine the relationship between brand attitude and recall a repeated measures ANOVA was used where Recall (yes, no) was added as a between-subject factor with Processing strategy.[6] The dependent measure here was brand attitude and the Recall factor was either the judged unaided or aided recall measure. The results for these two measures were virtually identical, so only the aided recall measure is presented.

The predicted Processing Strategy by Recall interaction was significant [$F(1,29) = 3.44$; $p < 0.05$],[7] and the means were in the predicted direction for the different Processing strategies (see Fig. 6.5). That is, considering both types of recall measures, subjects using a brand processing strategy showed no difference in brand attitudes as a function of recall, while subjects using a non-brand strategy evaluated products more positively when they were better recalled than when they were not recalled. This is as predicted, since with brand processing the subjects formed an evaluation of the advertised brand while they were exposed to the advertisement. When later asked to report this evaluation, they simply retrieved it from memory. Consequently, recall of the advertisement had no effect on the evaluation. With nonbrand processing, the individual did not form an evaluation of the advertised brand during exposure to the advertisement. When they are later asked to form an evaluation, they had to retrieve information about the brand and advertisement from memory to form this evaluation. Under these conditions recall of the advertisement had an effect on brand evaluations.

CONCLUSIONS

In this section, we first summarize the findings from this study concerning factors affecting both aided and unaided recall of advertisements. Then we

---

[6]Subjects whose recall was judged as "maybe" were included in the "yes" level of the Recall factor.

[7]Since the Recall factor and the Adtype factor are not orthogonal, the statistical significance of the results depends on the order in which the tests are made. The Recall factor and the Processing Strategy by Recall interaction were tested first for the results presented here. When the Recall factor and the Processing Strategy by Recall interaction were tested second, the interaction was only marginally significant.

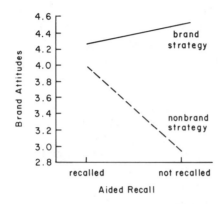

FIG. 6.5.   Brand attitudes by processing strategy and aided recall.

discuss the factors affecting brand attitudes and the relationship between brand attitude and recall. Finally, the generalizability of the results is discussed, along with future directions for exploring a recall/persuasion link in advertising.

Recall

In this study, only the Type of Advertisement was found to affect unaided recall. A significantly higher percentage of the advertisements in which an attribute was emphasized were recalled than advertisements in color or black and white. Slightly more advertisements were recalled under the brand processing manipulation than under the nonbrand processing manipulation, however, this difference showed only a trend toward significance.

For the aided recall measure, both Type of Advertisement and Processing Strategy affected recall. Subjects using a brand processing strategy recalled significantly more advertisements than subjects using a nonbrand processing strategy. Regardless of processing strategy, advertisements in which a product attribute was emphasized were recalled better than the color advertisements, which in turn, were recalled better than the black and white advertisements.

These results can be partially explained through the use of a network model of memory (Anderson, 1983a, 1983b). Within this model the nodes of the network are concepts and the arcs are linkages between concepts. The memory structure for a particular brand might consist of a brand node and a number of concepts or beliefs about the brand that are linked to the brand node (Fig. 6.6). One of these concepts may be the memory trace of an advertisement for the brand.

Recall, within this model, occurs through spreading activation. When someone thinks about a concept, such as a brand, the node representing that concept in memory is activated and activation then spreads to the nodes that are linked to the activated node. When the activation level of a particular node exceeds a threshold level, the contents of that node are recalled.

With a brand processing strategy, the individual will generally activate (or create) the appropriate brand or product node while processing information from the advertisement (Mitchell, 1983b). This increases the likelihood that a linkage will be formed between the brand or product node and a memory trace of the advertisement. With aided recall, the use of the brand or product name as a probe results in the activation of the brand or product node in memory. If a linkage has been formed between this node and a memory trace of the advertisement, the advertisement will probably be recalled.

With a nonbrand processing strategy, the individual will not activate (or create) the appropriate brand or product node in memory while processing the information from the advertisement so a linkage between this node and a memory trace of the advertisement probably will not be formed, or if it is, the link will be weak. Consequently, the use of a brand or product memory probe will not facilitate recall and aided recall will be approximately the same as unaided recall. In the study reported here, the subjects remembered approximately 50% of the test advertisements with unaided recall. With aided recall the subjects remembered around 80% of the test advertisements if they executed a brand processing strategy and 60% of the test advertisements if they executed a nonbrand processing strategy.

Since all the commercials were viewed under forced exposure conditions, these results indicate that recall is not a pure measure of whether or not the in-

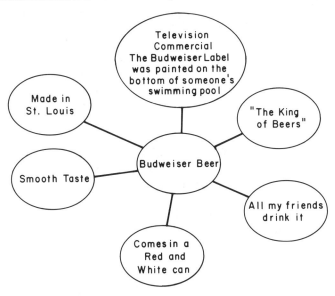

FIG. 6.6. Example of a hypothetic memory structure for Budweiser beer.

dividual attended to the advertisement. Clearly, in order to remember an advertisement, the individual must have attended to it, however, not all advertisements that are attended to are recalled. In this study, the type of advertisement also had an effect on recall.

Brand Attitudes

The type of advertisement affected brand attitudes only with a nonbrand processing strategy. With this type of processing, brand attitudes were more positive for products advertised in color and with an attribute emphasized than products advertised in black and white. This finding is as predicted, since the type of advertisement was expected to affect recall. With a nonbrand processing strategy individuals do not form an evaluation of the advertised product during exposure to the advertisement and must recall the advertisement to acquire information about the advertised brand in order to be persuaded. Also, as expected, no differences were found in brand attitudes by type of advertisement for the brand processing condition. This occurred because the different types of advertisements were designed to convey the same information about the advertised brand.

Recall and Brand Attitudes

What is of particular interest in the quest for clarification on the recall-persuasion link, is the effect of processing strategy on attitudes and recall. The advertisements used in this study were designed so the different types of advertisements would convey the same information about the product. Extensive pretesting of the advertisements indicated that each of them elicited slightly positive reactions. With a brand processing strategy, subjects should form similarly valenced brand attitudes when exposed to these advertisements, and accurately retrieve those attitudes when asked to evaluate advertised products (regardless of recall of other information). Our results are consistent with these hypotheses. With a nonbrand processing strategy, brand attitudes would not be formed during exposure to advertisements. When subjects are asked to evaluate a product, they must retrieve information from memory in order to form this evaluation. When subjects in this condition could remember an advertisement, they should have had more information available to form an evaluation. Since the advertisements were designed to convey positive information about the product, greater recall should reflect more positive evaluations. Given that advertisements with an attribute emphasized and color advertisements were remembered better than black and white advertisements with a nonbrand processing strategy, these results are also consistent with our hypotheses.

The examination of the effect of recall on brand attitudes after controlling for processing strategy and type of advertisement provided support for the hypothesis. The predicted processing strategy by recall interaction was significant and the means were in the predicted direction. There was virtually no difference in brand attitudes with a brand processing strategy on all the different recall measures. With a nonbrand processing strategy, however, the brand attitudes for advertisements that were recalled were more positive than brand attitudes for advertisements that were not recalled.

Generalizability of Results

In this study, we created conditions that would be most conducive to finding a relationship between recall and persuasion. The results indicated that a relationship existed, if at all, only when subjects executed a nonbrand processing strategy during exposure to the advertisements. Other factors unique to this study that were thought to affect this finding were the use of brands that were new to the subjects and advertisements that conveyed information that would cause a positive evaluation of the brand. The former condition is considered important because the subjects would have no previous information about the brand stored in memory and had not formed an attitude toward the brand. The latter condition is considered important because whatever information they were able to retrieve about the product from the advertisement would result in a positive evaluation of the product.

These conditions, of course, place severe restrictions on when recall of the advertisement might provide a valid measure of advertising effectiveness. It would limit the situations to those where consumers have not formed an attitude toward the brand, where they have little information about the brand, and have little motivation to process the information in the advertisement to form an evaluation of the brand. It is possible that these latter two conditions are not really binding. However, given the results under the brand processing condition, this does not seem likely.

What Does Recall Measure?

Although numerous industry research studies have identified demographic and context factors that affect recall, such as program type and position in program (Gibson, 1983), little attempt has been made to determine the micro-level factors affecting recall.

In this study, all the subjects were exposed to each advertisement, yet only a subset of all the test advertisements were recalled. A number of factors were found to affect whether or not an advertisement was recalled. One of these factors was the type of advertisement and the second was the processing strat-

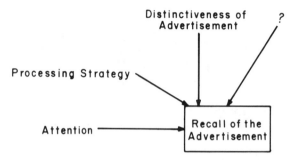

FIG. 6.7.   Factors affecting recall of an advertisement.

egy that the subject used during exposure to the advertisement. Advertisements with an attribute emphasized were recalled better and subject using a brand processing strategy showed better aided recall for the advertisements. In addition, our hypothesis that nonbrand processors would show correspondence in recall and persuasion, while brand processers would not, was supported.

If, as our data and previous investigations indicate, the recall/persuasion link is as tenuous as it appears, what does recall reflect? Based on the results of this study, several things can be inferred about advertisements that are recalled. Clearly, these advertisements are attended to and they tend to be more distinctive relative to other advertisements. In addition, subjects who were engaged in brand processing, focusing on the advertised product rather than the advertisement itself, recalled more advertisements. Consequently, attention to the advertisement is only one of the factors that affect recall (Fig. 6.7). At this point, there does not seem to be any strong empirical justification for implying, in general, that the advertisements that were recalled were more persuasive.

Several lines of investigation, however, could prove profitable in better understanding the factors underlying advertisement recall and persuasion. The analyses of the data collected in this study examined recall on an overall level. Further analyses will investigate individual components of recall, and their relevance to advertised product evaluation. Another factor left to explore involves the examination of these effects over time. Subjects in this study were asked for their evaluations of products and recall about advertisements after only a distractor task. It is expected that the use of a more realistic time lapse may accentuate the findings reported in this study so that the relationship between recall and evaluations under nonbrand processing conditions will be enhanced. Finally, the effect of attitude toward the advertisement on recall and evaluations should also be investigated using both immediate and delayed measures. Of importance here is whether more positively evaluated advertisements are more likely to be recalled and the effect of attitude toward the advertisement on evaluations in the nonbrand processing conditions.

SUMMARY

The results of this study cast some doubts on the validity of recall as a measure of advertising effectiveness. First, they suggest that a direct link between recall and persuasion will occur only under highly restrictive conditions. Second, they indicate that attention is a necessary, but not a sufficient condition for recall. In this study, other factors such as processing strategy and type of advertisement were found to affect recall. Finally, some advertisements that were persuasive were not recalled. With brand processing all of the products were evaluated positively, yet there was virtually no difference in the evaluations of brands whose advertisements were recalled versus those that were not recalled.

ACKNOWLEDGMENT

The authors would like to thank Linda Alwitt and Anthony Pratkanis for their comments on an earlier version of this paper.

REFERENCES

Anderson, J. R. (1983a). A spreading activation theory of memory. *Journal of Verbal Learning and Verbal Behavior, 22,* 261–295.

Anderson, J. R. (1983b). *The architecture of cognition.* Cambridge, MA: Harvard University Press.

Anderson, J. R. & Reder, L. M. (1979). An elaborative processing explanation of depth of processing. In L. S. Cermak & F. J. M. Craik (Eds.), *Levels of processing in human memory.* Hillsdale, NJ: Lawrence Erlbaum Associates.

Anderson, N. H., & Hubert, S. (1963). Effects of concomitant verbal recall on order effects in personality impression formation. *Journal of Verbal Learning and Verbal Behavior, 2,* 379–391.

Bransford, J. D., Barclay, J. R., & Franks, J. J. (1971). Sentence memory: A constructive versus interpretive approach. *Cognitive Psychology, 2,* 331–350.

Craik, F. I. M., & Tulving, E. (1975). "Depth of processing and the retention of words in episodic memory." *Journal of Experimental Psychology: General, 104,* 268–294.

Dosher, B. A. & Russo, J. R. (1976). Memory for internally generated stimuli. *Journal of Experimental Psychology: Human Learning and Memory, 2,* 633–640.

Dreben, E. K., Fiske, S. T., & Hastie, R. (1979). "The independence of evaluative and item information: Impression and recall order effects in behavior-based impression formation." *Journal of Personality and Social Psychology, 37,* 1758–1768.

Gibson, L. D. (1983). "Not recall." *Journal of Advertising Research, 23,* 39–46.

Greenhouse, S. W., & Geisser, S. (1959). On methods in the analysis of profile data. *Psychometrika, 24,* 127–152.

Greenwald, A. G. (1968). Cognitive learning, cognitive response to attitude change. In A. G. Greenwald, T. C. Brock, & T. M. Ostrom (Eds.), *Psychological foundations of attitudes,* New York: Academic Press, 147–170.

Hunt, R. R. & Mitchell, D. B. (1978). Specificity in nonsense orienting tasks and distinctive memory traces. *Journal of Experimental Psychology: Human Learning and Memory, 4,* 121–135.

Hyde, T. S. & Jenkins, J. J. (1969). Differential effects of incidental tasks on the organization of recall lists of highly associated words. *Journal of Experimental Psychology, 82,* 472–481.

Insko, C. A. (1964). Primary versus recency in persuasion as a function of the timing of arguments and measures. *Journal of Personality and Social Psychology, 69,* 381–391.

Jacoby, L. L. & Craik, F. I. M. (1979). Effects of elaboration of processing at encoding and retrieval: Trace distinctiveness and recovery of initial context," In L. S. Cermak & F. J. M. Craik (Eds.), *Levels of processing in human memory.* Hillsdale, NJ: Lawrence Erlbaum Associates, 1–21.

Jenkins, W. O. & Postman, L. (1948). Isolation and spread effect in serial learning. *American Journal of Psychology, 61,* 214–221.

Light, L. L., Kayra-Stuart, F., & Hollander, S. (1979). Recognition memory for typical and unusual faces. *Journal of Experimental Psychology: Human Learning and Memory, 5,* 212–228.

Mitchell, A. A. (1983a). Cognitive processes initiated by exposure to advertising. In R. Harris (Ed.), *Information processing research in advertising.* Hillsdale, NJ: Lawrence Erlbaum Associates.

Mitchell, A. A. (1983b). The effects of visual and emotional advertising: An information processing approach. In L. Percy & A. Woodside (Eds.), *Advertising and consumer psychology.* New York: Lexington Books.

Mitchell, A. A. (1984). Variables mediating advertising effects under different processing conditions. Working Paper, Graduate School of Industrial Administration, Carnegie-Mellon University, Pittsburgh, PA, 15213.

Mitchell, A. A., Gardner, M., & Russo, J. E. (1981). Strategy induced low involvement processing of advertising messages. Working Paper, Graduate School of Industrial Administration, Carnegie-Mellon University, Pittsburgh, PA, 15213.

Murdock, B. B., Jr. (1962). The serial position effect of free recall. *Journal of Experimental Psychology, 64,* 482, 488.

Norman, D. A. (1976). *Memory and attention,* New York, Wiley.

Norman, D. A., & Rumelhart, D. G. (1975). Memory for knowledge. In D. A. Norman, D. G. Rumelhart & the LNR Research Group, *Explorations in cognition,* San Francisco: Freeman.

Papageorgis, D. (1963). Bartlett effect and the persistence of induced opinion change. *Journal of Abnormal and Social Psychology, 67,* 61–67.

Ronis, D. L., Baumgardner, M. H., Leippe, M. R., Cacioppo, J. T., & Greenwald, A. G. (1977). In search of reliable persuasion effects: A computer controlled procedure for studying persuasion. *Journal of Personality and Social Psychology, 35,* 548–569.

Ross, H. L. (1982). Recall versus persuasion: An answer. *Journal of Advertising Research, 22,* 13–16.

Sachs, J. S. (1974). Memory in reading and listening to discourse. *Memory and Cognition, 2,* 95–100.

Sachs, J. S. (1967). Recognition memory for syntactic and semantic aspects of connected discourse. *Perception and Psychophysics, 2,* 437–442.

Schank, R. C. (1972). A theory of natural language understanding. *Cognitive Psychology, 3,* 552–631.

Stout, R. G. (1981). *Copy testing is only part of advertising research.* Paper presented at the Twelfth Annual Association for Consumer Research Conference.

Slamecka, N. J. & Graf, P. (1978). The generation effect: Delineation of a phenomenon. *Journal of Experimental Psychology and Human Learning and Memory, 4,* 592–604.

Taylor, S. E. & Fiske, S. T. (1978). Salience, attention, and attribution: Top of the head phenomena. In L. Berkowitz (Ed.), *Advances in experimental social psychology* (Vol. 11), New York: Academic Press.

Taylor, S. E., & Thompson, S. C. (1982). Stalking the elusive vividness effect. *Psychological Review, 89,* 155-181.

Taylor, S. E. & Wood, J. V. (1983). The vividness effect: Making a mountain out of a molehill? In R. Bagozzi & A. Tybout (Eds.), *Advances in consumer research* (VOL. X), Ann Arbor: Association for Consumer Research.

Wallace, W. P. (1965). A review of the historical, empirical, and theoretical status of the von Restorff phenomenon. *Psychological Bulletin, 63,* 410-425.

Watts, W. A., & McGuire, W. J. (1964). Persistence of induced opinion change and retention of inducing message content. *Journal of Abnormal and Social Psychology, 68,* 233-241.

Wilson, W., & H. Miller (1968). Repetition, order of presentation, and timing of arguments and measures as determinants of opinion change. *Journal of Personality and Social Psychology, 9,* 184-188.

Young, S. (1972). "Copy testing without magic numbers." *Journal of Advertising Research.*

APPENDIX A
CODING OF ADVERTISEMENT RECALL

Product Statement	Any statement that describes the product — how it performs or a particular characteristic of the product.
Advertisement Statement	Any statement that describes the advertisement — what the copy said or a description of the picture.

A Reliable Sleeper Effect in Persuasion: Implications for Opinion Change Theory and Research

Anthony R. Pratkanis
Carnegie-Mellon University

Anthony G. Greenwald
Ohio State University

INTRODUCTION

Attitude change agents are often concerned about the fruits of their labor after the passage of time. A government agency charged with litter control hopes that its anti-litter campaign will be effective long after its leaflets have been discarded. An advertiser hopes that the impact of a TV commercial persists through the interval between presentation and subsequent shopping trip. The pulpit preacher seeks a conviction of everlasting salvation and, not just momentary bliss from the congregation.

For the most part, research on persuasion finds that whenever opinion change occurs, it usually dissipates over time (see Cook & Flay, 1978 for a review). Over 50 years ago, researchers found a pattern of data opposite to this typical trend. This chapter tells the story of the history of this effect — termed the sleeper effect in persuasion.

The Discovery of the Sleeper Effect

In 1928 the Motion Picture Research Council commissioned a series of studies to investigate the effects of motion pictures on children. Peterson and Thurstone (1933) took up their charge by showing films about the Germans, gambling, prohibition, and other social issues to school children living in the midwest. They found that many of the films did indeed change children's attitudes with effects diminishing slightly over time. However, a pro-German film entitled *Four Sons* proved to be more effective after a six month delay than immediately after being shown to a group of Genoa, Illinois high schoolers. Peterson and Thurstone speculated that since Genoa did not have a movie theater, their experiment created considerable discussion, which was responsible for the delayed opinion change.

About 15 years later, the United States Army enlisted the aid of Hovland, Lumsdaine, and Sheffield to evaluate the effectiveness of its training films. They found that the film *The Battle of Britain* did change opinions in favor of the war effort. However, the film not only continued to be effective 11 weeks after it was shown, but actually produced more opinion change on a subset of opinion items. Hovland, Lumsdaine, & Sheffield, (1949) termed this a *sleeper effect* in persuasion.

The Sleeper Effect Defined

Figure 7.1 displays a hypothetical sleeper effect contrasted with two other common delayed persuasion findings. The top line shows the results of a message that produces initial yielding that dissipates over time — as noted previously, a very common finding. With a sleeper effect, the persuasive message results in little initial change followed by a delayed increase in impact. A sleeper effect should not be confused with a nonpersisting boomerang effect. In the latter case, a message results in immediate opinion change opposite to the direction advocated in the communication with this effect dissipating back to pre-message opinion. Without a pre-opinion or no-message control treatment, a nonpersisting boomerang effect may be mistaken for a sleeper effect.

Explanations of the Sleeper Effect

Over the course of its history, numerous explanations for the sleeper effect have been given. Hovland, Lumsdaine, and Sheffield (1949) provided four: (1) methodological artifact; (2) forgetting of a discounting cue; (3) delayed interpretation of message in a new context; and (4) delayed conversion of message details into an attitude. Festinger (1955) proposed an explanation similar to the one provided by Peterson and Thurstone (1933) — that recipients interact and discuss the message between the immediate and delayed opinion measures. Other suggested explanations of the sleeper effect include: the dissociation hypothesis (Hovland, Janis, & Kelley, 1953), psychodynamic theory of insight (Stotland, Katz, & Patchen, 1959; Stotland & Patchen, 1961), the Socratic effect (McGuire, 1960), Bartlett's reconstructive memory (Papageorgis, 1963), delayed reaction to a low-fear arousing message (Insko, Arkoff, & Insko, 1965), reactance theory (Brehm & Mann, 1975), delayed internalization of the values of a message (Rokeach, 1973), mere expo-

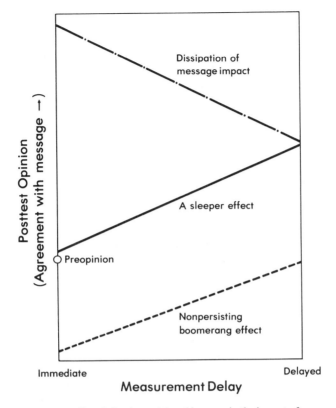

FIG. 7.1.   The sleeper effect defined as a delayed increase in the impact of a persuasive message.

sure theory (Crandall, Harrison, & Zajonc, 1976), dissipation of a fore-warning manipulation (Watts & Holt, 1979), the availability-valence hypothesis (Binns & Sternthal, 1981), and forgetting of negative reactions to an advertisement (Moore & Hutchinson, this volume).

THE HISTORY OF THE SLEEPER EFFECT
AS A LABORATORY FINDING

The Dissociation Hypothesis

In the early 1950s, research on the sleeper effect moved from the field to the laboratory setting. Also at this time (partly as a result of the influential monograph by Hovland, Janis, & Kelley, 1953), the sleeper effect became exclusively identified with the dissociation hypothesis. According to this hypothesis, a sleeper effect occurs when a persuasive message is presented with a discounting cue such as a counterargument or a low credible source. At short measurement delays both message content and discounting cue are present in memory. Recall of the discounting cue leads to a rejection of the message and opinion near pretreatment levels. Over time, the discounting cue and message topic become dissociated or separated in memory. At delayed opinion assessments, only the message content can be retrieved resulting in a delayed increase in persuasion or a sleeper effect.

Three studies (by Hovland & Weiss, 1951; Kelman & Hovland, 1953; Weiss, 1953) are often cited in social psychology textbooks as evidence for the dissociation hypothesis. In the Kelman and Hovland study (the results of which are given in Fig. 7.2), high school students listened to a message arguing for more leniency in the courts. The message was attributed to either a judge (high credible source), a juvenile delinquent (low credible source) or a member of the audience (neutral source). Opinions were measured immediately after hearing the message and 6 weeks later. Half of the subjects were reminded of the message source at the delayed measure. Kelman and Hov-

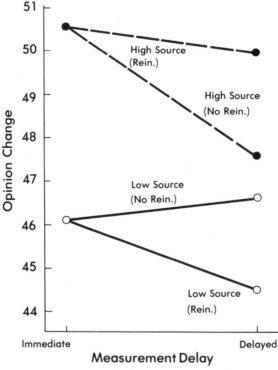

FIG. 7.2.   Opinion change as a function of measurement delay for a message from either a low or high credible source. The source was reinstated at the delay for half of the subjects. (Adapted from Kelman & Hovland, 1953).

land argued for a sleeper effect based on diminishing source effects compared to treatments where the source was reinstated.

The Existence of the Sleeper Effect Questioned

A comparison of Fig. 7.1 (the sleeper effect defined) and Fig. 7.2 (the results of the Kelman and Hovland study) most probably elicits this cognitive response from the reader, "I don't see a rising line in Fig. 7.2 like the sleeper effect in Fig. 7.1." Cook (1971), in an unpublished paper, was the first to draw attention to this discrepancy by distinguishing between absolute sleeper effects (a significant difference between the immediate and delayed measures, as in Fig. 7.1) and relative sleeper effects (more attitude change or less decay of message impact in a discounting cue group compared to a group that received the message under different conditions, as in Fig. 7.2). In a review of pre-1970 sleeper effect studies (later published in Cook, Gruder, Hennigan, & Flay, 1979), Cook frequently finds evidence for relative sleeper effects, but little evidence for absolute effects.

Gillig and Greenwald (1974) echoed Cook's (1971) concerns about the sleeper effect. In their studies, over 600 subjects received messages on such topics as the use of penicillin, medical check-ups, and vitamin C. These messages were attributed to a "nature therapist" (a low credible source). In seven replications, Gillig and Greenwald found one sleeper effect. This effect disappeared, however, when the data were pooled across replications. Gillig and Greenwald were not alone in having difficulty producing a reliable sleeper effect. Other studies pairing a discounting cue with an effective message that have failed to obtain a sleeper effect include: Chaiken (1980), Hennigan, Cook, and Gruder (1982), Maddux and Rogers (1980) and Whittaker and Meade (1968).

A Reawakening of the Sleeper Effect

Although no study had demonstrated an absolute sleeper effect, Gruder, Cook, Hennigan, Flay, Alessis, and Halamaj (1978) noted that no study had yet produced conditions that would be optimal for obtaining one. They reasoned that a sleeper effect would occur when: "(a) a persuasive message has substantial initial impact on attitudes; (b) this change is totally inhibited by a discounting cue; (c) the cue and message are dissociated over time; and (d) the cue and message are dissociated quickly enough so that the message by itself still has some impact when dissociation occurs" (Gruder et al., 1978, p. 1074).

Gruder et al. repeatedly produced sleeper effects when these logical conditions were met. Fig. 7.3 shows the results for two of the five discounting cue treatments (and appropriate controls) from Gruder et al.'s second study. In

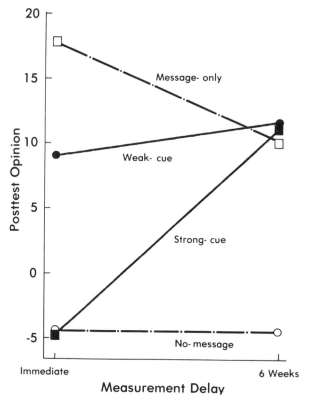

FIG. 7.3.   Opinion change as a function of measurement delay for a message paired with either a weak or strong discounting cue. A sleeper effect occurred with a strong discounting cue. (Adapted from Gruder et al., 1978).

this study subjects: (1) underlined as they read the main points of a long persuasive message arguing against the four day work week; (2) received a short discounting cue in the form of a counterargument; and (3) rated the trustworthiness of the message source before indicating their opinions on the topic. Subjects' delayed opinions were assessed 6 weeks later over the telephone. A sleeper effect was obtained using a strong discounting cue (declaring the message false, restating the conclusion and inducing reactance), but not with a weaker cue (merely declaring the message as false). Gruder et al.'s main point: Meeting their logical conditions is important for obtaining a sleeper effect.

The Computerized Persuasion Procedures

The vicissitudes of the sleeper effect are symptomatic of the unreliable nature of many persuasion findings. Ronis, Baumgardner, Leippe, Cacioppo, and Greenwald (1977) states:

Despite three decades of research, the state of knowledge on effects of persuasive communication is such that only the role of a few major variables in the persuasion process are established with confidence, and the effects of many variables that are widely assumed to be important in persuasion remain to be established. *How many variables are there for which persuasion effects are known confidently?* Little more than the fingers of one hand is needed to count them" (p. 548).

Over the past 10 years, we (see Baumgardner, Leippe, Ronis, & Greenwald, 1983; Pratkanis & Greenwald, 1984; Ronis et al., 1977) have been developing a computer-controlled persuasion procedure with the goal of obtaining reliable effects. These procedures are marked by the following characteristics: (a) the use of standardized procedures (to insure subjects work through materials in proper order, to reduce experimenter bias, etc,); (b) the presentation of many messages to a single subject (thus allowing the use of within-subject designs capable of detecting small, but nonetheless important effects); (c) the use of libraries of persuasive messages with known characteristics (to ameliorate idiosyncratic effects based on a single message); and (d) the ability to manipulate delay within a single session. The computer-controlled procedures also lower the cost and increase the efficiency of persuasion research. For example, routine tasks such as data and stimulus materials management are assigned to the computer.

Figure 7.4 gives a schematic representation of a typical computerized study. For example, in the first three studies by Pratkanis and Greenwald (1984), subjects were seated at a computer-controlled response box and video screen to view a sequence of text displays. The first series of displays provided instructions and practice with the system. Next subjects viewed a simulated TV show called "You Should Know." This show featured an emcee who introduced "letters written by previous viewers of the show" (20 persuasive messages) for the current audience (the subject) to evaluate. The 20 persuasive messages were 2 paragraphs in length and dealt with issues such as Puerto Rican statehood, coal as an energy source, and medical malpractice suits. Each message was paired with either its own discounting or accepting cue (a note attacking or bolstering the message source). Opinion about each message was assessed on a 15-point scale of agreement (1 = strongly disagree and 15 = strongly agree). Measurement delay was randomly determined for each topic presentation and calculated in terms of the number of intervening displays between a message and measure.

More Unreliable Sleeper Effects

By presenting many persuasive messages in a short period of time, the computerized procedures create high levels of associative interference (see Baumgardner et al., 1983). This makes the procedures well suited to investigate memorial processes such as those assumed by the dissociation hypothesis.

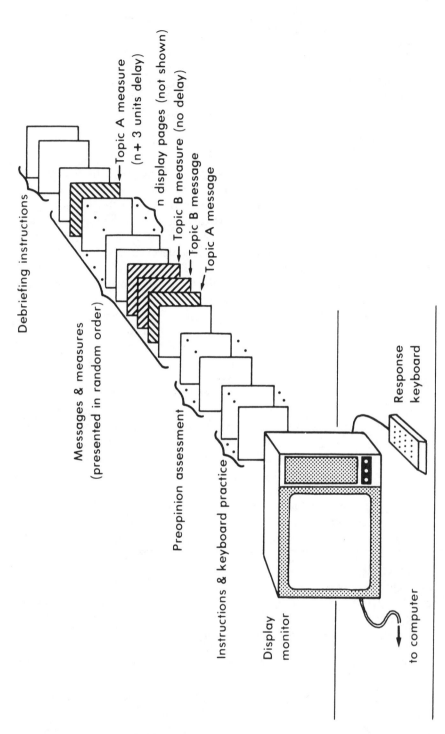

FIG. 7.4. A schematic representation of a typical computer-controlled persuasion study. (From Pratkanis & Greenwald, 1984).

The first set of sleeper effect studies to use the computerized procedures (summarized in Greenwald, Pratkanis, Leippe, & Baumgardner, 1984) obtained results similar to Gillig and Greenwald (1974). In 22 attempts only three sleeper effects were found—all of which failed to replicate.

The first study by Pratkanis and Greenwald (1984) further demonstrates the difficulty of obtaining a reliable sleeper effect. This study was designed to test the hypothesis that placing the discounting cue after the message was important for producing the Gruder et al. (1978) sleeper effect. Eighty subjects viewed 20 persuasive messages in a 2 (source: high or low credible) × 2 (timing of cue presentation: before or after) × 10 (measurement delay) design. The results indicated that messages paired with a high credible source were more readily accepted than when they were paired with a low credible source. However, these effects persisted throughout the experimental session and no reliable sleeper effect was obtained.

The Differential Decay Hypothesis

Our difficulty in obtaining a reliable sleeper effect motivated us to propose a new mechanism for producing the effect. Treating the discounting cue in the Gruder et al. study as an opposing persuasive message suggests that the sleeper effect may be another example of the primacy/recency effects first described by Miller and Campbell (1959). We hypothesized that the sleeper effect is based, not on a dissociation of source from message, but on a differential rate of decay of message and cue impact. According to the *differential decay* hypothesis, a sleeper effect occurs when the impact of a discounting cue dissipates more rapidly than the impact of the persuasive message. Thus, a sleeper effect is most likely to occur when an effective persuasive message is followed by a discounting cue. In this case, the discounting cue would limit immediate opinion change due to recency effects. At longer delays, the impact of a cue dissipates, yielding a delayed increase in the impact of a persuasive message.

Designing a Sleeper Effect

The inconclusiveness of our previous sleeper effect research also lead us to adopt a new research strategy, termed the *design approach* (see Greenwald et al., 1984, for more details). The design approach assumes that the sleeper effect, as a pattern of data, can be produced. Persuasion theory and methods should be strong enough to provide guidance for engineering the effect. In other words, one attempts to produce a sleeper effect much like an engineer produces a new minicomputer with prespecified functions or an advertising agency designs a campaign to accomplish certain objectives.

Using the design approach and the differential decay hypothesis, Pratkanis and Greenwald (1984) were able to develop operations for producing a reliable sleeper effect. One problem in their first study was the potential lack of message impact after a delay. To eliminate this problem Pratkanis and Greenwald (1984) instituted a procedure to strengthen message impact. In their second study, 20 subjects viewed 20 persuasive messages in a 3 (source: high, neutral, or low credibility) × 11 (measurement delay) design. The source was always given after the message. Message impact was strengthened by having subjects write down the argument they considered best for each message. For each topic, subjects: (1) received the message; (2) wrote down the best argument; (3) placed the argument in a "mailbox"; and (4) pressed a button to reveal the source of the message. This study also failed to produce a sleeper effect. Instead the message strengthening procedure increased the immediate message impact to the point of reducing the discounting effect of the low credible source.

The next study by Pratkanis and Greenwald reobtained a discounting effect by having subjects rate the trustworthiness of the source. Sixty subjects viewed 20 persuasive messages as in their second study. Again for each topic, subjects wrote down the one argument they considered best, placed the argument in the mailbox, and then pressed a button to reveal the message source. This time subjects also rated the trustworthiness of the source on a 15-point scale before going on to the next task.

Figure 7.5 presents the best fitting regression lines predicting opinion by delay for each treatment. This study obtained a sleeper effect of borderline significance (t (59) = 1.94, p = .06). The effect is significant if the data for three messages that did not produce persuasion are removed (t (59) = 2.06, $p < .05$). One anomaly is the finding of initial message discounting in the high credible source treatment. It appears that the source rating task eliminated the initial advantage of the high credible source found in previous computer studies. The trustworthiness rating indicates that subjects still perceived the high credible sources to be more trustworthy (M = 10.7) than the neutral (M = 7.1) or low credible sources (M = 5.6). One plausible interpretation of this result is that the source rating task drew attention to the persuasion attempt. This produced an immediate reactance to the message that later dissipated.

In an additional computerized study, Pratkanis and Greenwald (1984) successfully replicated these findings. This study was exactly like the previous one with the exception that stronger persuasive messages were employed. The results showed immediate discounting in both the high and low credible source treatments and a significant sleeper effect.

A Replication of the Gruder et al. Study

As another demonstration of the differential decay hypothesis, Pratkanis and Greenwald (1984) conducted an exact replication of the original Gruder

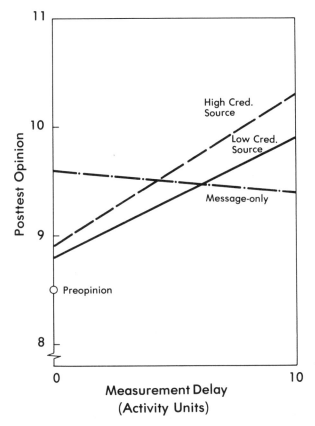

FIG. 7.5.   Opinion change as a function of delay for messages paired with low, neutral and high credible sources. Lines represent the best fitting regression equation for each treatment. A reliable sleeper effect was obtained. (From Pratkanis & Greenwald, 1984).

et al. (1978) study with some variations. In this study, 400 subjects received a booklet containing Gruder et al.'s 1000 word message arguing against the four day work week and their most effective discounting cue (a brief note from the editor restating the message conclusion and indicating that it was wrong). As in the Gruder et al. study, subjects underlined the important arguments in the message and rated the trustworthiness of the source before giving their opinions. Three different experimental treatments were employed: (1) the cue was given after the message (a direct replication of the Gruder et al. study), (2) the cue was given before the message, and (3) the cue was given after a shortened (300 word) version of the four day work week message. In addition, message-only and no-message controls were included. Opinions were assessed immediately after the message and after a 6 week delay by telephone. According to the differential decay hypothesis, a sleeper effect should occur when the cue is given after the message but not when it comes before. The shortened message treatment should produce a sleeper effect of smaller magnitude.

Figure 7.6 presents the results of this study. As in the original Gruder et al. study, a sleeper effect was obtained in the cue-after treatment (F (1,114) = 8.40, $p < .01$). The other two discounting cue treatments did not yield significant sleeper effects. Placing the cue before the message resulted in minimal discounting of the message with message effects persisting through the experiment. Using a shorter message followed by a cue resulted in an increase in persuasion at the delay, but this increase only approached significance (F (1,122) = 2.95, $p = .09$).

IMPLICATIONS OF A RELIABLE SLEEPER EFFECT

Theoretical Implications

Despite previous difficulties, two lines of research (the Gruder et al. study and the computerized persuasion research) have now converged on a single set of operations for producing a reliable sleeper effect. Sleeper effects were produced in these studies using the following operations: (1) subjects note the important arguments of a message, (2) receive a discounting cue after the message, and (3) rate the trustworthiness of the message source before the initial opinion assessment.

Our interpretation of these findings is based on the assumption of differential decay of message and cue impact. Like Miller and Campbell (1959), we assume that the persistence of persuasive impact for both cue and message can be described by a decay function over time and that net persuasive impact is determined by an additive combination of these two persistence functions. A sleeper effect occurs when the discounting cue has a strong immediate impact that dissipates more quickly than the impact of the message. The set of common operations established in these two lines of research can be viewed as one way of producing these empirical conditions. Thus it appears, according to the differential decay hypothesis, that the sleeper effect, far from being an exception, is just another example of the general finding that experimentally induced opinion change dissipates.

Methodological Implications

The computerized persuasion procedures were developed to improve the internal validity of persuasion research by attacking such problems as insufficient power to detect effects, unstandardized procedures and messages, and the inconvenience of investigating delayed effects. However, the novelty of

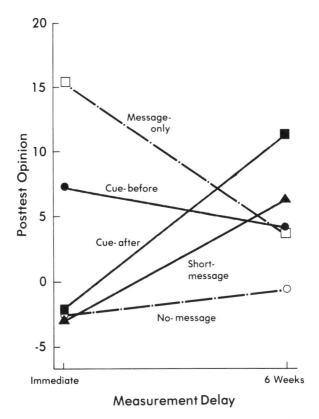

FIG. 7.6.   A successful replication of the Gruder et al. study. A sleeper effect occurs when the cue is given after the message, but not before. (From Pratkanis & Greenwald, 1984).

its procedures raises the issue of external validity — a question of recent concern in consumer research (see for example, Calder, Phillips, and Tybout, 1982; Ferber, 1977; Lynch, 1982). Although much of this debate centers on the use of students as subjects, the computerized persuasion procedures raise the issue of the external validity of the setting.

A long-standing maxim about laboratory research is that the ability to generalize findings depends on the similarity of laboratory to the "real world." Carl Hovland (1959) was one of the first to evaluate the correspondence between laboratory and field persuasion studies. He noted that laboratory studies tended to produce high levels of initial opinion change that dissipates whereas survey research uncovers much less persuasion. The two types of research differ on a number of dimensions including: size of a communication, setting, measurement delays, communicator credibility, postcommunication interactions, subjects and type of communications employed. According to

Hovland, these differences are more than adequate to account for the divergent experimental and survey findings. To the extent that these differences are important in persuasion, however, they should be incorporated into the laboratory study. Rather than conclude that laboratory research is inherently invalid, Hovland states that both approaches are needed for understanding persuasion.

A similar comparison of correspondences can be conducted between the computerized persuasion procedures and the "real world" of mass media. The most unique feature of the computerized persuasion procedures is the presentation of many messages in a short period of time to create a message-dense environment. As far back as 1932, Poffenberger noted that the advertising environment is dense with appeals of every variety. Other similarities between the computer procedure and mass media include: use of short messages like those for a 30-second spot or a news break, use of consumer and policy issues like those found in the mass media, and development of cover stories with real world analogs such as a TV talk show, a consumer affairs show, or a campus election. Differences include: the use of fictitious brand names, emphasis on text as opposed to visual information, self-paced reading, and frequent opinion assessments. Of course, some of these differences may not be apparent in all mass media settings. For example, magazine reading is self-paced, certain channels on cable TV primarily carry text, and with the advent of interactive cable television, frequent opinion assessment may become a reality. This illustrates one potential problem with relying on simple correspondence to evaluate laboratory research. Questions like, "Correspondence to what part of the real world?" and "What correspondences are important?" are difficult to answer. Perhaps the best strategy is to be aware of these differences. After all, today's oversight may be tomorrow's theoretical break-through.

Another, perhaps more fruitful method of evaluating the external validity of a laboratory procedure is to evaluate its theoretical contributions. Does it alert us to new phenomena and provide useful applications? One consistent finding from computerized persuasion studies is that cognitive functioning (such as attention and memory) decreases in the message-dense environment. Of course, this result is not limited to those studies using a computer. For example, Webb and Ray (1979) obtain similar results in their cluttered environment. One response for dealing with the overload of the message-dense environment is to develop information processing strategies. For example, Baumgardner et al. (1983) found that after an initial period of "socialization" to the computerized setting, subjects developed a strategy of picking up only needed information and ignoring the rest of the advertising. Such findings indicate that attentional processes are important in persuasion and has lead to the theorizing of the type put forth by Greenwald and Leavitt (this volume).

One additional, currently unexploited use of the message-dense environment is copy testing. Placing a test ad in a message-dense environment allows the measurement of the advertisement's attention-getting abilities and its relative persistence. These measures are obtained at relatively low costs.

Conclusions

After all these years of research, can we state when sleeper effects will occur? Many explanations of the sleeper effect have been proposed. Unfortunately, very few have been demonstrated to be reliable and the extent to which sleeper effects occur outside the laboratory has not been documented. A reliable sleeper effect has been obtained using operations suggested by the differential decay hypothesis. The specific operations used to produce a sleeper effect in the laboratory probably do not occur with any great frequency in natural settings. Given the pervasiveness of the decay of message impact, however, the differential decay of opposing persuasive materials can cause concern for attitude change agents.

The real value of laboratory research on the sleeper effect is not its production of a definitive interpretation of the real world, but its external *invalidity*. According to Mook (1983) it is often not the intention of laboratory research to describe the real world. "Artificial" findings are interesting because they demonstrate what can occur — even if it rarely does. For example, there is no real world analog of a high energy physics experiment. Nevertheless, the study is valuable in what it teaches about the structure of atoms.

Given that a laboratory researcher has near unlimited control over the message recipient and situation, it is indeed amazing that there has been so much difficulty in producing a reliable sleeper effect. The use of externally invalid procedures further demonstrates the difficulty in overcoming the natural tendency for experimentally-induced opinion change to decay. Despite the difficulty, it is reassuring that persuasion theory and research have gained the sophistication to produce such an unwieldy effect as the sleeper effect in persuasion.

ACKNOWLEDGMENTS

This research was supported by National Science Foundation Grants SOC 74-13436, BNS 76-11175, BNS 82-17006 and National Institute of Mental Health Grant MH 32317 all entitled Research in Persuasive Communications. Steven J. Breckler, Mahzarin R. Banaji, Andrew A. Mitchell, and Susan L. Schechtman provided valuable comments about the research.

REFERENCES

Baumgardner, M. H. Leippe, M. R., Ronis, D. L., & Greenwald, A. G. (1983). In search of reliable persuasion effects: II. Associative learning and persistence of persuasion in a message-dense environment. *Journal of Personality and Social Psychology, 45*, 524–537.

Binns, D., & Sternthal, B. (1981). *The sleeper effect as a test of the availability-valence hypothesis.* Unpublished manuscript, Northwestern University.

Brehm, J. W., & Mann, M. (1975). Effect of importance of freedom and attraction to group members on influence produced by group pressure. *Journal of Personality and Social Psychology, 31,* 816–824.

Calder, B. J., Phillips, L. W., & Tybout, A. M. (1982). The concept of external validity. *Journal of Consumer Research, 9,* 240–244.

Chaiken, S. (1980). Heuristic versus systematic information processing and the use of source versus message cues in persuasion. *Journal of Personality and Social Psychology, 39,* 652–766.

Cook, T. D. (1971). *The discounting cue hypothesis and the sleeper effect.* Unpublished manuscript, Northwestern University.

Cook, T. D., & Flay, B. R. (1978). The persistence of experimentally induced attitude change. In L. Berkowitz (Ed.), *Advances in experimental social psychology* (Vol. 11). New York: Academic Press, 1–57.

Cook, T. D., Gruder, C. L., Hennigan, K. M., & Flay, B. R. (1979). History of the sleeper effect: Some logical pitfalls in accepting the null hypothesis. *Psychological Bulletin, 86,* 662–679.

Crandall, R., Harrison, A. A., & Zajonc, R. B. (1976). *The permanence of the positive and negative effects of stimulus exposure: A sleeper effect.* Unpublished manuscript.

Ferber, R. (1977). Editorial: Research by convenience. *Journal of Consumer Research, 4,* 57–58.

Festinger, L. J. (1955). Social psychology and group processes. In C. P. Stone & Q. McNemar (Eds.), *Annual review of psychology* (Vol. 6). Stanford, CA: Annual Reviews, 187–216.

Gillig, P. M., & Greenwald, A. G. (1974). Is it time to lay the sleeper effect to rest? *Journal of Personality and Social Psychology, 29,* 132–139.

Greenwald, A. G., Pratkanis, A. R., Leippe, M. R., & Baumgardner, M. H. (1984). *Under what conditions . . . does theory obstruct research progress? (Lessons from the history of the sleeper effect).* Unpublished manuscript, Ohio State University.

Gruder, C. L., Cook, T. D., Hennigan, K. M., Flay, B. R. Alessis, C., & Halamaj, J. (1978). Empirical tests of the absolute sleeper effect predicted from the discounting cue hypothesis. *Journal of Personality and Social Psychology, 36,* 1061–1074.

Hennigan, K. M., Cook, T. D., & Gruder, C. L. (1982). Cognitive tuning set, source credibility, and attitude change. *Journal of Personality and Social Psychology, 42,* 412–425.

Hovland, C. I. (1959). Reconciling conflicting results derived from experimental and survey studies of attitude change. *American Psychologist, 14,* 8–17.

Hovland, C. I., Janis, I. L., & Kelley, H. H. (1953). *Communications and persuasion: Psychological studies of opinion change.* New Haven, CT: Yale University Press.

Hovland, C. I., Lumsdaine, A. A., & Sheffield, F. D. (1949). *Experiments on mass communications.* Princeton, NJ: Princeton University Press.

Hovland, C. I., & Weiss, W. (1951). The influence of source crediblity on communication effectiveness. *Public Opinion Quarterly, 15,* 635–650.

Insko, C. A., Arkoff, A., & Insko, V. M. (1965). Effects of high and low fear-arousing communications upon opinions toward smoking. *Journal of Experimental Social Psychology, 1,* 256–266.

Kelman, H. C., & Hovland, C. I. (1953). "Reinstatement" of the communicator in delayed measurement of opinion change. *Journal of Abnormal and Social Psychology, 48,* 327–335.

Lynch, J. G. (1982). On the external validity of experiments in consumer research. *Journal of Consumer Research, 9,* 225–239.

Maddux, J. E., & Rogers, R. W. (1980). Effects of source expertness, physical attractiveness, and supporting arguments on persuasion: A case of brains over beauty. *Journal of Personality and Social Psychology, 39,* 235–244.

McGuire, W. J. (1960). A syllogistic analysis of cognitive relationships. In M. J. Rosenberg, C. I. Hovland, W. J. McGuire, R. P. Abelson, & J. W. Brehm (Eds.), *Attitude organization and change: An analysis of consistency among attitude components.* New Haven: CT: Yale University Press, 65–111.

Miller, N., & Campbell, D. T. (1959). Recency and primacy in persuasion as a function of the timing of speeches and measurements. *Journal of Abnormal and Social Psychology, 59,* 1–9.

Mook, D. G. (1983). In defense of external invalidity. *American Psychologist, 38,* 379–387.

Papageorgis, D. (1963). Bartlett effect and the persistance of induced opinion change. *Journal of Abnormal and Social Psychology, 67,* 61–67.

Peterson, R. C., & Thurstone, L. L. (1933). *Motion pictures and the social attitudes of children.* New York: MacMillan.

Poffenberger, A. T. (1932). *Psychology in advertising.* New York: McGraw-Hill.

Pratkanis, A. R., & Greenwald, A. G. (1984). *In search of reliable persuasion effects: III. The sleeper effect is dead. Long live the sleeper effect.* Unpublished manuscript, Ohio State University.

Rokeach, M. J. (1973). *The nature of human values.* New York: The Free Press.

Ronis, D. L., Baumgardner, M. H., Leippe, M. R., Cacioppo, J. T., & Greenwald, A. G. (1977). In search of reliable persuasion effects: I. A computer-controlled procedure for studying persuasion. *Journal of Personality and Social Psychology, 35,* 548–569.

Stotland, E., Katz, D., & Patchen, M. (1959). Reduction of prejudice through arousal of insight. *Journal of Personality, 27,* 507–531.

Stotland, E., & Patchen, M. (1961). Identification and change in prejudice and in authoritarianism. *Journal of Abnormal and Social Psychology, 62,* 265–274.

Watts, W. A., & Holt, L. E. (1979). Persistence of induced opinion change and retention of the inducing message contents. *Journal of Personality and Social Psychology, 37,* 778–789.

Webb, P. H., & Ray, M. L. (1979). Effects of T.V. clutter. *Journal of Advertising Research, 19,* 7–12.

Weiss, W. (1953). A "sleeper" effect in opinion change. *Journal of Abnormal and Social Psychology, 48,* 173–180.

Whittaker, J. O., & Meade, R. D. (1968). Retention of opinion change as a function of differential source credibility: A cross-cultural study. *International Journal of Psychology, 3,* 103–108.

III PSYCHOLOGICAL PROCESSES DURING TELEVISION VIEWING

8 Online Cognitive Processing of Television

Daniel R. Anderson
University of Massachusetts, Amherst

INTRODUCTION

Academic research on television has involved a diverse assortment of disciplines, methods, and goals. The disciplines range from engineering to the humanities, the methods from signal analysis to critical analysis, and the goals from improved picture quality to political reform. Unquestionably, however, the mainstream disciplines of television research have been the social sciences, the major methods have been sociological or social psychological, and the goals have concerned television's social impact.

Despite the large role television plays in the economy and in how people spend their time, there has been relatively little academic research on its actual use. The research that has been done has been sociological in nature with the survey as the methodology of choice. Generally speaking, self reported characteristics of TV viewers (e.g., demographics, attitudes, product knowledge) are compared to self reported TV program choice. Assumptions are made that all content from programs reported watched is more or less uniformly absorbed, or assumptions about selected content are made on the basis of viewer or program characteristics. Neglected are the details of television viewing behavior itself. These details are of practical as well as theoretical importance.

Consider the problems faced by the producer of a television commercial, who must persuasively convey a certain amount of information about a product in an extremely limited time span. The costs of production and distribution of commercials, furthermore, make every single second of time a precious commodity. As such, the producer must make decisions about the temporal flow of visual and auditory information virtually on a frame by frame basis. Most published research on television in general and advertising in particular, however, reveals little of use to the producer in making the hundreds of large and small decisions about the temporal, conceptual, and artistic dynamics that ultimately determine the success of the production. Research useful in making such decisions would emphasize the *online* nature of television viewing. That is, the research would elucidate the moment by moment workings of attention, perception, comprehension, and affective components of watching television.

About ten years ago, my students and I began such a program of research on young children's online cognitive processing of television. This research was not designed with specific applications in mind, but rather, was designed as a means of studying the dynamics of attention and comprehension of multimodal discourse. Since then, our work, and that of a few other research groups, has produced a small but substantial body of data (c.f. recent edited volumes: Bryant & Anderson, 1983; Kelly & Gardner, 1981; Meyer, 1983). Much of this work not only helps clarify the online nature of TV viewing, but also provides a number of remarkably robust findings of general applicability for use in TV production.

In this chapter I describe the research, findings, and theory from my own research group as it applies to the production of short television segments such as commercials. The emphasis is on the dynamics of viewing behavior and cognition. Most of the research has been oriented toward young children, but many of the findings are at least heuristically applicable to adults.

A COMMENT ON METHODOLOGY AND THEORY

We work from the point of view that it is necessary to actually observe TV viewing behavior rather than depend on viewers' reports about their behavior, or, in the case of young children, parents' reports. Where such reports are used, we believe they should be validated to the degree possible. Our work, furthermore, is not primarily theoretically driven, since there is little relevant theory on the dynamic aspects of cognition, much less TV viewing. From these beginning principles, we do experimental research in the laboratory, and we also observe TV viewing in homes by means of automated time-lapse video equipment. Importantly, in both types of research, we encode the dynamics of the observed behavior, making extensive use of microcomputers for the task. As an example, consider visual orientation toward the TV set: Working from a videotape of the TV viewer, an observer presses a button connected to a microcomputer when the viewer looks at the TV screen and releases it when the viewer looks away. The computer stores the time from the exact beginning of the TV program of each button press and release. As such, a record of the temporal flow of TV viewing behavior can be related precisely to the temporal flow of the TV program itself (e.g., Levin & Anderson, 1976).

The goals of the research are to develop a set of reliable, empirically based principles of online cognitive processing of television. Using these principles, as well as research and theory outside the domain of television, the aim is to develop a strong theory of TV viewing. Ultimately, the goal is to extract principles that will prove of general applicability to the dynamics of cognitive functioning.

We have made substantial progress in achieving these goals: A number of reliable phenomena of TV viewing have been identified (cf. Anderson & Field, 1983). Using these phenomena as anchor points we have developed an initial theory of visual attention to television (Anderson & Lorch, 1983). Before discussing the details of visual attention, however, some of the dynamics of home TV viewing behavior are described.

A DESCRIPTION OF TELEVISION VIEWING AT HOME

Only three studies, each done a decade apart, have attempted to provide general descriptions of television viewing behavior: Each of these studies placed film or video equipment in homes for a period of one to several weeks. The observations from each study are strikingly consistent. The pioneering effort was that of Allen (1965) who placed time-lapse film cameras in 95 homes in Oklahoma in 1961, 1962, and 1963. The cameras shot the viewing area as well as the TV screen, shooting a frame every 15 sec. The second major study was reported by Bechtel, Achelpohl, and Akers (1972) who installed real time video cameras and microphones in 20 homes in Kansas during 1970. Despite the enormous efforts involved in data collection both the Allen (1965) and Bechtel et al. (1972) reports were sketchy, with few quantitative analyses of their results.

Ours is the third study to directly examine a substantial amount of TV viewing at home (Anderson, 1983). In this study (the data were collected during 1980 and 1981), time-lapse video equipment was placed in the homes of 106 families from metropolitan Springfield, Massachusetts. The families, each with a 5-year-old child, filled out extensive questionnaires concerning their TV viewing environment, viewing behaviors, and attitudes towards television. They also filled out two Nielsen-type viewing diaries a month apart with the second diary concurrent with the placement of the time-lapse video equipment. The automated video equipment shot the viewing area as well as the TV set, recording a video frame each 1.2 seconds. The equipment automatically began recording when the TV set was turned on, and stopped recording when the TV set was turned off. There were also two control groups of families who participated in all phases of the study but did not get equipment placed in their homes. One control group (41 families) was recruited in the same manner as the experimental group (i.e., they agreed to have equipment placed in their homes but were randomly selected as controls). The other group (102 families) was never told about the possibility of home camera placement. In addition to the experimental group and the two control groups, a fourth group consisted of 85 families who initially agreed to have equipment placed in their homes but who then backed out when it came to an actual placement. These families agreed to participate in all other aspects of the study. Comparisons between the four groups on 148 measures of demographics, self-reported viewing behavior, and psychological characteristics of the 5-year olds indicate no systematic differences. Thus, whatever selection biases there were in the subject sample, they appeared to be more due to volunteer research participation in general than to the use of cameras in the home. In general the sample is white, parents in their 20's and 30's, middle class (skilled blue collar, lower level white collar), rent or own an individual house, and have one color TV and one black and white TV. The camera group provided usable videotapes from 98 families (the remainder were lost due to technical problems); these videotapes contained 4960 hours of television-on time, and the viewing behavior of 270 children and 190 adults.

General Impressions of Behavior with Television.   When one spends many hours watching families watch television, some strong consistent impressions emerge. First, viewers engage in a great many activities concurrent with television viewing. The precise activities depend on the age and sex of the viewer, the time of day, day of the week, and the viewing environment (whether the TV is in the living room as compared to a kitchen, for example). If the TV is on during a weekday morning, viewers enter and leave the viewing area frequently, engaging in dressing, breakfast preparation, eating, getting ready for school, and so on. If TV is watched intently at this time, it is by the preschooler who does not need to go anywhere (unless news is on, in which case parents may look at it briefly, probably listening more than looking).

During the weekday daytime, the TV is likely to be used as a backdrop for household chores by the mother or as a background for play by young children. A daytime drama might, however, have the mother watching intently along with a school-age daughter if it is a nonschool weekday. Late afternoon finds the TV watched by school age children who frequently play games, read story books, roughhouse, or engage in some other play activity.

If TV is on during the early evening, the news forms a backdrop for dinner preparation, mealtime, or sometimes husband and wife together after dinner, often accompanied by a newspaper or magazine. Early prime time viewing is also accompanied by considerable social interaction between the parents and children. Exiting during the program and especially during commercials is frequent. Late evening viewing, often of adult-oriented drama or movies, involves much greater attention to the TV and less frequent exiting during commercials. When children are present, they are usually quiet and often fall asleep in front of the TV. Magazine, book, or newspaper reading is fairly common.

Weekend viewing usually involves much greater attention to the TV. Saturday morning finds the children more attentive than usual and correspondingly less likely to engage in concurrent play. Daytime viewing on the weekend is frequently done by the father watching sports, and evening viewing may be done in the context of social interactions (in which case less attention is paid to the screen).

In general, our impressions from these videotapes recorded in 1980–1 correspond well with impressions of Bechtel et al. (1972) and those of Allen (1965) from recordings made one and two decades earlier, respectively. An overwhelming impression is that television forms part of a family ecology. The times TV is turned on, the programs watched, and the concurrent activities appear to be highly regular and predictable within a family. The variability between families, on the other hand, is great.

Understanding the need to go beyond impressions, we are currently engaged in systematic quantitative analyses of our videotapes. Our first pass analyses are based on 55-min time-samples; future analyses of the tapes will be considerably more fine-grained. The next three sections are based on the first pass analyses. They establish basic normative data on: (1) visual angles and viewing distances of TV viewers; (2) age trends in visual attention to TV; and (3) initial estimates of the validity of viewing diaries.

Viewing Distances and Visual Angles.   An initial approach to understanding online cognitive processing of television concerns the nature of the perceptual display. As distinct from cinema, contemporary television usually presents a small screen with picture resolution such that fine visual detail cannot be perceived without a closeup shot. Viewers are free, moreover, to place themselves at various distances and visual angles with respect to the TV screen. There are, in fact, no published normative data on these issues.

We obtained detailed physical measurements of the viewing rooms and furniture for a subset of 78 families. With this information we prepared scale drawings of the viewing areas and noted on these drawings the position of each viewer during each time sample. From these records, we calculated various angles subtended by the TV screen from each viewer as well as the distance of the TV from each viewer.

We found, not surprisingly, that children in general sit closer to the TV than adults. Children's viewing locations were considerably more variable than adults, and the visual angle subtended by the TV screen horizontally averaged 12.4 degrees. The average visual angle was 7.3 degrees for adults. To put these observations in context, it should be pointed out that foveal (highly detailed) vision covers about 1.5 degrees whereas parafoveal vision (moderately detailed) covers about 10 degrees of the visual field (Ditchburn, 1973). Relevant to present concerns, children tend to place themselves at a viewing position optimal for rapid picture perception so that the TV screen nicely frames parafoveal vision, whereas adults' viewing positions appear to be more dictated by comfort. Adults view from furniture (usually placed on the room's boundaries) 84% of the time whereas children view from furniture only 51% of the time (Nathan, Anderson, Field, & Collins, unpublished data).

These visual angle and distance findings should be taken into consideration in the design of visual images, text, and commercial logos in terms of the demands they place on the viewer for resolution of visual detail. Requiring the viewer to discriminate fine visual detail may also require the viewer to change the arrangement of furniture in the viewing room. This issue is likely to be of special concern in preparation of images and text for videotex services, as well as for future generations of high resolution video screens where presentation of detailed images becomes possible.

In terms of the perceptual processing of visual images from television, it appears that eye-movements are probably not of great significance. Flagg (1978) has noted, for example, that even when child viewers are required to sit close to a TV such that the screen subtends 21 degrees of visual angle, fixations tend to cluster in the middle of the screen. With present day screen technology and production techniques, the viewer apparently apprehends scenes in a relatively wholistic manner, keeping the eyes fixed on the middle of the screen and letting scenes replace each other. The rapid sequential visual pacing of contemporary television, combined with producer tendencies to avoid visual "clutter," encourages such a perceptual strategy.

Based on these considerations, Anderson and Lorch (1983) have argued that the best measure of visual attention to television is visual orientation toward the screen as a whole rather than visual fixation to a part of the screen. Fortunately, visual orientation is fairly easily observed, whereas proper measurement of visual fixations requires elaborate equipment and methodology. In the remainder of this chapter, "visual attention" is used as equivalent to visual orientation.

Visual Attention and Time in the Viewing Room.   For the 98 families who provided scoreable videotapes, we noted the presence of each individual in the viewing room and whether or not the viewer was looking at the TV. No one was in the viewing room 13% of the time the TV was on; Allen (1965), in comparison, reported no audience during 19% of the TV-on time.

Figure 8.1 indicates percent visual attention to the TV (given that the viewer was in the room) as a function of age (Anderson, 1983; detailed analyses will be reported in a later paper: Anderson, Field, Lorch, Nathan, & Collins, unpublished data). There is a great increase in visual attention to TV during the preschool years, a leveling off of attention at about 70% during the school age years, and a significant decline in attention among adults. Figure 8.1 does not necessarily indicate the amount of attention that viewers pay to whole television programs. The reason for this is that viewers may leave the viewing room during programs and especially during commercials (we plan to analyze this exiting behavior in some detail in later work). Attention varies considerably, furthermore, from program to program, and as a function of time of day and day of the week.

Figure 8.2 indicates hours per day with television and hours per day looking at television as a function of age for these same families. In this case,

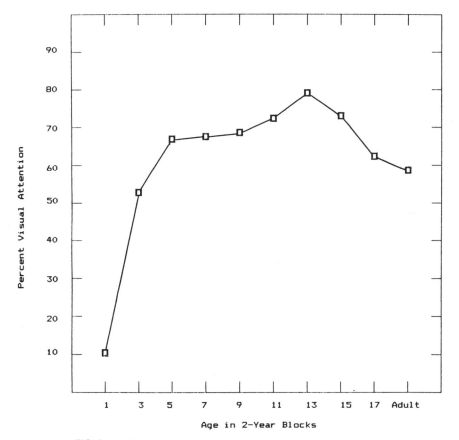

FIG. 8.1.   Visual attention to television at home as a function of age.

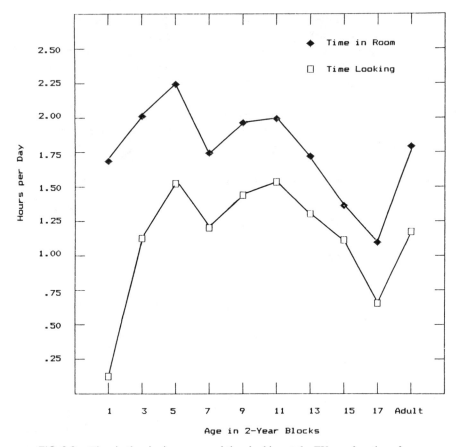

FIG. 8.2.   Time in the viewing room and time looking at the TV as a function of age.

there is a decrease in time spent in the viewing room among adolescents (as is also commonly found diary studies). There is a significant increase across the preschool years of hours looking at the TV; and a drop during middle and late adolescence. The preschool increase reflects the increase in visual attention to TV across the preschool years indicated in Fig. 8.1, and the decrease during adolescence reflects the reduction in time in the viewing room. The absolute value of viewing times shown in Fig. 8.2 is somewhat lower than those estimated by Nielsen nationally during the same time period. There are numerous possible reasons for this discrepancy which we are currently exploring.

The home observation attention data nicely replicate age trends in percent visual attention found in laboratory studies (Alwitt, Anderson, Lorch, & Levin, 1980; Anderson & Levin, 1976; Anderson, Lorch, Field, & Sanders, 1981; Calvert, Huston, Watkins, & Wright, 1982). Combined with survey and other observational work (Carew, 1980; Schramm, Lyle, & Parker, 1961), the evidence converges that television viewing rapidly increases through the preschool years until it is well established by about four or five years of age. Visual attention then remains at a relatively high level until adulthood when it drops significantly.

We have interpreted the age trends in attention as related to the perceived comprehensibility and redundancy of TV. During the preschool years television becomes increasingly understandable and therefore worthy of attention. During the school-age years much of TV is optimally comprehensible, but during adulthood a good deal of TV is predictable and redundant, requiring relatively little active attention (Anderson & Lorch, 1983; Anderson & Smith, in press). Given the change in cognitive demands of television viewing at different ages, it is a reasonable guess that the use of television changes as well. Csikszentmihalyi and Kubey (1981), for example, find adults report TV viewing as relaxing and involving relatively little active mental activity. Anderson and Lorch (1983), on the other hand, have argued that for young children, TV viewing is an active and demanding cognitive activity.

Validity of Parents' Estimates of TV Viewing. The viewing diary is a major commercial instrument by which home television viewing is assessed. One of our purposes in collecting the in-home observational data was to determine the validity of viewing diaries. At this time we have analyzed parents' reports of their 5-year-olds' viewing in relationship to the children's actual presence and visual attention to the TV. Table 8.1 presents the diary estimates (in average hours per day), the actual observed time in the room, and the time looking at the TV. Also presented are correlations of the diary estimates with the actual observations. It is quite clear that the concurrent diary measure provides an excellent estimate of time spent with television, but is less useful for estimating time looking at television. Several notes of caution should be sounded here: We have not yet analyzed diary accuracy in terms of

TABLE 8.1
Observed 5-Year Old Viewing Compared to Parent Diaries

	Time in Room	*Time Looking*	*Diary*
mean[a]	2.30	1.58	2.05
r [b]	.82(94)**	.67(90)**	
t [c]	2.85(95)*	5.94(91)**	

[a]Hours per day.
[b]Correlation (degrees of freedom) with diary
[c]t-test (degrees of freedom) comparison with diary
$*p < .01$
$**p < .001$

the viewership of particular programs. The parents' knowledge that the cameras would be used to verify their accuracy, furthermore, may have made them keep more careful diaries. The diaries of our control groups appear to contain far more sloppy and ambiguous records than those of the camera groups. It is likely, therefore, that the validity estimates given in Table 8.1 represent maxima rather than typical values. Nevertheless, the viewing diary can, in some circumstances at least, provide a reasonably valid estimate of time spent with television.

VISUAL ATTENTION TO TELEVISION

In a movie theater the viewer sits in a chair in a dark room oriented toward a screen subtending perhaps 40 degrees. Visual attention to the film is probably on the order of 95%. At home the viewer is usually in a lighted environment affording opportunities for a variety of activities other than looking at the 10 degrees on the (average) TV screen. It is not suprising, therefore, that TV viewers look at and away from the TV screen many times in the course of a viewing session. We find, for example, that children who view with toys or with other children available look at and away from the TV from 150 to 200 times an hour. The vast majority of these looks are short. For 5-year-olds watching *Sesame Street,* for example, we find that over 60% of looks are less than 5 sec in length; looks as long as a minute are relatively infrequent. The data for college students watching self-selected prime time television (in an environment allowing homework, magazine reading, puzzle solving, etc.) is quite similar in this respect to that of the young children. A TV producer, especially the producer of commercials, thus faces a formidable task in ensuring attention, comprehension, and involvement of the viewer.

Much of our research has been directed toward understanding the variability in visual attention, trying to account for the factors that cause a viewer to look at the screen, maintain looking, look away, and maintain inattention. If a producer can gain a fundamental understanding of the principles underlying these periods of attention and inattention to television, and if the relationship of attention to comprehension processes is understood, then the producer is better prepared to make decisions about the conceptual flow and pacing of the production. Our work on the dynamics of TV viewing suggests three major principles: Attention is guided by comprehension processes; audio monitoring occurs during periods of inattention; and a process called attentional inertia serves to drive attention across content boundaries.

Attention is Guided by Comprehension Processes.   Attention to television is maintained by the meaning the content has to the viewer, and fluctuations in attention are to some extent determined by the degree to which the content is optimally comprehensible. If the material is overly comprehensible and predictable, as when it has been seen before, attention will be terminated, and so also will attention be lost if the program is incomprehensible (as much of television is for very young children).

This sensible assertion sounds odd only when the alternative is considered. Many writers in both popular and professional literatures have declared that viewers, especially children, pay attention to television because of its unique formal production characteristics such as editing features, pans, zooms, visual movement, special effects, and the like (e.g., Lesser, 1977; Mander, 1978; Moody, 1980; Singer, 1980; Winn, 1977). It is these presumed powerful effects on attention of production features that have led many popular writers to give television labels such as "plug-in-drug." At least for young children, this perspective is flatly wrong. The lines of evidence are numerous and, in essence, the research indicates that young children pay attention to parts of TV programs that are to them comprehensible and generally do not pay attention to parts of television that are incomprehensible. There is as yet no evidence that young children will watch incomprehensible video material which incorporates supposedly attention-trapping production features. In other words, television does not control a child's attention independent of his or her understanding of the content.

It is this principle that explains the dramatic increase in attention to television across the preschool years (Fig. 8.1); children pay more attention to television as more of it becomes understandable. Throughout the school age years, as children master the cinematic codes and conventions of television, and as their world knowledge and receptive vocabulary increases, television provides optimally paced information about the world (both real and unreal) beyond their immediate experience and attention is therefore maximal. Among adults, television viewing is an overlearned experience and much of television becomes redundant and predictable so that TV readily forms a backdrop or a context for a variety of activities beside paying active attention. In all cases, however, paying attention is fundamentally under control of comprehension processes. On the whole, the medium provides no "silver bullets" by which the viewer's attention can be maintained independent of the content and its basic meaning to the viewer. This is not to say that humor, suspense, excitement, and many other attributes of entertainment are irrelevant to attention. Rather, optimal comprehensibility is a necessary ingredient in the effectiveness of these attributes in maintaining attention.

The first evidence for this position was reported by Lorch, Anderson, and Levin (1979). We found that 5-year-olds' visual attention to given portions of *Sesame Street* were positively correlated with their comprehension of those portions. Experimental manipulations of visual attention (by including or excluding toys as part of the viewing environment), on the other hand, had no effect on comprehension. Lorch, et al. (1979) concluded that the children were sensitive to variations in program comprehensibility, paying attention to those parts of the program that were most understandable. We suggested that, contrary to popular opinion, comprehension processes drive attention rather than the reverse. The findings of the Lorch et al. (1979) study were later replicated by Pezdek and Hartman (1983) who came to essentially the same conclusion.

Anderson, Lorch, Field, and Sanders (1981) pursued the comprehension-driven attention hypothesis by examining the relationship of dialogue concreteness to visual attention to *Sesame Street* by 3- and 5-year-old children. We rated each utterance of 15 different programs as having "immediate" or "nonimmediate" referents. An immediate utterance referred to an object, action, or state of being that was visually or auditorally present. A nonimmediate utterance referred to objects, events or states displaced in time or space. Based on psycholinguistic research, we reasoned that immediate utterances should be more comprehensible to preschool children than nonimmediate utterances and should therefore receive greater attention. Analyzing visual attention in the exact presence of each utterance type, we found that immediate utterances indeed received greater visual attention than nonimmediate utterances.

Anderson et al. (1981) provided a further verification of the comprehension guided attention principle. We experimentally distorted the comprehensibility of *Sesame Street* segments by: (1) rearranging scenes within the segments so that the scenes occurred in random order; or by (2) reversing each utterance so that it occupied the same video frames but ran backward (thus retaining voice quality and rough lip-synch); or by (3) using foreign dialogue (Greek) substituted for the normal English. Each of these distortions reduced comprehensibility without changing the structure of formal features. The results were straightforward: As compared to normal segments, the distorted segments received substantially reduced attention from preschool children. This reduced attention occurred despite the fact that the video techniques, pacing, sound effects, and voice qualities remained undisturbed. Even at early ages TV viewers are sensitive to the content of a TV program; they pay much less attention to incomprehensible content regardless of how attractively it is produced. For older children and adults, of course, the comprehensibility of the content by itself probably accounts for less of the variability of attention than in young children, since for the older viewers most of television is easily understood. Indeed, overly comprehensible programming probably accounts for more loss of attention than incomprehensible material. Nevertheless, the demonstration that in young children attention to TV is strongly guided by comprehension processes suggests that the *meaning* of the content is more important in maintaining attention than its packaging.

An obvious question arises as to how a viewer knows to pay attention at certain points of critical interest in a TV program if the viewer is not already paying attention. We and others (Alwitt, Anderson, Lorch, & Levin, 1980; Collins, 1979; Lesser, 1974; Wright & Huston, 1981) have suggested that the viewer monitors the audio for attributes that "mark" the presence of critical content. This constitutes the second major principle of online cognitive processing of television.

Audio Monitoring During Visual Inattention.   When visually inattentive, viewers make heavy use of the audio to guide their full attention back to the TV. At least among children, however, visually inattentive viewers do not fully attend to the audio at the level of meaningful content. This is revealed by detailed studies of retention of audio information in relationship to visual attention. Children were much more likely to recall auditory material if they were looking at the screen at the time the material was presented. This effect holds even when the video provides no relevant information in support of the audio (Field, 1983; Lorch et al., 1979).

Instead of listening carefully when not looking, children monitor the audio for sound qualities that are predictive of comprehensible, entertaining, and appropriate content. As an example, consider the auditory attributes of adult men's voices and children's voices. Adult men's voices consistently suppress the onset of visual attention in children who are inattentive at the time the voices occur; that is, men's voices maintain *inattention* to the TV. Children's voices, on the other hand, consistently elicit visual attention (Alwitt et al., 1980; Anderson & Levin, 1976; Calvert, et al., 1982). Our interpretation of these and numerous other related findings is that, through experience with the medium, children have learned that certain audio attributes are predictive of child-oriented comprehensible content, and that other attributes are predictive of adult-oriented content. By monitoring the audio for such predictive auditory cues, the child is able to divide attention between TV viewing and other activities such as toy play. In this way the child devotes full attention only to those portions of programs that are likely to yield comprehensible content of interest to children. On American television, adult men's voices are ubiquitous and, by and large, are predictive of relatively abstract, difficult to understand, adult-oriented content. Children's voices, on the other hand, virtually never occur except when the content is meant for children (see Alwitt et al. 1980, for details of these and other effective auditory attributes). While the equivalent research on auditory attention elicitors and suppressors has not been done for adult TV viewing, it is likely that this early-acquired viewing strategy is maintained. With increasing medium experience, and with changing interests, however, the adult likely adopts somewhat more differentiated and sophisticated auditory monitoring strategies, including monitoring the audio for key words and phrases of interest.

From these first two principles, attention maintained by involvement with content, and attention initiated by auditory cues that have been learned to be predictive of a particular type of content, television viewing is seen to be a rational and somewhat strategic form of processing information. A consequence of this strategy is that inattentive viewers are quite stereotyped in terms of the points in a program at which their attention is brought back to the screen. As an example of this phenomenon, we found that the probability of two preschoolers (viewing separately) initiating a look at the same *Sesame Street* program at the same time (within a 3 sec time window) was .41 whereas the probability of terminating a look at the same time was .17 (Anderson, Lorch, Smith, Bradford, & Levin, 1981). Viewers thus tend to respond in the same way at the same times to the auditory cues that they have learned are predictive of interesting content. Viewers are relatively idiosyncratic, however, as to when they look away from the screen. This follows insofar as they tend to be cognitively engaged in comprehending the content of the program when they are looking at the TV. Since individual differences in background, cognitive abilities, experiences, and interests affect interpretation of content, there are greater differences between viewers as to just when a program becomes overly predictable, incomprehensible, or just plain boring.

Attentional Inertia.   So far I have described TV viewing as a cycle of paying attention to interesting, optimally comprehensible content, followed by terminating attention when the content becomes overly predictable or incomprehensible, then monitoring surface features of the audio during inattention, and eventually coming back to full attention when appropriate auditory cues indicate that renewed attention might be rewarded with interesting, optimally comprehensible content. There is every reason to believe that these attention-inattention cycles are reasonably descriptive of adult TV viewing as well as that of children, although the confirming research is largely lacking.

The story is, of course, not complete. The two principles discussed above describe only the broad temporal flow of online cognitive processing of television. There are various logical reasons why additional mechanisms underlying attention to television are required. Consider the nature of the television stimulus. It is an edited medium such that scenes, images, actions, and dialogue succeed each other often at a rapid pace. The montage by which a TV program is constructed demands by convention numerous inferences of time, space, action, and character psychology if the viewer is to have a connected mental representation of the flow of depicted events and their interrelationships. For example, a standard cinematic sequence might show an exterior daytime shot of a skyscraper succeeded by an interior shot of a modern corporate office. The viewer is expected to immediately make the spatiotemporal inference that the interior scene is inside the skyscraper and that it is still daytime. Literally hundreds of such inferences are required to comprehend even such a lightweight program as *Dukes of Hazzard* (cf. Anderson & Smith, 1984), and they are often demanded in commercials.

We examined the ability of young children to make the routine cinematic inferences necessary to achieve connected comprehension of television. Using stop-animation techniques, we prepared short animated segments showing dolls moving and conversing in buildings and on streets. Each segment incorporated camera actions or edits requiring an inference of space, time, deleted but implied action, or character perspective (the world as seen through the eyes of one of the characters). After a child viewed a segment, he or she was asked to reconstruct the action and dialogue using the actual dolls and sets. The technique works exceedingly well for assessing young children's comprehension of TV. For 4-year-olds, the results indicated that inferences of implied actions were easiest, inferences of time were most difficult, and inferences of space and character perspective were of intermediate difficulty. Anderson and Smith (1984) make the argument that the overall performance was impressive: "...the four-year-olds performed at 70% of their visual baseline reproductions (reproducing explicit actions which require no inferences) and the seven-year-olds at 88% of their baseline."

It is clear from these results that television viewing requires active inferential cognition by children. Although even preschoolers are moderately competent in inferential decoding of filmic syntax, their failures to comprehend cinematic transitions cumulatively gives them a fragmented comprehension of lengthy televised narratives (e.g., Collins, Wellman, Kenniston, & Westby, 1978). With age and viewing experience, however, the child more rapidly and automatically makes the bridging inferences necessary to achieve connected comprehension. Often, however, the appropriate bridging inferences cannot be immediately made (for a variety of reasons) and the program becomes at least temporarily incomprehensible. This is especially true for young children but also likely happens with adults (as in a too clever avant garde editing sequence). Normally, attention would be terminated, but often it is not. Why? An answer lies in the phenomenon of attentional inertia.

The longer a viewer continuously maintains visual attention to television, the more likely it is that he or she will continue to do so. Conversely, the longer it has been since a viewer last looked at the TV, the less probable it is that he or she will look back. These phenomena are illustrated in Fig. 8.3 for one 3-year-old child (who was observed viewing a heterogeneous variety of children's programs and commercials) and in Fig. 8.4 for one college student (who watched 4.5 hours of self-selected prime time television). These figures are representative: Every viewer we have analyzed shows the attentional inertia effect (Anderson, Alwitt, Lorch, & Levin, 1979). A look (or nonlooking pause) is more likely to survive the longer it has already been in progress. Note the time course of attentional inertia: After a look or pause has been in progress for about 15 seconds, the likelihood of changing attentional state diminishes substantially.

We have been exploring the functional significance of attentional inertia.

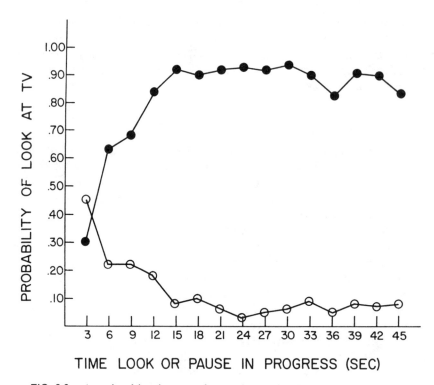

FIG. 8.3.   Attentional inertia curves for one 3-year-old television viewer. Figure reprinted from Anderson and Field (1983).

The first issue we examined was whether it is solely a reflection of increasing cognitive involvement with particular content throughout the time course of a look at TV. Consider looks that are in progress at the time one content unit ends and another begins (as, for example, the transition from a TV program to a commercial). Normally, at these content transitions, attentive viewers have a strong tendency to look away from the TV and inattentive viewers tend to look at the TV (Alwitt et al., 1980). The question here is whether this tendency to terminate attention at content boundaries interacts with time the look was in progress prior to the content boundary. If attentional inertia represents a form of attentional arousal that goes beyond cognitive involvement with immediate content, then we would expect that the longer a look has been in progress prior to a content boundary, the longer it will remain in progress after the content boundary. If, on the other hand, a change in content eliminates attentional inertia, there should be no relationship between look length prior to and after a content boundary.

To test the relationship, we examined the visual attention of 149 3-year-olds and 150 5-year-olds who each watched an hour of *Sesame Street*. Each *Sesame Street* program is in magazine format such that it consists of approxi-

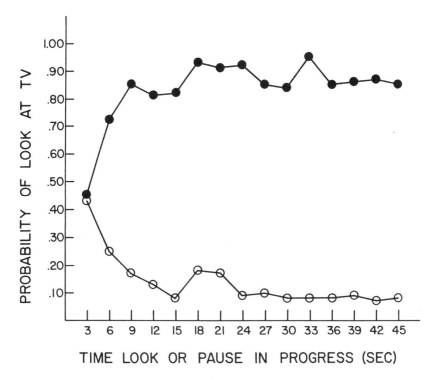

FIG. 8.4.   Attentional inertia curves for one 20-year-old television viewer. Figure reprinted from Anderson and Field (1983).

mately 40 segments which average 90 seconds in length. For each look which was in progress at the time a segment boundary occurred, we compared the length of time it remained in progress after the segment boundary to the amount of time it was in progress prior to the segment boundary. The results are in Fig. 8.5: The longer, on the average, it remained in progress prior to the segment boundary the longer it remained in progress after the segment boundary. Attentional inertia serves to drive attention across segment boundaries and thus exists somewhat independently of involvement with particular content. This effect is relevant to the producer of commercials since it should be apparent that the attention value of the program just preceding the commercial will be quite influential in determining whether attention will be driven across the content boundary or be terminated by that boundary.

We are currently involved in a series of studies to determine whether information acquisition from TV is enhanced as a function of attentional inertia. One question we addressed is whether a viewer becomes less distractible as attentional inertia builds up. In one study we observed 30 3-year-olds and 30 5-year-olds viewing *Sesame Street* in a room equipped with attractive toys. During the viewing session, on a rear-projection screen to the side of the TV

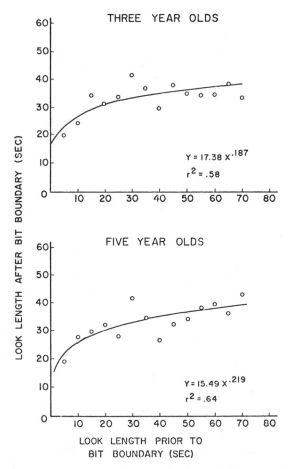

FIG. 8.5.   Average time a look remains in progress after a bit boundary as a function of time the look is in progress prior to the bit boundary. Figure reprinted from Anderson and Lorch (1983).

set, a computer aperiodically presented a slide for 4.0 sec, the onset of each slide accompanied by a loud "beep." Concurrently the viewer's visual attention to the TV and to the slide distractor was monitored. The important analysis in this experiment compared the distraction power of slides that were presented after a look at the TV was in progress for only a short time (15 sec or less) or after a relatively longer time (greater than 15 sec). The effect of look length was substantial: The probability of being distracted from the TV if a look had progressed for 15 sec or less was .30, whereas the probability of being distracted during look lengths greater than 15 sec, was .15. Viewers were thus half as distractible from the TV if they had been continuously looking more than 15 sec (Anderson, Lorch, & Field, unpublished data). We conclude that not only does attentional inertia tend to drive looks across content boundaries, but it also renders the viewer less distractible.

We have a working theoretical position on the nature of attentional inertia (Anderson & Lorch, 1983; Anderson & Smith, 1984) that is coherent with the two principles of TV viewing described earlier in this paper, namely, comprehension-guided attention and audio-monitoring inattention. We suggest that attentional inertia acts as a kind of attentional "glue" which provides cognitive continuity across a temporally extended flow of audiovisual discourse. If, in the recent past, the discourse has been significant and optimally comprehensible, an attentional arousal to the medium of discourse builds up which is above and beyond the cognitive involvement with the content of the discourse. When the receiver of the discourse encounters conceptual gaps (bridging inferences not immediately available), or when the source of discourse temporarily fails (as when a speaker pauses), or when the topic changes, attentional inertia provides a temporal bridge of continued active cognitive processing of the discourse medium. If, on the other hand, in the recent past the medium has not been a source of optimally comprehensible and significant information, attentional inertia does not build up. In this case, any momentary incoherence of content, or temporal gap, or unavailability of a bridging inference, or change of topic may lead to a lapse of attention.

IMPLICATIONS FOR PRODUCTION AND
FUTURE DIRECTIONS

The television commercial is a brief segment of content inserted in the audiovisual flow that is unrelated to the content surrounding it. The audience consists of individuals who vary in: (1) world knowledge, predisposition, and interest in the product; (2) concurrent activity while "watching" television; and (3) attentional state at the beginning of the commercial. With a few exceptions, the audience has no prior interest in watching the commercial. With these notions in mind, I now draw out a few practical implications of our work on the online cognitive processing of television.

First, given that the time of day and day of the week the commercial is broadcast is a prime consideration in any advertising strategy, consideration should be given to visual attentiveness and concurrent activities in each time slot. Weekday early morning audiences, for example, are far less likely to be visually attentive as they prepare for the day's activities. It is at this time, nevertheless, that they are involved with, and likely thinking about, food (as they prepare and eat breakfast), clothing (as they dress, often in front of the TV set), personal grooming (as they wash, shave, put on makeup, etc.), and transportation (as they prepare to leave for work or school). They are also likely preparing and discussing the day's activities, including shopping lists.

These commercially significant activities go on frequently with television as a background and as a locus of occasional full attention. The weekday morning is thus an interesting challenge and opportunity for the advertiser. The challenge is in getting the audience's attention in the face of competing activities, and the opportunity is to communicate with the audience at a time when it may be most receptive to messages about a variety of products. The producer's concern with the audience's concurrent activities and associated involvements should extend, of course, to all other time periods, days of week, and seasons.

Beyond awareness of the audience's concurrent activities, the three principles of online patterns of attention should be taken into consideration in commercial design. These principles are comprehension-guided attention, audio-monitoring inattention, and attentional inertia.

The principle of comprehension-guided attention underscores the importance of the content. Detailed consideration of the viewer's world knowledge and inference processes required for comprehension must be combined with consideration of their needs and interests. Fundamentally, the commercial must address an issue of concern to the viewer in order to hold attention. Knowing the audience is therefore of primary importance in designing the message. This is particularly relevant in communicating with children, where concerns and interests may vary widely as a function of age. This general point, I suppose, has long been obvious to advertising copy writers. It takes considerable talent to make mundane products so interesting and exciting that the viewer is held in rapt attention. As far as production features are concerned, there is at this time remarkably little evidence that visual production features are in and of themselves of great importance in maintaining attention to television (cf. Anderson, Lorch, Field, & Sanders, 1981). In fact, one production feature, the extended zoom, reliably terminates visual attention in children (Alwitt et al., 1980; Anderson & Levin, 1976; Calvert et al., 1982; Susman, 1978). This is not to say that visually interesting image and graphics are irrelevant; rather, the same general principle of comprehensibility holds. Abstract art, for example, may entrance the knowledgeable art connoisseur but not the less informed general public.

No matter how skillfully the content of a commercial addresses the audience's interests, the producer must realize that a large portion of the audience will not be paying attention to the TV at the onset of the commercial. This makes the production of the audio of crucial significance to the overall design of the program. It is important to realize, moreover, that audio monitoring by inattentive viewers is to some extent at the level of sound attributes, such as voice qualities. Viewers have learned that some audio attributes reliably predict content change or (to them) interesting content. Some attributes, however, are learned as associated with uninteresting content and actually suppress attention. For young viewers, men's voices are a prime example.

Given that an auditory cue is appropriately placed early in a commercial, the producer must also be aware that a large portion of the audience may just initiate full attention several seconds into the segment. This portion of the audience will have missed the very beginning of the segment. If that beginning is crucial to general comprehension of the message, much of that newly attentive audience will be lost again. After all, the majority of looks at TV are under 5 sec in length.

Finally, attentional inertia is a pervasive factor of cognition that can work both for and against the advertiser. It should be quite obvious that the context in which a commercial is placed will have important implications as to whether the beginning of the segment is watched, if indeed the segment is watched at all. A highly involving program will draw audience attention into the beginning of a commercial. The converse is also true; a program that requires little attention produces some resistance against attention being drawn back to the TV (see the lower functions in Figs. 8.3 & 8.4). There is an interesting tradeoff here: Intensely involving program content is probably good for the advertiser in terms of attention, but for many viewers, TV provides a backdrop for other activities. These viewers may avoid highly involving programs because they interfere with concurrent activities or with general relaxation. The attentional inertia principle also implies that nesting a commercial behind another commercial will likely produce lower attention unless the prior commercial is particularly effective in holding attention. In general, the producer should consider the attentional states of the audience through each second of the commercial, reflecting on the consequences of attention gained or attention lost at each point.

Researchers, of course, have not even come close to specifying all of the temporal dynamics involved in the online cognitive processing of television. After all, such research has been going on for barely a decade, and the number of active laboratories is small. In our work we plan to examine numerous aspects of attentional inertia, auditory attention, processing of montage, and the perceived temporal structure of audiovisual narrative. We will also carry out detailed quantitative analyses of home TV viewing behavior including behavior during commercials. I am quite optimistic about the future of this research. Although the work is expensive and often technically difficult, the effects are large and reliable, and the discoveries of fundamental significance both in practical application and in contributing to a basic understanding of human cognition.

ACKNOWLEDGMENTS

The research described here was supported by grants from the National Science Foundation, The National Institute of Mental Health, the W. T. Grant Foundation, Children's Television Workshop, and the John and Mary Markle Foundation. I would like to thank Patricia Collins, Diane Field, and John Nathan for contributing their observations from many hours of watching families watch television.

REFERENCES

Allen, C. (1965). Photographing the TV audience. *Journal of Advertising Research, 14,* 2–8.

Alwitt, L. F., Anderson, D. R., Lorch, E. P., & Levin, S. R. (1980). Preschool children's visual attention to television. *Human Communication Research, 7,* 52–67.

Anderson, D. R. (1983). *Home television viewing by preschool children and their families.* Paper presented at the Society for Research in Child Development biennial meeting.

Anderson, D. R., Alwitt, L. F., Lorch, E. P., & Levin, S. R. (1979). Wathing children watch television. In G. A. Hale & M. Lewis (Eds.), *Attention and cognitive development.* New York: Plenum.

Anderson, D. R., & Field, D. E. (1983). Children's attention to television: Implications for production. In M. Meyer (Ed.), *Children and the formal features of television.* Munich: Saur.

Anderson, D. R., Field, D. E., Lorch, E. P., Nathan, J. G., Collins, P. A., unpublished data.

Anderson, D. R., & Levin, S. R. (1976). Young children's attention to *Sesame Street. Child Development, 47,* 806–811.

Anderson, D. R., & Lorch, E. P. (1983). Looking at television: Action or reaction? In J. Bryant & D. R. Anderson (Eds.), *Children's understanding of television: Research on attention and comprehension.* New York: Academic Press.

Anderson, D. R., Lorch, E. P., & Field, D. E., unpublished data.

Anderson, D. R., Lorch, E. P., Field, D. E., & Sanders J. (1981). The effects of TV program comprehensibility on preschool children's visual attention to television. *Child Development, 52,* 151–157.

Anderson, D. R., Lorch, E. P., Smith, R., Bradford, R., & Levin, S. R. (1981). Effects of peer presence on preschool children's television viewing behavior. *Developmental Psychology, 17,* 446–453.

Anderson, D. R., & Smith, R. (1984). Young children's TV viewing: The problem of cognitive continuity. To appear in F. J. Morrison, C. Lord, & D. F. Keating (Eds.), *Applied developmental psychology.* New York: Academic Press.

Bechtel, R. B., Achelpohl, C., & Akers, R. (1972). Correlates between observed behavior and questionnaire responses on television viewing. In E. A. Rubinstein, G. A. Comstock, & J. P. Murray (Eds.), *Television and social behavior* (Vol. 4), *Television in day-to-day life: Patterns of use.* Washington, D.C.: U.S. Government Printing Office.

Bryant, J., & Anderson, D. R. (Eds.) (1983). *Children's understanding of television: Research on attention and comprehension.* New York: Academic Press.

Calvert, S. L., Huston, A. C. Watkins, B. A., & Wright, J. C. (1982). The relation between selective attention to television forms and children's comprehension of content. *Child Development, 53,* 601–610.

Carew, J. (1980). Experience and the development of intelligence in young children at home and in day care. *Monographs of the Society for Research in Child Development, 45,* No. 187, 1–89.

Collins, W. A. (1979). Children's comprehension of television content. In E. Wartella (Ed.), *Children communicating: Media and the development of thought, speech, and understanding.* Beverly Hills, Cal.: Sage.

Collins, W. A., Wellman, H., Keniston, A. H., & Westby, S. D. (1978). Age related aspects of comprehension and inference from a televised dramatic narrative. *Child Development, 49,* 389–399.

Csikszentmihalyi, M., & Kubey, R. (1981). Television and the rest of life: A systematic comparison of subjective experience. *Public Opinion Quarterly, 45,* 302–315.

Ditchburn, R. W. (1973). *Eye-movements and visual perception.* London: Oxford University Press.

Field, D. (1983). *Children's television viewing strategies.* Presented at the Society for Research in Child Development biennial meeting, Detroit.

Flagg, B. N. (1978). Children and television: Effects of stimulus repetition on eye activity. In J. W. Senders, D. F. Fisher, & R. A. Monty (Eds.), *Eye movements and the higher psychological functions.* Hillsdale, N.J.: Lawrence Erlbaum Associates.

Kelly, H., & Gardner, H. (Eds.) (1981). *Viewing children through television.* San Francisco: Jossey-Bass.

Lesser, G. S. (1974). *Children and television: Lessons from Sesame Street.* New York: Academic Press.

Lesser, H. (1977). *Television and the preschool child.* New York: Academic Press.

Levin, S., & Anderson, D. (1976). The development of attention. *Journal of Communication, 26*(2), 126–135.

Lorch, E. P., Anderson, D. R., & Levin, S. R. (1979). The relationship of visual attention to children's comprehension of television. *Child Development, 50,* 722–727.

Mander, J. (1978). *Four arguments for the elimination of television.* New York: William Morrow.

Meyer, M. (Ed.) (1983). *Children and the formal features of television.* Munich: Saur.

Moody, K. (1980). *Growing up on television.* New York: New York Times.

Nathan, J. G., Anderson, D. R., Field, D. E., & Collins, P. A., unpublished data.

Pezdek, K., & Hartman, E. (1983). Children's television viewing: Attention and comprehension of auditory versus visual information. *Child Development, 54,* 1015–1023.

Schramm, W., Lyle, J., & Parker, E. B. (1961). *Television in the lives of our children.* Stanford, Calif.: Stanford University Press.

Singer, J. L. (1980). The power and limitations of television: A cognitive-affective analysis. In P. H. Tannenbaum (Ed.), *The entertainment functions of television.* Hillsdale, N.J.: Lawrence Erlbaum Associates.

Susman, E. J. (1978). Visual and verbal attributes of television and selective attention in preschool children. *Developmental Psychology, 14,* 447–461.

Wright, J. C., & Huston, A. C. (1981). Children's understanding of the forms of television. In H. Kelly & H. Gardner (Eds.), *Viewing children through television.* San Francisco: Jossey Bass.

Winn, M. (1977). *The plug-in drug.* New York: Viking Press.

9 EEG Activity Reflects the Content of Commercials

Linda F. Alwitt
Leo Burnett U.S.A.
Chicago, Illinois

INTRODUCTION

In recent years there has been an increased interest in electroencephalographic (EEG) measurement of brain activity as a way to learn more about how advertising works. There have been several studies of EEGs of people watching television commercials (for reviews see Stewart & Furse, 1983 or Ray & Olson, 1983). Many of the studies have been concerned with issues such as EEG differences in hemispheric laterality between print advertising and television commercials. The question of what aspects of commercial content are reflected by EEGs has not been addressed.

The purpose of the current analysis is to search for events in commercials that may trigger EEG responses of a person viewing those commercials. This analysis can be useful for two areas of concern about EEG research on advertising. First, it can answer some technical questions about how EEGs can be used to examine reactions to an on-going real-life event like a television commercial. It can guide us to the brain sites and frequency bands most likely to reflect responses related to the content of television commercials. Second, it can help us learn more about how advertising works. The specific aspects of a commercial that are reflected by EEG measures of the brain's activity may suggest to us what parts of a commercial are relevant, what parts are attended to, what parts mean something to the viewer.

The data for this analysis are from a Marketing Science Institute sponsored pilot study of EEG responses to television commercials, which was designed by Jerry Olson and Bill Ray of Pennsylvania State University with input from several sponsoring companies. Olson and Ray recorded EEGs of thirty people while they watched a television talk show which included twelve commercials. They are currently preparing a report of this research, using the commercial as the unit of analysis. The current analysis differs from Olson and Ray's analyses in that it uses two-second segments of the commercials as the unit of analysis.

In order to explore the relationship between the content of commercials and EEG-detected brain activity that occurs when a person watches the commercials, the following approach was used:

First, the twelve commercials were coded for the presence or absence of certain events such as cuts, zooms, brand name mention, or humor. Second, two brain sites and three frequency bands were chosen as those most likely to show a relationship to events coded in the commercials. Third, the coded events were related to the EEG parameters via regression analyses.

There are two main questions of interest:

1. How well does the coded content of the commercials account for variability in the EEG parameters?
2. Which events coded in the commercials best account for the variability in EEG amplitude at each brain site and frequency band?

METHOD

The EEG data for these analyses are from the Olson and Ray study. The EEG data were collected from fifteen men and fifteen women aged 18–55 years who were all right-handed as they watched twelve commercials embedded in a television talk show. All thirty subjects were at least occasional users or purchasers of the product categories advertised in the twelve commercials.

The EEGs were recorded from right and left frontal, parietal, and temporal sites. They were analyzed via a Fourier analysis of fifteen two-second epochs of each commercial for each of five frequency bands: delta, theta, alpha beta1 and beta2. Details of the data collection and Fourier analysis are discussed by Olson & Ray (in preparation).

There were two commercials for each of six product categories: three drink products, a food, a durable product, and a personal product. Commercials for five of the product categories were for the same brand, and one commercial emphasized product attributes while the other was a mood or image commercial. The commercials for the sixth product category were for two different brands.

Subjects were tested individually in a small room. They watched television as the electrodes were attached in order to get used to the surroundings and the television, and then watched the talk show and commercials.

Content of Commercials

The events coded from the content of the commercials were chosen in order to test four hypotheses about the classes of events which are likely to be reflected by EEGs. These hypotheses are:

1. EEG activity is evoked by physical events in a commercial such as cuts, zooms, closeups, and music. We might expect EEG responses to changes in stimulation, and perhaps to concrete events.

2. EEG activity is evoked by brand and message events such as brand name mention, specific messages about the brand, visual of brand in use, and product or package shots. EEG responses may be triggered by events that are relevant to the viewer. A viewer who watches a TV commercial may have a predisposition to take in information about brand or message. Brand and message information is relevant to the goals of the commercial and to the current state of the viewer.

3. EEG activity is evoked by viewer reactions to the commercial such as acquiring information, seeing an emotional moment, seeing a relationship between the characters in the commercial, seeing a realistic depiction, or humor. EEG responses might be triggered either by the event of being stimulated or by the subject's consideration of the implication of that event for himself. That is, EEG responses may be driven by the viewer's reaction to the stimulating event rather than by the stimulating event itself.

4. EEG activity is evoked by the medium used to communicate such as a speaker on screen, a voiceover or speaker off-screen, or words superimposed on the visual. The medium rather than the message may influence EEG responses.

Table 9.1 defines each of the events coded from the content of the twelve commercials.

Fourteen of the events were coded by two raters while three were coded by five or six raters. All twelve commercials were coded for a single event at one time before they were coded for another event. The order in which commercials were coded was randomly varied. All raters were professional advertising researchers who were accustomed to analytically viewing a wide range of types of commercials. Coding was carried out with the help of an APPLE computer. The rater watched each commercial and pressed a key on the APPLE terminal in the presence of the event to be coded. The APPLE computer program segmented the commercial into two-second epochs which were equivalent to the two-second epochs over which the EEG data was integrated. Whether or not the event occurred was recorded for each two-second epoch of each commercial. For the fourteen "simple" events, only epochs for which both raters were in agreement were recorded as "present." For the three

TABLE 9.1
Definitions of Events Coded in Commercials

Physical	
Cuts	Cuts or dissolves from one scene to another.
Zooms	Camera shot zoom in or out.
Music	Presence of music.
Closeups	Closeup visual shots relative to other shots in commercial.
Brand Message	
Brand name mention	Audio mention of name of advertised brand.
Specific message	Specific product/brand message outside context of commercial narrative flow.
Brand in use	Visual of brand being used as intended to be used.
Product shot	Visual of product/brand; package shots.
Reactions	
Meaningful units	Moment when commercial fits together for rater, makes sense and gives some information about the brand, the message or the narrative.
Relationship	Two or more people in any relationship; both need not be visually present at same time; implied relationships and explicit relationsips.
Touching	Two people on screen touch each other or vocalize feelings about each other.
Realistic	Moments when people in commercial look and act like real people rather than like actors acting.
Emotional moment	Moments when people in the commercial experienced an emotion.
Humor	Moments when rater thought something was humorous.
Communication Media	
Speaker on screen	Visual of speaker speaking
Super	Words superimposed over picture on screen
Voice over	Off-screen speaker speaking

more complex events, the average "presence" rating was recorded for each epoch of each commercial.

Reliability for these fourteen events was estimated by phi coefficients, which ranged from .74 to .93, averaged across commercials for the events. If reliability for an event in a commercial fell below .70, it was recoded. Table 9.2 shows the frequency of occurrence and reliabilities of all coded events.

Three of the coded events, all concerned with viewer reactions to the commercials, require some comment because they are more complex than are the others and more difficult to rate. "Realistic moments" are defined as parts of a commercial that show life "as it really is." They are moments when people in the commercial act as they do in real life and not like actors playing a part. "Emotional moments" are defined as times in the commercial when the characters experienced an emotion such as joy, humor, affection, dismay, etc. Emotional moments were judged not only by what was depicted in the commercial but also by whether or not the rater was moved by the event in the commercial. "Meaningful units" are defined as moments when the commercial fit together so that the rater could understand the brand message or the emotional message of that scene. It was a moment when the rater learned something about the events in the commercial. Events similar to "meaningful

TABLE 9.2
Frequency of Occurrence and Reliability of Coding Events in Commercials

Commercial Content	Mean	Standard Deviation	Range	Reliability
Physical				
Cuts	7.67	4.08	3 — 14	.87
Zooms	4.50	4.58	0 — 14	.90
Music	8.67	7.66	0 — 15	.88
Closeups	7.67	3.26	4 — 15	.74
Brand Message				
Brand name mention	4.42	2.61	1 — 10	.91
Specific message	3.25	1.91	0 — 6	.93
Brand in use	5.50	3.63	0 — 13	.87
Product shot	5.53	2.67	2 — 10	.90
Reactions				
Meaningful units*	4.81	1.06	3.5 — 6.6	.50
Relationship	7.25	6.55	0 — 15	.86
Touching	2.08	3.58	0 — 10	.93
Realistic*	4.94	4.84	0 — 13.5	.41
Emotional moment**	2.38	3.29	0 — 8.4	.55
Humor	2.08	3.23	0 — 9	.77
Communication				
Media				
Speaker on screen	3.83	5.61	0 — 13	.87
Super	2.92	2.64	0 — 10	.96
Voice over	8.42	5.37	0 — 15	.90

*Mean of 6 ratings.
**Mean of 5 ratings.

units" have been studied by Newtson (1973, 1976), who suggests that boundaries between perceived events reflect changes in the flow of events shown in a video presentation.

"Realistic moments" and "meaningful units" were coded by six raters each, and "emotional moments" was coded by five raters. For these more complex events, the order of coding commercials was balanced or partially balanced across raters so that the two commercials for the same product category were rated in sequence but the order of product categories differed for each rater. Reliabilities for these ratings were estimated by an analysis of variance approach (Rosenthal, 1982), and are shown in Table 9.2. The lower reliabilities of these three events reflects the difficulty of coding them. They were included, however, because they are an attempt to measure a set of variables that is quite relevant to our purpose, reactions to events in a commercial.

EEG Measures

Based on a preliminary analysis of the EEG data, two brain sites were chosen, the frontal area and the parietal area. The temporal area was not included in this analysis because it is less variable over time, and would be less appropriate for an initial examination of the effect of commercial content on EEG.

Three EEG frequency bands were chosen for this analysis, alpha (8–12 hz), beta 1 (12–16 hz), and beta 2 (16–28 hz). These frequency bands are less likely to be contaminated by eye movement artifacts than are the lower frequency bands and are the bands that have been used in most advertising effects studies.

The EEG parameters were absolute Fourier coefficients, a measure of the amplitude of EEG voltage for each frequency band at each brain site. There are large individual differences in any psychophysiological measure including EEG (Stewart & Furse, 1983), and there are various techniques available to control for these differences (Olson & Ray, 1982). In the current analysis, EEG parameters were standardized for each brain site of each respondent.

The EEG responses of viewers were related to the commercial content on an aggregate basis; standardized EEGs were aggregated across respondents. Aggregating the data should maximize relationships between commercial content and EEG, compared to individual data (O'Grady, 1982). However, by aggregating the data, a number of variables unrelated to commercial content, which probably contribute to EEG variability, could not be considered. Variables such as respondent sex, age, interest in the advertised product and relevance to past experience could not be taken into account when the data was aggregated over respondents. These variables are, to some degree, independent of commercial content but they are very likely to influence the EEG parameters. They contribute to the error term for the purposes of the current analysis.

However, one non-content variable that may be related to commercial content could be controlled in the current analyses — the hemisphere from which the EEG was recorded. Hemispheric differences do account for some EEG variability at some brain sites and for some frequency bands. Since the current analysis is concerned with effects of commercial content, most of the analyses were carried out on data from which effects of hemispheric differences were statistically removed by a two-level regression. The first regression used an EEG parameter as the dependent variable and hemispheric differences as the independent variable. The residual EEG parameters were the dependent variable in a second regression in which commercial content events were the independent variables. Hemispheric differences are considered as a secondary issue later in this chapter.

RESULTS

Hemispheric differences account for more of the variance in EEG parameters at the frontal than at the parietal brain site, and for more of the variance in the beta2 frequency band than in the alpha or beta1 frequency bands. Table 9.3 shows the percentages of variance for each brain site and frequency band which are accounted for by differences between the right and left hemispheres. As mentioned above, the residual EEG parameters are used in the following analyses.

How Well is Commercial Content Reflected by EEG Parameters?

The seventeen events coded in the twelve commercials account for between 6 and 15% of the variance in EEG activity for the two brain sites and three frequency bands. These percentages are shown in row 1 of Table 9.4.

TABLE 9.3
Contribution of Hemispheric Differences to
Variability of Brain Wave Parameters

Percentage of Variance due to Hemispheric Differences

	Brain Site:	
Frequency Band	*Parietal*	*Frontal*
Alpha	0.02%	5.26%*
Beta 1	0.02	7.69*
Beta 2	7.85*	22.54*

$*p < .0001$

TABLE 9.4
Effects of Commercial Content on Brain Wave Parameters at each Brain Site and
Frequency Band — Hemisphere Effects Removed

	Beta Weights					
	Parietal			Frontal		
	Alpha	Beta 1	Beta 2	Alpha	Beta 1	Beta 2
% Variance accounted for by model [a]:	15%*	9%*	11%*	14%*	6%*	7%*
Commercial Content						
Physical						
Cuts	−.10	−.09	.02	−.16*	−.09	−.04
Zooms	.01	.07	.00	.00	.05	−.04
Music	−.17*	−.08	−.07	−.01	−.01	−.01
Closeup	.03	−.04	−.10	−.07	−.10	−.04
Brand/Message						
Brand name mention	−.13*	−.12*	−.11*	−.05	−.01	−.13*
Specific message	.14*	.05	.09	.09	.05	.06
Brand in use	−.29*	−.20*	−.26*	−.20*	−.16*	−.13*
Product shot	−.07	.02	−.08	−.02	−.09	−.10
Reactions						
Meaningful Unit	−.02	−.02	.00	−.03	.06	.07
Relationship	.01	−.06	−.16*	−.01	−.04	−.11
Touching	−.05	−.09	−.09	−.05	−.08	−.18*
Realistic	−.02	.03	.14	−.06	−.02	.24*
Emotional moment	−.14	−.01	−.05	−.14	−.04	−.03
Humor	−.01	−.08	−.06	.03	.03	.05
Communication Media						
Speaker on screen	−.16*	−.13	−.18*	−.05	−.18*	−.17*
Super	.08	.02	−.02	.02	.02	.00
Voice over	−.24*	−.24*	−.14*	.02	−.24*	.00

*p < .05
[a]adjusted for df

The reliability of these estimates was checked by computing regressions on each half of the sample of thirty respondents (randomly assigned within sex). The amount of variance accounted for at each of the two brain sites and three frequency bands is significantly greater than zero for both halves of the sample, although the proportion of variance accounted for by each half-sample differs. The same predictor events were significant in both half-samples. This result suggests that commercial content is likely to be reflected in the EEG parameters, and the reliabilities of the particular predictor events are reasonably good.

The amount of variance accounted for by the coded events is much smaller when events are combined into classes that conform to the four hypothesized classes of events that might influence EEGs. Those classes of events are: physical, brand/message, cognitive — emotional reactions, communication media. This result suggests that, although events coded in the study may logically fit together, they do not form a coherent nor a complete description of the hypothesized classes of influential events. For example, although "brand name mention" and "brand in use" both convey information about the advertised brand, EEG reactions differ to these two events in commercials.

The seventeen coded events were also combined into classes depending on whether they were conveyed by audio, video, or both. This grouping did not account for as much variance in the EEG as was accounted for by the seventeen commercial content events. This result suggests that audio-visual paths of communication do not seem to capture the essence of events that might trigger EEG responses.

What Events in a Commercial are Reflected by EEG Parameters?

Four classes of events were hypothesized to influence EEG parameters: physical events like "cuts," brand/message events like "brand name mention," cognitive or emotional reactions, and communication media like "speaker on screen." As can be seen in Table 9.4, the coded events within a commercial that influence EEG parameters vary by brain site and frequency band. Table 9.4 shows beta weights for each of the seventeen coded events for all six brain site-frequency band combinations. Only one event is consistently related to both brain sites at all three frequency bands — visuals of the brand in use. For the parietal brain sites, seven of the twelve possible brand/message events and five of the nine possible communication media events show a relationship to EEG parameters, as indicated by significant beta weights in the regressions. Only one of the twelve possible physical events and one of the eighteen possible cognitive-emotional reactions show a significant relationship to EEG. These results suggest that the influence of commercial content on EEG may be primarily due to brand/message events and to communication media or how these messages were conveyed.

For the frontal brain sites, four of the twelve possible brand/message events and three of the nine possible communication media events show a relationship to EEG parameters, as indicated by significant beta weights in the regressions. Only one of the twelve possible physical events and two of the eighteen possible cognitive-emotional reaction events were significantly related to EEG. For the frontal brain site, events that trigger EEG responses come from all four hypothesized classes of events. The results suggest the frontal sites are less likely than are parietal sites to reflect any events we coded, but especially brand or message related information from the commercial.

The results of this analysis are consistent with previous descriptions of the functions of the parietal and frontal areas of the brain (Luria, 1973; Pribram, 1971). The parietal brain is supposed to coordinate information and evaluate it in tems of its relevance to the viewer. The commercial events which contributed to parietal EEG involve the goal of the commercial, telling about and selling the advertised brand. One of the functions of the frontal brain is supposed to be control of emotional behavior (Pribram, 1971; Tucker, 1981). Results of the current analysis are consistent with an emotional function for the frontal brain; two emotional events in the commercials (touching and realistic moments) contributed to frontal EEG.

Delayed EEG Reactions to Some Aspects of Commercial Content

Viewers may react quickly to certain events in a commercial but more slowly to other events. Slowed reactions should result in a stronger relationship between an event in a commercial and EEG when the response to an event is lagged by one or more epochs. This way of measuring lagged EEG effects is also influenced by the duration of the event in the commercials. To examine the possible influence of slowed reactions to events in commercials, the events in each commercial were correlated with EEG parameters at lags of 0–5 two-second epochs. As an example, the correlations for parietal alpha at each lag are shown in Table 9.5. For each brain site-frequency band combination, the lag with the highest significant correlation was chosen as the independent variable in a regression in which EEG was the dependent variable. The "default" lag was zero. For example, the underlined correlations in Table 9.5 were entered into the regression for parietal alpha.

Lagged events were included in regression models in order to consider the effects of slow reactions to some events in the commercials. What does this add to our knowledge about the effect of commercial content on EEGs? A comparison of the percentage of variance explained in EEG parameters by delayed reactions in row 1 of Table 9.6 to that explained by immediate reactions to events in row 1 of Table 9.4 shows that including different response times to coded events in the analyses does not substantially change the amount of influence on frontal EEGs for any frequency band but there is a small increase in the influence on parietal EEGs for all three frequency bands.

Respondents did seem to have slower EEG reactions to some events in the commercials. The clearest example is zooms. Zooms take place over time, and are sometimes difficult to perceive at first; a delayed reaction to zooms,

TABLE 9.5
Correlation of Events in Commercial at Different Delays with Parietal Alpha

Commercial Content	LAG					
	0	1	2	3	4	5
Physical						
Cuts	−.21*	−.02	−.05	−.14	−.18*	−.05
Zooms	.02	.21*	.32*	.31*	.28*	.10
Music	−.16*	−.16*	−.15*	−.09	−.09	−.09
Closeups	−.14	−.14	−.15*	−.17*	−.14*	.03
Brand/Message						
Brand name mention	−.10	.09	.06	.11	.05	.00
Specific message	.13	.18*	.16*	−.01	−.02	−.04
Brand in use	−.26*	−.24*	−.13	−.05	−.01	−.09
Product shot	.06	.17*	.07	−.07	−.08	.02
Reactions						
Meaningful Unit	−.07	−.05	.15*	.00	−.04	−.00
Relationship	−.14	−.19*	−.14*	−.06	−.07	−.11
Touching	−.13	−.18*	−.11	−.07	−.14	−.10
Realistic	−.14	−.18*	−.13	−.07	−.02	−.05
Emotional moment	−.17*	−.09	−.01	−.04	−.08	−.08
Humor	−.04	−.04	.14	.01	.00	−.08
Communication Media						
Speaker on screen	.00	−.04	.14	.16*	.11	.10
Super	.15*	.14*	.07	−.07	−.07	−.01
Voice over	−.05	.01	−.02	−.07	−.01	−.01

*p < .05

TABLE 9.6
Effects of Events in Commercials at Different Delays on Brain Wave Parameters at
each Brain Site and Frequency Band-Hemisphere Effects Removed

	Beta Weights					
	Parietal			Frontal		
	Alpha	Beta 1	Beta 2	Alpha	Beta 1	Beta 2
% Variance accounted for by model [a]:	18%*	10%*	14%*	15%*	6%*	8%*
Commercial Content						
Physical						
Cuts	− .09	− .08	.03	− .15*	− .08	− .01
Zooms	.17*	.10	.11	.05	.04	− .12*
Music	− .12	− .10	− .11	− .02	− .03	− .03
Closeup	.05	− .03	− .12*	− .08	− .10	− .06
Brand/Message						
Brand name mention	− .11*	− .11*	− .10	.04	− .02	− .12*
Specific message	.18*	.12*	.17*	.13*	.06	.11
Brand in use	− .25*	− .19*	− .23*	− .20*	− .15*	− .08
Product shot	− .03	− .00	− .10	− .05	− .06	− .10
Reactions						
Meaningful Unit	− .09	− .02	− .02	− .07	.05	.05
Relationship	.03	− .08	− .13	− .04	− .02	− .03
Touching	− .06	− .07	− .05	− .03	− .05	− .12
Realistic	− .06	.03	.12	− .08	− .02	.19*
Emotional moment	− .14	− .01	− .06	− .13	− .07	− .06
Humor	.00	− .08	− .04	.03	.02	.04
Communication Media						
Speaker on screen	− .08	− .12	− .21*	− .07	− .19*	− .14
Super	.09	.01	− .02	.01	− .08	.02
Voice over	− .23*	− .24*	− .14*	.00	− .25*	.04

*$p < .05$
[a]adjusted for df

then, is not surprising. When delayed zooms were included in the regression model, zooms appeared to influence EEG parameters for parietal alpha and frontal beta 2. Specific brand messages are another possible example of slower EEG reactions. The immediate EEG response to specific brand message is only present for parietal alpha. However, a two-second delayed EEG response to specific messages is present for all three parietal frequency bands and for frontal alpha. Table 9.6 shows beta weights for differently lagged events for all six brain site-frequency band combinations.

In summary, while delayed reactions to events in commercials should be considered in assessing the effect of commercial content on EEG, these effects appear to be small and may be due to the duration of the events in the commercial as well as to delayed reactions of the viewers.

Influence of Commercial Content on Right and Left Hemispheres

The analyses reported so far excluded the influence of hemispheric differences on EEG parameters because these effects are not part of the content of commercials. However, one might want to know whether an event in a commercial influences EEG parameters more in one hemisphere than in the other. This problem was approached in two ways. First, regressions that included hemispheric differences were compared with regressions on residual EEGs after hemispheric difference effects had been removed. Table 9.7 summarizes the regressions with hemispheric difference effects included for all six brain site-frequency and combinations. Table 9.7 can be compared with Table 9.4, which shows the summary of regressions after hemispheric difference effects had been removed.

As one would expect from the effect of hemispheric differences at different brain site-frequency band combinations (See Table 9.3), more EEG variance is accounted for in parietal Beta2 and all frequency bands at the frontal brain site when hemispheric differences are included. However, whether or not hemispheric differences are considered, the same coded events in the commercials influence EEGs at each of the brain site-frequency band combinations. This result suggest that none of the events in the commercials are reacted to differently in the two hemispheres.

The second approach to looking for hemispheric differences in reactions to the different events in commercials was to examine the interactions between each event and hemispheres in analyses of variance. None of the interactions for any event with hemisphere were significant for any site or frequency band. To the extent that we are willing to accept the null hypothesis, these results suggest that the events coded in the commercials in this study are not reacted to differently by the right and left hemispheres.

TABLE 9.7
Effects of Commercial Content on Brain Wave Parameters at each Brain Site and Frequency Band-Hemisphere Effects Included

	Beta Weights					
	Parietal			Frontal		
	Alpha	Beta 1	Beta 2	Alpha	Beta 1	Beta 2
% Variance accounted for by model [a]:	15%*	9%*	18%*	18%*	12%*	28%*
Commercial Content						
Physical						
Cuts	−.10	−.09	.02	−.15*	−.08	−.04
Zooms	.01	.07	.00	.00	.05	−.04
Music	−.17*	−.08	−.07	−.00	−.01	−.01
Closeups	.03	−.04	−.09	−.07	−.09	−.04
Brand/Message						
Brand name mention	−.13*	−.12*	−.11*	−.05	−.01	−.11*
Specific message	.14*	.05	.09	.09	.05	.05
Brand in use	−.29*	−.20*	−.25*	−.20*	−.15*	−.11*
Product shot	−.07	.02	−.08	−.02	−.08	−.09
Reactions						
Meaningful Units	−.02	−.02	.00	−.03	.06	.06
Relationship	.01	−.06	−.15*	−.01	−.04	−.10
Touching	−.05	−.09	−.09	−.05	−.08	−.15*
Realistic	−.02	.03	.13	−.06	−.02	.21*
Emotional moment	−.14	−.01	−.05	−.13	−.04	−.03
Humor	−.01	−.08	−.06	.03	.03	.05
Communication Media						
Speaker on screen	−.16*	−.13	−.17*	−.05	−.18*	−.15*
Super	.08	.02	−.02	.02	.02	.00
Voice over	−.24*	−.24*	−.13*	.02	−.23*	.00
Hemisphere	.01	−.01	−.28*	.23*	.28*	.47*

*$p < .05$
[a]adjusted for df

Although we have no evidence from these analyses that there are hemispheric differences in how events in commercials affect EEGs, it is too soon to reject the idea. Hemispheric differences are very small (Donchin, Kutas, & McCarthy, 1977) and may be reflected in processes people use to perceive and comprehend events rather than in storing the events themselves (Kinsbourne, 1982). If some events in a commercial call for a different kind of processing than do other events, there may indeed be hemispheric differences in EEG responses to different events. However, these differences might have to be detected by a method sensitive to processing of events within different contexts.

DISCUSSION

Events in a commercial appear to merely tickle the brain waves; they do not scratch it vigorously. When one considers the complexity of brain events, it is impressive that commercial content can be shown to have any effect on EEG measures of brain reactions. With the one exception of a visual of a brand in use, which appears to influence EEG at both sites and all frequency bands, *different* aspects of commercial content are reflected by EEGs at each of the brain site-frequency combinations. Brand and message events and how they are communicated appear to have more of an effect on parietal EEG than do physical events and emotional-cognitive reactions. The classes of events which are reflected by frontal behavior are less clear.

The analyses reported in this paper demonstrate that commercial content is related to EEG but is not clear just what the relationship means. A negative correlational relationship between EEG and an event in the commercials could mean there is a positive reaction or it could mean there is a negative reaction by the viewer. Further, an EEG reaction could represent attention, memory, relevance, puzzlement, admiration, astonishment, and so forth. Not enough is known about how EEG reflects functions of the brain to allow us to interpret correlations of commercial events with EEG parameters in a simple way. The Olson and Ray study, which is the source of the EEG data reported in this paper, includes measures of verbal reactions to the commercials, and those reactions might be used to interpret the relationship between content and EEG parameters. That analysis is not presented in this paper.

The degree to which commercial content can account for EEG variability is significant but relatively small in these analyses. There are several possible reasons for the small effect. First, the only non-content variables considered were hemisphere differences and individual differences for a given brain site (via standardization of data). Other non-content variables such as age or interest in the advertised product may well influence the EEG parameters. Second, EEG measures the gross activity of the brain. It may not be sensitive to complex events such as those coded for the commercials of this study. Almost all of the recent studies of psychological functions and electrophysiology of the brain measure evoked potentials (Hillyard & Kutas, 1983), which may be a more sensitive neurophysiological correlate of behavior. A related point is that, while regression analysis depends on the reliability of the variables in the regression, we have no measure of the reliability of EEG parameters for the same stimulation conditions. Indeed, it would be difficult to obtain "test-retest" reliability because one would expect EEGs to change when an event is repeated (John & Schwartz, 1978). Third, the seventeen events coded in the commercials used in this study may not adequately sample the events which influence EEG. A different set of events might be able to explain more of the variance in EEG parameters. Also, although most of the events could be reliably coded in the commercials, complex events such as emotional and cognitive reactions were less reliably coded.

CONCLUSIONS

The results of this analysis can be useful in deciding which brain sites and frequency bands are most likely to yield information about reactions to advertising. For example, the parietal alpha EEG parameters seem to be a likely place to seek reactions to brand and message content of a commercial. The frontal beta 2 parameters might be a likely place to seek reactions to executional variables. The results also suggest that content is not necessarily responded to differently by the two hemispheres (although *processes* used to respond to content may well differ in the hemispheres).

The results of this analysis are an encouraging first look at the relationship between ongoing events and EEG-recorded brain reactions. The topic certainly warrants future research.

ACKNOWLEDGMENTS

I thank Jerry Olson, Bill Ray and Susan F. Taylor for providing the EEG data in a form which was manageable to analyze, and Burt Leiman for help in the process of coding events in the content of the commercials.

REFERENCES

Donchin, E., Kutas, M., & McCarthy, G. (1977). Electrocortical indices of hemispheric utilization. In S. Harnad, R. W. Doty, L. Goldstein, J. Jaynes, and G. Krauthamer (Eds.), *Lateralization in the nervous system.* New York: Academic Press.

Hillyard, S. A., & Kutas, M. (1983). Electrophysiology of cognitive processing. *Annual Review of Psychology, 34,* 33–61.

John, E. R., & Schwartz, E. L. (1978). The neurophysiology of information processing and cognition. *Annual Review of Psychology, 29,* 1-29.

Kinsbourne, M. (1982). Hemispheric specialization and the growth of human understanding. *American Psychologist, 37,* 411-420.

Luria, A. R. (1973). *The working brain.* New York: Basic Books.

Newtson, D. (1973). Attribution and the unit of perception of ongoing behavior. *Journal of Personality and Social Psychology, 28,* 28-38.

Newtson, D. (1976). *Meaning in ongoing behavior: The second derivative of movement.* Paper presented at annual meeting of American Psychological Association, Washington, D.C.

O'Grady, K. E. (1982). Measures of explained variance: cautions and limitations. *Psychological Bulletin, 92,* 766-777.

Olson, J. C., & Ray, W. J. (1982, September). *Toward an understanding of psychophysiological responses to advertising: A progress report on the MSI 'brain wave study.'* Paper presented at annual conference of the Advertising Research Foundation, Chicago, Illinois.

Olson, J. C., & Ray, W. J. (in preparation). Analysis of EEG responses to advertising.

Pribram, K. (1971). *Languages of the brain.* Englewood Cliffs, N.J.: Prentice-Hall.

Ray, W. J., & Olson, J. C. (1983). Perspectives on psychophysiological assessment of psychological responses to advertising. In L. Percy & A. Woodside, (Eds.), *Advertising and consumer psychology,* Boston: Lexington Press.

Rosenthal, R. (1982). Conducting judgment studies. In K. R. Scherer, & P. Ekman, (Eds.), *Handbook of methods in nonverbal behavior research.* Cambridge: Cambridge University Press.

Stewart, D. W., & Furse, D. H. (1982). Applying psychophysiological measures to marketing and advertising research problems. In J. H. Leigh & C. R. Martin Jr. (Eds.), *Current issues and research in advertising.* Ann Arbor, Michigan: University of Michigan.

Tucker, D. M. (1981). Lateral brain function, emotion, and conceptualization. *Pyschological Bulletin, 89,* 19-46.

IV INVOLVEMENT

10 Cognitive Theory and Audience Involvement

Anthony G. Greenwald
Clark Leavitt
Ohio State University

CONSUMER BEHAVIOR CONCEPTIONS OF INVOLVEMENT

Many of the paths followed by consumer psychologists in recent analyses of audience involvement emanate from an article that appeared in *Public Opinion Quarterly* in 1965, by Herbert Krugman. Krugman's thesis was offered partly in reaction to then-accepted views (e.g., Bauer, 1958; Klapper, 1960) that persuasive communications depended for their impact on the active processing efforts of the audience. Krugman's seminal observation was that there are

> two entirely different ways of experiencing and being influenced by mass media. One way is characterized by lack of personal involvement. . . . The second is characterized by a high degree of personal involvement. By this we do *not* mean attention, interest, or excitement but the number of conscious "bridging experiences," connections, or personal references per minute that the viewer makes between his own life and the stimulus.

> . . . with low involvement one might look for gradual shifts in perceptual structure, aided by repetition, activated by behavioral-choice situations, and *followed* at some time by attitude change. With high involvement one would look for the classic, more dramatic, and more familiar conflict of ideas at the level of conscious opinion and attitude that precedes changes in overt behavior. (p. 355)

Krugman's distinction between two types of involvement and his assertion that both types can be associated with effective advertising (albeit via different routes) have stood up remarkably well in light of subsequent research. Also, Krugman's conception of " 'bridging experiences,' connections, or personal references" turns out to correspond well to a contemporary account of the dependence of memory on variations in the learner's cognitive elaboration of incidentally encountered information (Anderson & Reder, 1979; Craik & Tulving, 1975).

Before examining the cognitive psychological concepts that bear on involvement, we briefly review the variety of interpretations of involvement that have appeared in the consumer behavior literature since Krugman's 1965 article. This review, grouped in terms of ideas concerning antecedents, consequences, and mediating processes of involvement, is neither exhaustive nor evaluative. One justification for not being evaluative is that there is little direct conflict (and much complementarity) among the views presented.

Antecedents of Involvement

The determinants of involvement that have been most emphasized in prior treatments are communications media, product characteristics, and personality differences. Krugman focused on the role of media, observing that advertising on television typically does not attract high levels of involvement. Several other theorists, influenced by Howard and Sheth's (1969) concept of importance of purchase, have observed that involvement should increase to the extent that products have salient distinguishing attributes (Hupfer & Gardner, 1971; Lastovicka & Gardner, 1979; Ray, Sawyer, Rothschild, Heeler, Strong, & Reed, 1973; Robertson, 1976). Product characteristics can be treated either as situational or personality determinants of involvement, depending on whether one assumes that reactions to product attributes are relatively constant or, rather, importantly conditioned by individual differences among consumers. Houston and Rothschild (1977), although locating the effect of product characteristics as a personality variable (their concept of enduring involvement), explicitly recognize both situational and personality determinants (their distinction between situational and enduring involvement).

Consequences of Involvement

Two themes are apparent in treatments of the consequences of involvement — that different types of communication effects occur for high and low involvement, and that high involvement is associated with greater resistance to persuasion than low involvement.

As already mentioned, Krugman (1965) convincingly argues that communication impacts are not confined to high-involvement persuasion situations. With high involvement, Krugman argues, a communication should act most directly to modify beliefs (that is, verbalizable propositions). By contrast, with low involvement the impact should be more on perceptions (that is, on sensory organizations such as brand logos or package configurations), and should occur more gradually, being effective only with repeated exposures.

Sherif and Hovland's (1961) analysis of ego-involvement was influential in leading to the recognition that high involvement could be associated with resistance to (rather than acceptance of) persuasion. On that theme, Robertson (1976) notes that, even though low-involved consumers might not show much *direct* impact of advertising communications on beliefs, they might be induced more easily than highly involved consumers to try a new product or brand. The consequence is that, for the low-involved consumer, attitude change should be more likely to occur after trial, rather than being directly influenced by communication. The theme that different levels of involvement are associated with different *sequences* of impacts on the familiar attitude components of affect, behavior, and cognition has been developed especially by Ray et al. (1973), with further elaboration by Calder (1979).

Processes of Involvement

Krugman identifies high involvement with a specific cognitive process that he calls "personal connections" or "bridging experiences." A quite different conception of the cognitive mediation of involvement appears in analyses influenced by Sherif and Hovland's (1961) theory that involvement is interpretable as the linkage of new information to central (ego-involved) attitudes (cf. Ostrom & Brock, 1968). That is, by tapping into regions of strong belief, high involvement yields resistance to cognitive change, or a narrowing of the range of acceptable opinion positions (i.e., of the latitude of acceptance). A third interpretation of involvement appears in Houston and Rothschild's proposal that consumer decision processes increase in complexity (their dimension of response involvement) with increasing importance. A more recent process interpretation of low vs. high involvement is Petty and Cacioppo's (1981) distinction between peripheral and central routes to persuasion. Finally, Mitchell (1979) conceives involvement as a high level of arousal, or drive, similar to Burnkrant and Sawyer's (1983) interpretation in terms of information processing intensity.

Summary

There is consensus that high involvement means (approximately) personal relevance or importance. Further, it is generally accepted that communication influences can occur with either low or high involvement, and that the mechanism of communication impact for low involvement is different from that for high involvement. However, theorists have shown little agreement regarding the theoretical mechanism of involvement. They have interpreted it, alternately, in terms of extent of personal connections (Krugman), linkage to central values (Sherif & Hovland), sequence of impact on attitude components (Ray et al.), complexity of decision-making (Houston & Rothschild), peripheral vs. central cognitive processes (Petty & Cacioppo), and level of arousal (Mitchell).

Because of this lack of consensus about the processes underlying variations in involvement, there remains considerable uncertainty about how to apply the concept of involvement in predicting consumers' responses to variations in marketing strategy. This uncertainty takes the form, for example, of some interpretations that predict greater cognitive change (Krugman; Ray et al.), and some that predict greater resistance to cognitive change (Sherif & Hovland; Ostrom & Brock), with high involvement. We take it as our major task to identify, in terms of psychological theory, the processes that constitute variations in involvement.

ATTENTION, LEVELS OF PROCESSING, AND INVOLVEMENT

Some Preliminary Distinctions

Audience vs. Actor Involvement.   An audience is engaged in acquiring knowledge, whereas an actor uses knowledge that has been acquired previously. One might be tempted to say that a person engaged in action is "more involved" than is one who is ("passively"?) receiving information. However, further consideration suggests that this conclusion is not generally valid. For example, the football fan who is in the audience at a crucial game, may reasonably be described as being very highly involved — perhaps more involved than are some of the players. This observation justifies a distinction between knowledge-acquiring and knowledge-using types of involvement, to which we refer, respectively, as audience and actor involvement. The present analysis focuses mostly on audience involvement, which is the type that is more directly relevant to analyzing the effects of advertising messages.

Capacity vs. Arousal as Components of Involvement.   Recent treatments of the concept of attention (esp. Kahneman, 1973; Posner & Boies, 1971) have established an important distinction between arousal and expended capacity. Arousal (or alerting) designates a state of activation or excitement that facilitates the performance of well-learned responses. Capacity (or attentional effort), on the other hand, is a limited resource that must be used to focus on a specific task, and is needed in increasing amounts as the cognitive complexity of a task increases. Both arousal and capacity are relevant to phenomena of involvement. That is, a person can be involved in the sense of being aroused or excited, and can also be involved in the sense of effortfully attending to some task or message. Arousal and capacity are only partly related. In particular, the cognitive capacity available for a task appears to increase with increasing arousal, but only up to moderate levels of arousal. High levels of arousal interfere with cognitive activity. (This is the Yerkes-Dodson effect — see Hasher & Zacks, 1979; Kahneman, 1973).

In this treatment, we identify involvement much more closely with the cognitive capacity aspect of attention than with arousal. This choice was made primarily in order to relate increasing involvement to increasingly strong effects of advertising messages. That is, procedures that increase the attentional capacity allocated to a message make the message both more memorable and potentially more persuasive. (Arousal, on the other hand, appears not to be related in a direct way to either memorability or persuasive impact.)

Levels of Processing

In an influential paper, Craik and Lockhart (1972) proposed that the level, or depth, to which an incoming message is processed determines the durability of memory for it. Subsequent research — even though leading to some modification of this formulation (Baddeley, 1978; Cermak & Craik, 1979; Craik & Tulving, 1975) — has continued to support the general principle that memory for an event depends on the amount and nature of cognitive activity that accompanies it. Our interpretation of audience involvement incorporates this general principle. We identify, as levels of involvement, four qualitatively different forms of cognitive activity that (i) require increasing levels of attentional capacity, (ii) use increasingly complex representational systems, and (iii) produce increasingly strong effects on memory.

Levels of Involvement

Figure 10.1 gives our analysis of levels of audience involvement. The four levels differ in the abstractness of symbolic activity that occurs in the analysis of an incoming message. The progression from preattention, the lowest level, through elaboration, the highest, is accompanied by increasingly abstract analyses, which are assumed to require increasing allocation of capacity. *Preattention* uses little capacity. The second level, *focal attention,* uses modest capacity to focus on one message source, and to decipher the message's sensory content into categorical (object, name, word) codes. Further capacity is required for *comprehension,* which analyzes speech or text by constructing propositional representations of it. The fourth level of involvement, *elaboration,* uses still more capacity to enable the integration of message content with the audience member's existing conceptual knowledge.

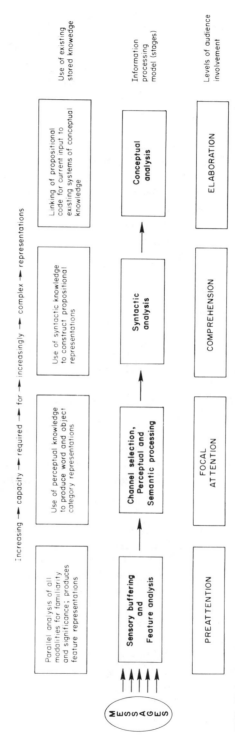

Increasing → capacity → required → for → increasingly → complex → representations

| Parallel analysis of all modalities for familiarity and significance; produces feature representations | Use of perceptual knowledge to produce word and object category representations | Use of syntactic knowledge to construct propositional representations | Linking of propositional code for current input to existing systems of conceptual knowledge | Use of existing stored knowledge |

| Sensory buffering and Feature analysis | Channel selection, Perceptual and Semantic processing | Syntactic analysis | Conceptual analysis | Information processing model (stages) |

| PREATTENTION | FOCAL ATTENTION | COMPREHENSION | ELABORATION | Levels of audience involvement |

FIG. 10.1. Four levels of involvement, indicating relationships to sequential stages of information processing, and use of increasingly complex representational systems.

Relation to Other Information Processing Approaches

In addition to being related to psychological treatments of attention and levels of processing, the present analysis has a close relation to the well known information processing approach to persuasive communication (Hovland, Janis, & Kelley, 1953; McGuire, 1969). In the information processing view, persuasion depends on sequential steps of attention to, comprehension of, and acceptance of a message. The Fig. 10.1 conception can be regarded as an extension of this earlier view by (i) adding preattention as another stage, or level, of processing, (ii) characterizing the difference among levels in terms of attentional capacity and levels of processing, and (iii) relating the levels to increasingly abstract systems of mental representations.[1]

RESEARCH PROCEDURES AND LEVELS OF INVOLVEMENT

Table 10.1 relates Fig. 10.1's four levels of involvement to a variety of procedures that have been used in laboratory research. The contents of Table 10.1 are presented more fully in the following for each of the five areas of research described in the table. References to reviews of the relevant literature are not given in the text, but can be found in the rightmost column of the table.

Orienting Responses

When a novel or unfamiliar stimulus is initially presented, it elicits an orienting response, which consists of mild physiological arousal together with physical orienting of receptors toward the source of stimulation. The orienting response corresponds to focal attention being directed toward the novel stimulus. If the same stimulus is repeated several times, it ceases to elicit the orienting response. The elimination, or *habituation,* of the orienting response corresponds to a reduction of involvement from focal attention to preattention. Orienting response can be elicited also by familiar stimuli that are specially significant, such as one's own name, or by cues that predict the occurrence of affectively significant events.

Selective Listening

Selective listening research uses the shadowing task, in which the subject repeats a verbal message aloud as it is being heard. This task commands focal

---

[1]Burnkrant and Sawyer (1983) also relate involvement to depth of processing and capacity. Their treatment differs from the present approach in that they treat involvement as varying along a continuum of intensity, rather than having qualitatively distinct levels.

TABLE 10.1
Research Procedures Related to Levels of Involvement

Research Areas	Levels of Involvement				Sources
	Preattention	*Focal Attention*	*Comprehension*	*Elaboration*	
Orienting Responses	repeated stimulus presentation (habituation of the orienting response)	loud, colorful, moving, novel, unexpected, or affect-evoking stimulus			Berlyne (1960); Kahneman (1973); Lynn (1967)
Selective Listening	message presented in unattended channel	message presented in attended channel (shadowing task)			Moray (1970); Neisser (1967); Norman (1976)
Levels of Processing		sensory orienting tasks	semantic orienting tasks	self-reference orienting tasks	Cermak & Craik (1979); Craik & Lockhart (1972); Kuiper & Rogers (1979)
Cognitive Elaboration		message that lacks context needed for comprehension	message that has context enabling comprehension	self-generated elaboration; visual imaging	Anderson & Reder (1979); Bransford & Johnson (1973)
Persuasion	strong distraction; very familiar message; unimportant message	moderate distraction; moderately familiar message	mild distraction; credible source; agreeable message; novel message	cognitive responding; disagreeable message; ego-involvement	Greenwald (1968); McGuire (1969); Petty, Ostrom, & Brock (1981); Sherif, Sherif, & Nebergall (1965)

attention, and also effectively prevents focusing on any concurrent auditory message. Thus, a second message that is presented simultaneously with the shadowed message remains at the level of preattention. Further, the cognitive demands of repeating one message and rejecting a second may use enough capacity to prevent the subject's involvement in the attended message from progressing to any level of involvement higher than focal attention.

Levels of Processing

Research on levels of processing in memory uses procedures, referred to as *orienting tasks,* that constrain the nature of a subject's processing of experimental stimuli. The design of orienting tasks assumes that events are ordinarily processed by means of a number of optional cognitive operations. The more operations applied to the analysis of any event, the "deeper" is the processing of that event. Some tasks — for example, judging whether a word is printed in uppercase or lowercase — are intended to use only sensory analyses. These require only the focal attention level of involvement. The more demanding task of judging whether or not two words are synonyms is assumed to require semantic analysis in addition to sensory analysis; it is placed at the comprehension level in Table 10.1. A more complex orienting task obliges subjects to judge whether or not each of a series of trait adjectives accurately describes the subject's personality. This self-reference task, which requires judgments based on the relation of stored knowledge about oneself to current input, has been placed in the column for the highest level of involvement in Table 10.1, elaboration.

Cognitive Elaboration

In some recent studies of human memory, the levels-of-processing conception of a sequence of processing stages has been supplemented by the assumption that encountered events give rise to propositional representations. Greater cognitive elaboration of an event consists of generating a greater number of proposition representations based on the event. Among the relevant research procedures are ones that have been used to vary comprehension of a message. For example, Bransford and Johnson wrote stories that were virtually incomprehensible without additional context, such as a title for the story, or a picture that showed the action being described. Reading such stories without the needed context effectively constrained subjects' involvement to the focal attention level, permitting little or no comprehension or elaboration. Addition of the context permitted comprehension. Still greater involvement (elaboration) can be achieved by instructions that induce the subject to generate visual imagery or additional story details that supplement a provided text.

Cognitive Responses in Persuasion

In recent years, the *cognitive response* approach has been influential in research on the persuasion process. In this approach the audience is conceived as an active processor of the persuasive message. Research procedures that encourage active cognitive responding – for example, explicit instructions to respond verbally to the message, or instructions to improvise a message from materials provided by the experimenter – correspond to the elaboration level of involvement. This active cognitive responding also occurs when a communication is ego-involving, and especially when it presents a disagreeable opinion, in which case elaboration takes the form of counterarguing.

The presence of a mild distractor may occupy enough attentional capacity to interfere with cognitive responding, while still permitting comprehension. Examples of such mild distraction that have been used in persuasion research include accompanying a spoken persuasive message with an irrelevant film of abstract art, or asking the message's audience to form an impression of the speaker's personality. Messages that are known to be agreeable, or ones that are presented by trustworthy sources, or ones that are difficult (but not impossible) to understand, may all be received at the comprehension level, without elaborative cognitive responding.

In order to lower the level of involvement further to focal attention the experimenter can use messages that are moderately familiar, or are accompanied by sufficient distraction to disrupt comprehension, or are constructed so as to be incomprehensible. Involvement may be reduced still further to the level of preattention by using distractors that are sufficiently strong to draw focal attention to another source, or by using messages that are either very familiar or very unimportant.

LEVELS OF REPRESENTATION

Figure 10.2 relates the four levels of audience involvement to a broader conception that includes mental representations and performance controls at four levels. The four levels of involvement are portrayed, in Figure 10.2, as successive stages of event analysis, providing access to qualitatively different representation systems at increasing levels of complexity and abstraction. With the aid of this levels-of-representation (LOR) analysis, the effects of advertising communications can be analyzed into three functions involving mental representations: (i) the role of communications in activating existing mental representations, (ii) the role of communications in forming new representations, and (iii) the role of these representations in the control of action. Before attempting to apply the LOR analysis to advertising communications, we review the major known phenomena concerning these functions of mental representations.

Principles of Message Analysis

Factors that influence the level of analysis of incoming messages have been well studied using the laboratory procedures that were described in Table 1. The results of these studies can be summarized in terms of four principles.[2]

1. *Bottom-up (data-driven) processing.* When a level of analysis detects indications of significant message content, the next higher level of analysis is invoked.

2. *Top-down (concept-driven) processing.* Analysis at the level of comprehension or elaboration may reveal that the message is unimportant. As a consequence, the use of capacity for comprehension may be suspended, and attention directed elsewhere.

3. *Competence (data) limitation.* Analysis is limited to a low level if the content of a message cannot be analyzed at a higher level—for example, words may be in a foreign language, they may be presented too rapidly, or they may be masked by noise.

4. *Capacity (resource) limitation.* Because high levels of analysis demand the limited resource of attentional capacity, analysis of one message at a high level necessarily limits the level of analysis that can be applied to some other message.

These four principles interact in determining the effective level of analysis. Consider, for example, the complex situation of an automobile driver who is (i) listening to a story being told by a passenger while (ii) watching for an upcoming highway exit, (iii) monitoring the road and nearby vehicles, and (iv) hearing a radio news description of areas of exceptional traffic congestion. Each of these four message sources contains cues that could, if it were the only message, evoke (by a bottom-up process) focal attention. A high level of analysis is needed to choose (by a top-down process) the message that merits greatest capacity allocation, in this case (let us assume) the traffic report. Analysis of the other messages must be reduced to a preattentive level for the moment (capacity limitation). Regrettably, however, the masking noise of a truck alongside causes much of the report to be unanalyzable at the propositional level (data limitation). If this example seems fabricated in its complexity, consider the much more mundane example of a person who is at home, watching television and cooking a meal when the telephone rings. The

---

[2]Expository presentations of the concepts of bottom-up, top-down, data-limited, and resource-limited processes are available in Norman (1976).

point of such illustrations is that adults easily and effectively manage the direction of attention in situations of substantial informational complexity.

Principles of Memory Formation

The following four principles describe the relationship between analysis at different levels and the formation of memory representations. The first three principles have been established by empirical research, whereas the fourth is a theoretical expectation based on the LOR model of Fig. 10.2.

5. *Preattentive amnesia.* Preattentive analysis monitors background stimulation for the occurrence of novel or significant events, and includes sensory buffering — that is, brief sensory persistence of visual or auditory inputs. Sensory buffering makes it possible to switch attention to, and identify, an event *after* it has ceased to stimulate receptors. Despite these very important forms of preattentive analysis, there is no generally accepted evidence of any enduring (i.e., memory) effects of preattentive analysis. Rather, establishment of memory traces appears to depend on analysis at (at least) the level of focal attention.[3]

6. *Differential mnemonic efficiency of levels.* The higher the level of analysis accorded to an event or message, the fewer exposures required to achieve some criterion of memory for it. This differential efficiency has been demonstrated by research in both the levels-of-processing and cognitive elaboration traditions. It has also been established tentatively that the probability of remembering an event is directly related to the capacity allocated to its processing (Tyler, Hertel, McCallum, & Ellis, 1979; but cf. Zacks, Hasher, Sanft, & Rose, 1983). Accordingly, the greater mnemonic efficiency of higher levels of analysis may be, in effect, the return on the greater investment of attentional capacity required for their use.

7. *Differential availability of representations.* The higher the level of a memory representation, the less its retrieval depends on triggering by external cues. Two types of memory research provide strong support for this principle. First, studies of memory for prose text show very poor learning (e.g., lack of recognition) for text that is missing important clues to comprehension (and so, cannot — by data limitation — be analyzed and retained at the propositional level). Research using simpler verbal materials (e.g., single nouns or adjectives) has shown that conceptual activities — such as relating the to-be-remembered words to past experiences — substantially improves the likelihood of recalling the words without external cues (free recall).

8. *Developmental ordering of levels.* The ability to use levels of representations develops (presumably as a joint product of innate potential and expe-

---

[3]There are, however, some controversially claimed mnemonic effects of preattentive analysis — see Kunst-Wilson and Zajonc (1980), and Wilson (1979), but see also Obermiller (1983).

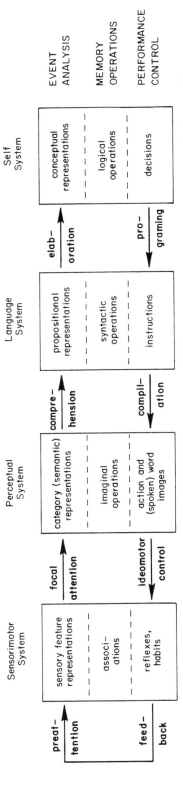

FIG. 10.2. Levels of representation. This diagram shows how levels of involvement (successive left-to-right, labeled arrows) are conceived as providing access to increasingly complex representational systems. Also, the hypothesized role of these representational systems in memory operations and performance control is indicated.

233

rience) in the order of categories, then propositions, then conceptual interpretations. The periods at which these successive levels of representation
become established are, very approximately, infancy (categories), childhood
(propositions), and early adolescence (interpretations).

Principles of Performance Control

Similarly to event representations, performance-control representations are
assumed to be qualitatively distinct at the different levels. Regrettably, the
psychological lexicon of response terms (in contrast with that for stimulus
terms) is not well enough developed to provide unique designations for performance control representations at the four levels, or for the transforma-
tions that link levels in the descending direction. Figure 10.2 suggests re-
ferring to the four levels of performance control representations, respectively, as habits, action images, instructions, and decisions.

The lack of established terms for performance control is a consequence of
the relative lack of research on performance mechanisms in recent cognitive
psychology. (Note that the areas of research that were summarized in Table
10.1 deal with stimulus analysis and memory, to the neglect of performance
control.) Of the following principles of performance control, the first two are
hypothesized applications of the general principles of the LOR approach;
only the third is empirically well-established.

9. *Parallel operation.* The linear arrangement of levels in Fig. 10.2 implies
that activation of a higher level must be preceded by activation of all lower
levels. If it is assumed that activated lower levels remain active during an
attentional episode, then all levels up to the highest one activated may be involved simultaneously in the control of performance.

10. *Performance efficiency.* Given that higher levels require more of a
limited resource (attentional capacity), interests of efficiency will be served if
performance is controlled at the lowest level that is competent in a given situation. Therefore, if effective controls for some performance exist at several
levels, activation of levels (and, correspondingly, the locus of performance
control) should not proceed beyond the lowest competent level.

11. *Regression of control levels.* As a consequence of the differential efficiency principle (Principle 6), repeated practice in any situation should establish representations at progressively lower levels. Applying also the performance efficiency principle (Principle 10), practice should reduce the effective
level at which performance is controlled. There exists substantial empirical
support for this regression-of-control principle, in research on conditioning
(Germana, 1968) and on the acquisition of complex skills (Anderson, 1982).

Complexities of Application

Unfortunately, application of the LOR analysis in predicting performance
effects of advertising communications is complex. This complexity is a con-

sequence of (i) the assumption that performance can be controlled from (up to) four levels of representation, and (ii) the fact that multiple, competing performance-relevant cues are likely to be present in relevant consumer behavior situations. Consider, for example, the shopper pausing before the supermarket breakfast cereal shelf. The shopper might (i) execute well practiced package-removal *habits,* (ii) act in imitation of a brand-selection *action image* that has been encountered repeatedly in advertising, (iii) follow a specific *instruction* of a shopping list, or (iv) make an on-the-spot *decision* based on price after narrowing the choice to several brands that have sufficiently nourishing ingredients. Which of these levels controls action is determined jointly by such factors as existing brand preferences, haste to complete the shopping trip, prominence of price information in the display, the number of brands available on the shelf, and whether the cereal is to be consumed by the shopper or someone else. (Note that some of these factors may be quite independent of advertising influences.) Given the potential complexity of even this most ordinary of consumer choice situations, effective use of the LOR model will require assumptions that permit simplification of analysis.

APPLICATIONS TO ADVERTISING AND CONSUMER BEHAVIOR

Memory for Advertising Copy

The level of involvement required of an audience varies as a function of complexity of the advertising message (copy). "Image" advertising, which links the brand name with attractive objects, requires only focal attention; sentence-length slogans or assertions about brand attributes (which can only be effective if they achieve propositional representation) require comprehension; and ads that call for inferences about brand quality based on sequences of persuasive arguments, require the elaboration level of involvement.

In accord with the differential availability principle (Principle 7), the conditions under which advertisement copy can be retrieved should vary with the level of analysis it receives on exposure. Representations based on elaboration-level analysis should be readily available without external cues (i.e., they should be free-recallable). By contrast, retrieval of representations based on focal-attention analysis should depend on encounter with external cues that have been well associated with the to-be-retrieved image.

These memory implications of the LOR model suggest two principles for the design of advertising copy. First, *proper design requires a match between the desired conditions of retrieving the copy and the level of involvement it obtains from the audience.* If, for example, it is desired that copy be retrievable by free recall, audience involvement must reach the elaboration level. Second, *audience involvement must be at the minimal level required by the com-*

plexity of the copy. Thus, an ad that compares attributes of the advertised brand with those of competitors — and, therefore, calls for inferential activity in order to permit conclusions about brand quality — requires audience involvement at the elaboration level. Combining these two design principles, one should design an advertisement to achieve audience involvement at the higher of (i) the level suitable to assure the desired conditions of retrieval, or (ii) the level demanded by the complexity of the copy's content. For greatest efficiency of advertising impact, it should be desirable for these two constraints to target the same level.

Affective, Attitudinal, and Evaluative Effects of Advertisements

Advertisement copy is often intended to influence brand valence — that is, the attractiveness of the brand to the audience. Brand valence is represented in different ways at each level of representation. At the level of feature representations, valence takes the form of associations of features of the brand to stimulus features that, either innately or by previous conditioning, elicit affective reactions. At the category/image level, positive valence is represented by associations to liked objects or activities. At the proposition level, positive valence consists of propositional linkages to evaluatively favorable concepts, or by symbolically encoded intentions to use the brand. Finally, at the conceptual level, positive valence consists of beliefs about the brand's instrumentality in achieving personal goals.

The same considerations that relate levels of audience involvement to the design of advertising copy for memory apply to the design of copy for influencing brand valence. That is, the appropriate level of audience involvement is jointly constrained by complexity of the desired brand-valence representation and the desired conditions of retrieval.

Hierarchical Conceptions of Influence Sequences

The Hierarchy of Effects.   In an influential treatment, Ray et al. (1973) related variations in audience involvement to variations in the sequence of communication impacts on affect, cognition, and behavior. In their analysis, high involvement produces a *learning hierarchy of effects,* in which the communication directly produces cognitive change, which in turn can produce affective change and then behavior change. In their *low involvement hierarchy,* cognitive change again occurs first, but is followed by behavior change, with affect being the last component to change.

The LOR model agrees with Ray et al. in expecting variable sequences of communication effects to depend on level of audience involvement. In the LOR conception, the effects that can occur in variable sequence are not the classical affect-behavior-cognition triumvirate but, rather, the effects on representations at the four levels (features, categories, propositions, and conceptual interpretations). The first level impacted by an advertisement depends on the level of audience involvement. If, for example, an advertisement elicits elaboration-level involvement its initial impact is at the conceptual level. Repetitions of the ad should result in representations being established at lower levels, in accord with the regression principle (Principle 11). In contrast, an advertisement that elicits only focal attention initially impacts on the category level of representations. However, after repetitions sufficient to establish (say) action image representations that can control behavior, derivative representations may form at higher levels. For example, a person who has been influenced via image advertising to purchase a particular brand might later infer the existence of an intention to purchase that brand and may discover, further, some linkage of this brand choice to personal goals. This would be an example of acquisition of higher-level representations of brand-favorable action following, rather than preceding, acquisition of a lower, category-level representation. (Note that this sequence of increasing levels of impact fits with predictions of cognitive dissonance theory, self-perception theory, and attribution theory.)

Multiple Concurrent Effects of Advertising

An advertisement on television may include some or all of: (i) a sequence of pictures, (ii) a spoken message, (iii) printed words, (iv) music, and (v) dramatized action. This complex package of events has the potential to produce concurrent changes on representations at all levels. This makes possible the design of advertising to produce multiple effects — different effects on representations at different levels. Equally, it makes it possible for an advertisement that is designed to produce an effect at a specific level of representation to produce unintended effects at other levels. As a consequence, in trying to assess the impact of ads, one should look not only for intended effects on (say) recall of propositional information about brand attributes, but also for possible effects on affective reactions, brand recognition, and evaluative cognitive reactions to the message. It is especially important to monitor effects at the lower levels of representation if it is planned to give the audience many exposures to the same advertisement.

CONCLUSION

At the beginning of this chapter, we noted the wealth of existing theoretical treatments of consumer involvement, and their lack of agreement on a process interpretation of involvement. This chapter has presented a process interpretation that treats variations in involvement as correlated variations in attentional capacity and level of processing allocated to a message. We have tried to justify this model in two ways — first, by showing that it is consistent with several bodies of findings from cognitive psychological research of the past two decades and, second, by indicating how it fits with a broader cognitive psychological conception of levels of representation (LOR).

The LOR model offers, perhaps, an embarrassing wealth of possibilities for application to consumer behavior. Applications that need to consider effects mediated by up to four levels of analysis, memory, and performance control have the potential of being prohibitively complex. We can note, as one possibility for dealing with that complexity, that analyses with the LOR model become simpler as fewer levels are involved. This is, perhaps, a tempting justification for the intelligent manager to devise campaigns that attempt to confine consumer analysis, memory, and performance controls to low levels of involvement/representation. At the same time, it is apparent that rapid, dramatic effects of advertising campaigns on consumer behavior can be achieved only by attempting to appeal to, and modify, representations at high levels.

ACKNOWLEDGMENT

Preparation of this chapter was facilitated by NIMH grant MH–31762 ("Attention and preparation in rapid performance") to the first author, by NIMH grant MH–32317 and NSF grant BNS 82–17006 (both titled "Research in persuasive communication") to the first author, and by a Dean's Research Professorship award by OSU's College of Administrative Science to the second author. The first half of this chapter summarizes a theoretical approach recently reported by Greenwald and Leavitt (1984).

REFERENCES

Anderson, J. R. (1982). Acquisition of cognitive skill. *Psychological Review, 89,* 369–406.

Anderson, J. R., & Reder, L. M. (1979). An elaborative processing explanation of depth of processing. In L. S. Cermak & F. I. M. Craik (Eds.), *Levels of processing in human memory.* Hillsdale, N.J.: Lawrence Erlbaum Associates.

Baddeley, A. D. (1978). The trouble with "levels": A re-examination of Craik and Lockhart's framework for memory research. *Psychological Review, 85,* 139–152.

Bauer, R. A. (1958). Limits of persuasion. *Harvard Business Review, 36,* 105–110.

Berlyne, D. E. (1960). *Conflict, arousal and curiosity.* New York: McGraw-Hill.

Bransford, J. D., & Johnson, M. K. (1973). Considerations of some problems of comprehension. In W. G. Chase (Ed.), *Visual information processing.* New York: Academic Press.

Burnkrant, R. E., & Sawyer, A. G. (1983). Effects of involvement and message content on information-processing intensity. In R. J. Harris (Ed.), *Information processing research in advertising.* Hillsdale, NJ: Lawrence Erlbaum Associates.

Calder, B. J. (1979). When attitudes follow behavior: A self-perception/dissonance interpretation of low involvement. In J. C. Maloney & B. Silverman (Eds.), *Attitude research plays for high stakes*. Chicago: American Marketing Association.

Cermak, L. S., & Craik, F. I. M. (Eds.) (1979). *Levels of processing in human memory*. Hillsdale, N.J.: Lawrence Erlbaum Associates.

Craik, F. I. M., & Lockhart, R. A. (1972). Levels of processing: A framework for memory research. *Journal of Verbal Learning and Verbal Behavior, 11,* 671–684.

Craik, F. I. M., & Tulving, E. (1975). Depth of processing and the retention of words in episodic memory. *Journal of Experimental Psychology: General, 104,* 268–294.

Germana, J. (1968). Psychophysiological correlates of conditioned response formation. *Psychological Bulletin, 70,* 105–114.

Greenwald, A. G. (1968). Cognitive learning, cognitive response to persuasion, and attitude change. In A. G. Greenwald, T. C. Brock, & T. M. Ostrom (Eds.), *Psychological foundations of attitudes*. New York: Academic Press.

Greenwald, A. G., & Leavitt, C. (1984). Audience involvement in advertising: Four levels. *Journal of Consumer Research, 11,* 581–592.

Hasher, L., & Zacks, R. T. (1979). Automatic and effortful processes in memory. *Journal of Experimental Psychology: General, 108,* 356–388.

Houston, M. J., & Rothschild, M. L. (1977). *A paradigm for research on consumer involvement*. Unpublished working paper, Graduate School of Business, University of Wisconsin, Madison.

Howard, J. A., & Sheth, J. N. (1969). *The theory of buyer behavior*. New York: Wiley.

Hovland, C. I., Janis, I. L., & Kelley, H. H. (1953). *Communication and persuasion*. New Haven: Yale University Press.

Hupfer, N. T., & Gardner, D. M. (1971). Differential involvement with products and issues: An exploratory study. In D. M. Gardner (Ed.), *Proceedings, association for consumer research*. College Park, Md.: Association for Consumer Research.

Kahneman, D. (1973). *Attention and effort*. Englewood Cliffs, N.J.: Prentice-Hall.

Klapper, J. (1960). *The effects of mass communication*. New York: Free Press.

Krugman, H. E. (1965). The impact of television advertising: Learning without involvement. *Public Opinion Quarterly, 29,* 349–356.

Kuiper, N. A., & Rogers, T. B. (1981). Encoding of personal information: Self-other differences. *Journal of Personality and Social Psychology, 37,* 499–514.

Kunst-Wilson, W. R., & Zajonc, R. B. (1980). Affective discrimination of stimuli that cannot be recognized. *Science, 207,* 557–558.

Lastovicka, J. L., & Gardner, D. M. (1979). Components of involvement. In J. C. Maloney & B. Silverman (Eds.), *Attitudes research plays for high stakes*. Chicago: American Marketing Association.

Lynn, R. (1967). *Attention, arousal, and the orientation reaction*. Oxford: Pergamon.

McGuire, W. J. (1969). The nature of attitudes and attitude change. In G. Lindzey & E. Aronson (Eds.), *Handbook of social psychology* (2nd ed., Vol. 3). Reading, Mass.: Addison-Wesley.

Mitchell, A. A. (1979). Involvement: A potentially important mediator of consumer behavior. In W. H. Wilkie (Ed.), *Advances in consumer research* (Vol. 6). Ann Arbor, Mich.: Association for Consumer Research.

Moray, N. (1970). *Attention: Selective processes in vision and hearing*. New York: Academic Press.

Neisser, U. (1967). *Cognitive psychology*. New York: Appleton-Century-Crofts.

Norman, D. A. (1976). *Memory and attention* (2nd ed.). New York: Wiley.

Obermiller, C. (1983). *An experimental investigation of repetition and processing task as determinants of recognition and evaluation of noncommunication stimuli*. Unpublished Ph.D. dissertation, Ohio State University.

Ostrom, T. M., & Brock, T. C. (1968). Cognitive model of attitudinal involvement. In R. P.

Abelson et al. (Eds.), *Theories of cognitive consistency: A sourcebook*. Chicago, Ill.: Rand McNally.

Petty, R. E., & Cacioppo, J. T. (1981). *Attitudes and persuasion: Classic and contemporary approaches*. Dubuque, Iowa: Wm. C. Brown.

Petty, R. E., Ostrom, T. M., & Brock, T. C. (Eds.) (1981). *Cognitive responses in persuasion*. Hillsdale, N.J.: Lawrence Erlbaum Associates.

Posner, M. I., & Boies, S. J. (1971). Components of attention. *Psychological Review, 78,* 391–408.

Ray, M. L., Sawyer, A. G., Rothschild, M. L., Heeler, R. M., Strong, E. C., & Reed, J. B. (1973). Marketing communication and the hierarchy of effects. In P. Clarke (Ed.), *New models for mass communication research* (Vol. 2). Beverly Hills, Calif.: Sage.

Robertson, T. S. (1976). Low-commitment consumer behavior. *Journal of Advertising Research, 16,* 19–27.

Sherif, M., & Hovland, C. I. (1961). *Social judgment*. New Haven: Yale University Press.

Sherif, M., Sherif, C. W., & Nebergall, R. (1965). *Attitude and attitude change: The social judgment-involvement approach*. Philadelphia: Saunders.

Tyler, S. W., Hertel, P. T., McCallum, M. C., & Ellis, H. C. (1979). Cognitive effort and memory. *Journal of Experimental Psychology: Human Learning and Memory, 5,* 607–617.

Wilson, W. R. (1979). Feeling more than we know: Exposure effects without learning. *Journal of Personality and Social Psychology, 37,* 811–821.

Zacks, R. T., Hasher, L., Sanft, H., & Rose, K. C. (1983). Encoding effort and recall: A cautionary note. *Journal of Experimental Psychology: Learning, Memory, and Cognition, 9,* 747–756.

11 The Effect of People/Product Relationships on Advertising Processing

Peter Cushing
Melody Douglas-Tate
Leo Burnett, U.S.A.

INTRODUCTION

In simple terms, most models of the communication process consider source, message, media or environment (context), and receiver characteristics as variables that affect receiver response. Or as Laswell (1948) put it, the communication process can be described as "Who . . . says what . . . in what channel . . . to whom . . . with what effect." While all of these things are deemed important in understanding the communication process, the bulk of research in advertising has traditionally been oriented towards what it is about advertising (including the source, message, and the media) that affects consumers' choice processes, rather than characteristics of the consumer (receiver).

For example, early research on persuasion done by learning theorists focused on characteristics of the message, source, and the context that impede or enhance message acceptance by the receiver. Studies of different types of appeals (e.g., Janis & Feshbach, 1953; McGuire, 1964), source credibility (e.g. Hovland & Weiss, 1951), order effects (e.g. Hovland et al., 1957), as well as attention getting devices such as vividness (see Taylor & Thompson, 1982, for a review), all deal with non-receiver characteristics that affect communication response.

Similarly, information processing researchers have focused on aspects of the communication process other than receiver characteristics. While information processing is conceptually a consumer oriented perspective on the decision making process, research has typically dealt with both message and contextual factors that impact on how a communication message affects de-

241

cision making. Effects of message structure (e.g. Kahneman & Tversky, 1979; Bettman & Zins, 1979), amount of information (e.g. Hendrick, Mills, & Kiesler, 1968; Jacoby, Speller, & Kohn, 1974), time constraints and distraction (e.g. Wright, 1974) are all studies of how message organization or context affects response.

Finally, in involvement theory as well, although it is recognized that the extent to which a person is personally involved in a decision making process affects the way a decision is made, research has dealt primarily with issues, affecting involvement that are external to the consumers. Involvement has been postulated to be a function of the type of medium (e.g., Krugman, 1965, 1967), or a function of the product category (e.g., Vaughn, 1979). It has even been expressed as a function of advertising itself (e.g., Batra & Ray, this volume). Again we have a stream of research that has dealt with what is said and through what medium, and not with receiver characteristics.

But let's back up a moment. Can we really understand how advertising works by just looking at who says what and in what context? Can we, if we know the source and context of a message, the structure of the message, the situation in which a message is received, and the medium of the message, expect to know how a piece of advertising will work? Obviously not in all cases. It depends also on who the receiver is. People do not all respond the same to advertising just as they do not all approach purchase decisions in the same way.

Certainly some research has considered receiver characteristics (e.g., motivation research of the 1950's, and psychographic or "lifestyle" research of the late 60's and early 70's). However, most of the receiver characteristics studied were rather general, broad variables (e.g. demographics, personality, category usage, etc.) that were only weakly linked theoretically to people's specific responses to communication. Instead of adding to a general framework for understanding the process of persuasive communication, these variables were treated as mediating influences on behavior that necessarily must be controlled to reduce individual variation in response. Variables that are reflective more directly of specific types of purchase behavior have not been well studied. Variables that relate to individual orientation towards buying need to be incorporated into a communication model, since it is these predispositions that are likely to affect receiver reaction to other communication variables.

Thus, in terms of a model of persuasive communication, the one link that seems to not have been well studied is "to whom do you say it," and how these receiver characteristics interact with other communication variables. Specifically, in any given purchase situation, what characterizes the way a person approaches a purchase decision, and how does this affect responses to advertising (and other communication variables). This research takes a step towards understanding these relationships.

PEOPLE/PRODUCT RELATIONSHIPS

As mentioned earlier, theorists have largely recognized "involvement" as being an important determinant of the way people respond to advertising and make decisions. But what does the term mean? While "involvement" has been used in a number of different ways, its most common usage seems to be that involvement reflects the importance of the product category to a consumer, and that further, categories can be classified in terms of whether they are "high involvement" or "low involvement" categories.

Recently, however, researchers have begun to realize that the orientation people have towards products and product purchases is a more complex issue. Vaughn (1979) has argued that classification of categories should not only be in terms of product involvement, but should also be in terms of whether the general orientation towards the category is emotional (feeling) vs. cognitive (thinking). Others have suggested that involvement or importance could have temporal aspects as well (e.g., Houston & Rothschild, 1978) and depends on whether it is an immediate goal or central need that is being satisfied (Bloch & Richins, 1983).

We would submit that, in general, a person's orientation towards a product (what we would call people/product relationships) depends on how the product fits into that person's life. Category Involvement or importance is just one aspect of how a product fits into a person's life. Other dimensions can include such things as variety seeking behavior, experimentation, price sensitivity, brand commitment, and product knowledge. Table 11.1 shows a nonexhaustive list of dimensions descriptive of people/product relationships.

While the importance of this has been recognized through lifestyle research

TABLE 11.1
Dimensions of People/
Product Relationships

- Category involvement

- Brand commitment

- Brand Differentiation

- Variety seeking and experimentation

- Information seeking

- Communication with others

- Attribute/characteristic consideration

- Product knowledge

- Price interest

- Time allocated to decisions

(e.g., Wells & Tigert, 1971), it is only recently that people have attempted to provide structure for the way products are linked to or fit into people's lives (e.g. Gutman, 1982; Olson & Reynolds, 1983). In general it is believed that the type of relationship depends on a person's set of experiences, values, and perceived consequences related to product usage. We would hypothesize that these can differ across both people and across product categories. Thus, different people may have different relationships with the same product (a similar point has been made by Tyebjee, 1979). Further, we believe the same person can have different relationships across different products. Earlier research at LBCo has provided evidence that both these things are true.

Finally, we believe that people use advertising in different ways, depending on the type of relationship they have with a product. Thus, the understanding of relationships and how they affect responses to advertising is important for developing advertising strategy and copy.

The purpose of this research, then, is twofold: (1) to identify various types of relationships people have with products, and (2) to relate these to responses to advertising and discuss how these responses link to brand purchase attitudes.

Sample and Data Collection

For this study we drew a sample of 960 respondents who had been recruited as participants in the LBCo copy testing program. While not fully representative of the U.S. as a whole (they were predominantly white, married females, between the ages of 20–55, who were somewhat upscale in terms of income and education), they still represented a fairly diverse set of respondents. Each respondent was shown one and only one of a total of 32 commercials, which resulted in 30 respondents per commercial. These commercials covered a range of 16 consumer product categories (e.g., food, paper, household, personal care, etc.). All respondents were users of the category for which they were shown advertising.

Respondents were then asked two sets of questions. Responses to advertising were measured using LBCo's Viewer Response Profile (VRP) which is a battery of 61 items designed to measure a wide range of both execution and product related reactions to advertising. These have been applied and analyzed thousands of times and have been found to be extremely reliable and useful in diagnosing responses to advertising (e.g., Schlinger, 1979). A list of some of the dimensions the VRP measures is in Table 11.2.

The second set of questions consisted of 35 items designed to measure, on a 6-point scale, various dimensions of people/product relationships. Dimensions measured are those listed in Table 11.1, and include category involvement, brand commitment, variety seeking, information seeking, attribute consideration, and price interest. This battery was labeled the Buying Style Profile (BSP).

TABLE 11.2
Dimenions of the Viewer
Response Profile (VRP)

- Brand Purchase Attitudes

- Cognitive Interest

- Emotional Response

- Stimulation

- Confusion

- Familiarity

- Relevance

- Antagonism

- Differentiation

Group Identification

The first step of our analysis consisted of identifying various types of relationships people have with products. This was accomplished through a combination of clustering techniques which grouped people on the basis of their responses to the buying style questions. Results from a Q-analysis, which clusters people based on inter-people correlations, were cross-tabbed against results from a K-means clustering procedure, which clusters people based on Euclidean distances. Groups containing at least 100 people were kept for further analysis. This was done since it was felt that differences in patterns of responses as well as differences in the magnitudes of individual responses were important for determining our groups.

Based on this procedure, we were able to identify four groups of people, representing four types of people/product relationships. These were labeled "Involved Brand Loyalists," "Involved Information Seekers," "Uninvolved Brand Switchers," and "Routine Brand Buyers." Table 11.3 shows the mean scores for each of the groups on a number of descriptive items. General descriptions of these groups follow.

Group Descriptions

As mentioned previously, one of the key factors included in our Buying Styles questionnaire was "Category Involvement." Sample items loading on this factor include: "This product is important for me," "This product makes my life better," "This product is a necessity," etc.

Not surprisingly, these items did discriminate among the groups in predicted ways. Both the Involved Brand Loyalists and the Involved Information Seekers were found to be highly involved in the category, while the Rou-

TABLE 11.3
Group Means on Selected BSP Items
(6-point scale: 6 = Strongly Agree, 1 = Strongly Disagree)

	Involved Brand Loyalist	Involved Information Seekers	Uninvolved Brand Switchers	Routine Brand Buyers
This product is really a necessity, not a frill.	5.00	4.50	3.97	4.30
This product makes my life better.	4.45	4.61	3.57	3.50
I have a favorite brand.	5.76	4.73	3.58	5.11
I always buy the same brands without thinking.	4.57	2.91	2.60	3.99
I don't need the best brand. Something less than the highest quality suits my needs.	1.81	2.25	3.71	3.06
I use different brands depending on the occasion or purpose I have in mind.	1.76	3.99	3.43	2.39
I wait until I am at the store to decide what brand to buy.	1.09	2.48	4.11	1.79
I am always looking for something better.	3.10	5.05	4.02	3.30
I like buying new brands.	1.86	4.11	3.88	2.47
There are several brands I really like.	1.99	4.33	4.35	2.92
When I buy, I take a lot of different things into account.	3.51	4.62	3.23	2.70
I look for ways to cut the cost of the product.	2.49	3.44	4.08	3.20

tine Brand Buyers and the Uninvolved Brand Switchers were relatively less so. On a 6-point scale, the average item scores for the Involved Brand Loyalist and the Involved Information Seekers were 5.0 and 4.9 respectively, while for the Routine Brand Buyers and the Uninvolved Brand Switchers they were 4.2 and 4.1 respectively. This pattern was the same across all items used to measure category involvement.

However, category involvement by itself is not sufficient to describe the types of relationships people have with products, nor is it sufficient to explain different people's reactions to advertising. The following are descriptions of each of the four groups in terms of dimensions other than category involvement.

Involved Brand Loyalist

In addition to being highly involved in the category, these people show strong attachment to their brand. They agree much more than others to items such as "I have a favorite brand," "I make sure the person shopping knows what brand to buy," and "I don't buy a product if I can't find my favorite brand." Probably because of this attachment, they do not show much interest in experimenting with new brands, and do not claim to be looking for anything better than what they have. They disagree more than others with statements such as "I like to try new brands for variety," "I like several brands," and "I am looking for something better."

They claim to want the best brand (implying they feel they already have it). Despite this, they believe themselves to have only moderate amounts of knowledge about the product, and do not claim to take a lot of things into account when they buy.

In sum, the Involved Brand Loyalists are highly involved with both the category and their brand. However, their seeming lack of desire to gain more information (despite the fact that they want the best brand) suggests that their commitment to a brand is more on an emotional versus rational level. These strong feelings of emotional attachment may well guide their purchase habits.

Involved Information Seekers

These people, like the Involved Brand Loyalists, say they are highly involved in the product category. Unlike the Brand Loyalist, however, they appear to be much less commited to a single brand. While they may say they have a favorite brand, they tend more to have a set of acceptable brands, often to be used for different occasions. Relative to the Brand Loyalists, they agree more to statements such as "There are several brands I really like," and "I use different brands depending on the occasion or purpose I have in mind." Further, relative to the Brand Loyalists, they seem to care more about performance than the brand name, and appear willing to change their brand set if they find a better brand. Consequently, they think of themselves as informed shoppers who seek out information to make their decisions—by paying attention to advertising, talking to other people, and even by experimenting with new brands.

In sum, Involved Information Seekers seem to relate to brands in a functional, rather than an emotional way. This is not to say that they are not susceptible to emotional appeals, but that their emotional attachment is more with the category than with any specific brand. For this reason, they are primarily interested in assessing how well a brand performs, and appear willing to seek out information (from advertising, other people, brand trial, etc.) in order to make what they believe to be "the rational decision."

Uninvolved Brand Switchers

Unlike the two groups above, people in this group are not highly involved in the product category. Behaviorally, they seem to exhibit some of the same characteristics as the Involved Information Seekers. They claim they like several brands, and take turns among those they like. Further, they say they like buying new brands and often try new brands for variety. However, product performance is not a key issue for them, so long as it performs at some minimum level. They say they don't need the best brand and aren't really fussy about the product. Further, they are not users of information. Relative to the Information Seekers, they say they don't take much into account when they buy, they don't ask others for information, and they don't attend to advertising. More than any other group, they seem not to have a favorite brand, making their decision at point of purchase often on the basis of price.

In sum, these people currently have little interest in the category. Despite the fact that they are regular users in the category, they appear content with some minimum level of performance—anything beyond that does not seem important to them. They use little information in their purchase decisions, buying primarily on the basis of price and, perhaps to some extent, ease of purchase (e.g., they are not likely to go out of their way to make a purchase, even on deal).

Routine Brand Buyers

Like the Uninvolved Brand Switchers, the Routine Brand Buyers are relatively uninvolved in the category. Further, they say they do not make highly informed purchase decisions, claiming that they don't know what is in the products they buy, that they don't take lots into account when the buy, and that they don't pay attention to advertising.

Unlike the "Brand Switchers," however, they do seem to stick with one brand. They say they have a favorite brand, and will not buy a sale brand other than their regular brand. In addition, they appear not to be interested in experimenting with other brands to find a better brand. More than others they seem not to care about the product, and their brand purchases appear to be based more on routinized behavior than anything else.

In sum, these people apparently buy the same brand on the basis of habit and without any strong emotional attachment. They don't seek out information to make their decisions (even price appears unimportant), and don't generally try brands other than their current brand. They probably buy brands more on the basis of familiarity (largely through habitual experience) than anything else.

Responses to Advertising

Table 11.4 gives a summary of each of the four groups in terms of the buying style dimensions. As explained, people do differ in terms of category involvement or importance. However, other factors, such as brand commitment, interest in trying new products, interest in product features and performance, information seeking, etc., all combine to describe different types of relationships people have with products. We would expect that these different relationships would affect how people react to and process advertising; i.e., there should be different avenues to persuasion for different types of relationships.

For the Involved Brand Loyalists, who seem to relate to their brand emotionally rather than rationally, we would expect that advertising for their brand would act primarily to reinforce these emotional attachments. We also would hypothesize that they would be the most resistant to competitive advertising, especially if it's based solely on a rational, attribute-oriented appeal. For competitive appeals to have any persuasive power, we believe they must somehow elicit a positive emotional response in order to break down and ultimately supplant the existing emotional relationship.

TABLE 11.4
Types of Relationships

High Category Involvement	Low Category Involvement
Involved Brand Loyalists	Routine Brand Buyers
• Care about brand • Want the best • Have a favorite brand • Do not use other brands	• Do not care about product/ brand • Do not need best • Have a favorite brand • Do not use other brands
Involved Information Seekers	Uninvolved Brand Switchers
• Care about category • Want the best • Try variety of brands • Seek information	• Do not care about brand/ product • Do not need best • Use variety of brands • Respond to price

The Involved Information Seekers, on the other hand, are oriented towards acquiring information to make "rational" decisions. Because of their desire for information, and their willingness to switch brands if something "better" comes along, we would expect them to be more responsive, and act more favorably towards advertising in general, irrespective of whether or not it is for their favorite brand. Further, we would expect that advertising that provided information would be the most effective for this group.

We would also expect that the two uninvolved groups would be less overtly influenced by advertising, in general. For the Uninvolved Brand Switcher, it seems likely that promotions, in-store displays, and to some extent advertising oriented towards value, would have the largest impact on their purchase behavior. They appear to make their purchase decisions in-store, and largely on deal. In the long term, it may be possible to use advertising to precipitate changes in their relationship by increasing the overall salience of the category (e.g., by connecting the category or brand with some other related category known to be important to these people).

Finally, the Routine Brand Buyers' behavior seems to fit most closely to Krugman's (1965) description of "Low Involvement," since they appear to buy more on the basis of familiarity than anything else. One function of advertising, then, might be to increase the awareness and saliency of a particular brand at a pre-conscious level over repeated exposures. For this group, too, it may be possible to change their relationship over time by connecting the category to another, more important (to them), category.

ANALYSIS OF GROUP RESPONSES TO ADVERTISING

As previously stated, people's responses to advertising were measured via the battery of 61 items known as the Viewer Response Profile (VRP). Thus, we are dealing with people's verbalized perceptions about the advertising viewed, and not with the manipulation of advertising appeals. Further, because we have a small number of respondents for any one commercial (30 per commercial), we cannot analyze group differences at the individual commercial level. Instead, our analyses are limited to more general group differences across commercials. Because we compared groups according to their responses across 32 commercials, we standardized each VRP item within each commercial. That is, for each commercial, each VRP item was set to a mean of zero and a standard deviation of one. This was done to rule out the possibility that any observed group differences could be attributed simply to differences among commercials.

Finally, it should be noted that the analyses were done only on respondents who were shown commercials for brands other than their favorite. Since reactions to advertising are expected to differ between advertising that is for one's favorite brand and advertising that is not, respondents who viewed ads for their favorite brands were eliminated from the analyses.

Results

In order to see if groups did differ in terms of their responses to advertising, we compared the mean VRP scores (standardized within each commercial) across all four groups. Not surprisingly, there were significant differences for 54 out of 61 VRP items. As one might expect, the most striking difference is that the Involved Information Seekers show more favorable responses across all dimensions. They are more stimulated, less antagonized, less confused, and show more positive attitudes towards brand purchases. Average item scores on the VRP dimensions are shown in Table 11.5 for each of the four groups.

However, more important to us was shedding some light on the following two issues. First, on a relative basis, would different groups respond favorably to different ads? That is, would ads received favorably relative to other ads for one group, be the same ads for other groups. The extent to which this is not the case (i.e., an ad is relatively effective for one group, but not for another), suggests the need for different appeals for different groups.

The second issue deals with the identification of those different appeals. What is it about advertising that affects people's evaluative responses differently?

TABLE 11.5
Group Mean Scores on VRP Dimensions
(Average Item Score)

	Involved Brand Loyalist	Involved Information Seekers	Uninvolved Brand Switchers	Routine Brand Buyers
Brand Purchase Attitudes	4.14	4.91	4.30	3.98
Cognitive Interest	3.31	4.11	3.36	3.09
Emotional Response	3.33	3.90	3.17	3.04
Stimulation	3.51	4.34	3.60	3.21
Confusion	2.06	1.97	2.11	2.29
Familiarity	2.94	2.63	2.80	2.91
Relevance	4.64	4.98	4.56	4.44
Antagonism	2.33	1.94	2.37	2.49
Differentiation	3.79	4.30	3.67	3.44

To address the first issue we used the VRP dimension "Brand Purchase Attitudes" to assess favorability of response. Sample items found repeatedly to be reliable indicators of this dimension include: "During the commercial I thought about how that product might be useful to me," "The commercial made me feel the product is right for me," and "The commercial strengthened my favorable views about the brand." Our task, then, was to ascertain if the patterns of brand purchase attitudes scores across commercials remained the same for all four groups.

Since our interest here was in differences in *patterns* of responses, rather than absolute score differences, we standardized brand purchase attitude within each group. Commercials were then ranked for the total sample in terms of these standardized brand purchase attitude scores. Because our sample sizes were too small to do analyses based on individual commercials, we collapsed commercials into quartiles consisting of eight commercials each. Quartile means were then compared across the groups.

Figure 11.1 shows the results of this comparison. Since each group has equal means and variances of brand purchase attitude (due to standardization), we would expect a series of flat parallel lines if they had the same patterns of responses. However, this is clearly not the case.

For example, the Involved Brand Loyalist rates the first quartile significantly higher than any other group. Also, the difference between the first and second quartile is significantly greater for the Involved Brand Loyalist than for any other group. Other differences exist, which in sum, all suggest that people are indeed affected by different things in advertising.

What actual aspects of advertising are affecting people differently we can't say, since we are unable to do an analysis at the individual execution level. We are, however, able to offer some perspective on what it is about people's *perceptions* of ads that seems to relate to their brand purchase attitudes.

We had hypothesized earlier that Information Seekers should respond more favorably to informational or attribute oriented advertising, while the Brand Loyalists would be more likely to respond to more emotionally oriented image appeals. We had also made some hypotheses about the two uninvolved groups (e.g., how advertising might be used to change their orientation over time). However, the VRP items are not appropriate measures for these hypotheses. Hence hypotheses about these groups are not considered in this analysis.

In order to test the hypotheses concerning the two involved groups, we related the VRP dimensions labeled "Cognitive Interest" and "Emotional Response" to brand purchase attitudes. Cognitive interest, as the name suggests, was used to measure the extent to which people responded on a cognitive level. Likewise, emotional response was used to measure the extent to which people responded on an emotional level. Sample items measuring cognitive interest include: "I learned something from the commercial that I

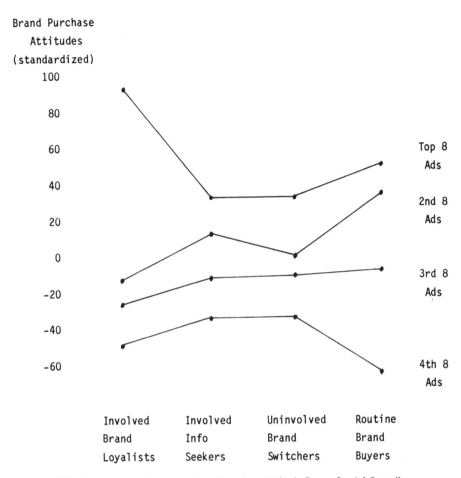

FIG. 11.1.   Group Means on Brand Purchase Attitude Scores for Ad Quartiles.

didn't know before," "The commercial gave me a new idea," and "I would be interested in getting more information about the product." Sample items measuring emotional response include: "I felt as though I was right there in the commercial experiencing the same thing," "The commercial made me 'feel' rather than 'think,' " and "It made me feel warm."

A regression model was postulated which expressed brand purchase attitudes as a function of cognitive interest, emotional response, and a dummy variable coded to represent the two groups (Information Seekers and Brand Loyalists). The full model included all main effects, and all two-way and three-way interactions. Results are listed in Table 11.6.

As expected, emotional response and cognitive interest were significant predictors of brand purchase attitudes. Also, there were significant group differences (as measured by the dummy variable "Brand Involvement") in

TABLE 11.6
Regression Results — Dependent Variable Is
Brand Purchase Attitudes

Parameter	Estimate	Std. Error
ER	.22**	.077
CI	.51**	.079
BL	−.31**	.095
ER*CI	−.26**	.058
BL*ER	.12	.099
BL*CI	.04	.099
BL*ER*CI	.16*	.076

$**p<.005$
$*p<.05$
KEY: ER = emotional response
             (standardized 6-point scale)
       CI = cognitive interest
             (standardized 6-point scale)
       BL = brand loyalty
             (dummy variable coded:
             1 if Brand Loyalist
             0 if Information Seeker)

brand purchase attitudes; the Information Seekers had higher overall brand purchase attitudes than the Brand Loyalists. This was expected since respondents had viewed commercials that were not for their favorite brands, and the Information Seekers are more favorably disposed towards trying different brands than are the Brand Loyalists.

We found that there were no significant two-way interactions between groups and the cognitive interest or emotional response variables on brand purchase attitudes. However, there was a strong negative two-way interaction between emotional response and cognitive interest. That is, the effect of either of the independent advertising response variables (emotional response or cognitive interest) on brand purchase attitudes decreases as the score of the other independent advertising response variable increases. Importantly, as indicated by the significant three-way interaction, this two-way interaction was much stronger for the Information Seekers than for the Brand Loyalists.

To illustrate these interactions, we looked at those respondents who scored relatively high (top third) or low (bottom third) on both cognitive interest and emotional response. This gave us four conditions for each group (high-high, high-low, low-high, low-low). Within each of these conditions, group means were calculated for both cognitive interest and emotional response. Predicted values (from the regression equation) for brand purchase attitudes were plotted for each group against these means in Figures 11.2a and b.

Within the range of our data, we see that, for the Information Seekers, cognitive interest is always positively related to brand purchase attitudes. Further, when cognitive interest is high, brand purchase attitude is always high, irrespective of whether emotional response is high or low. Emotional response does seem to relate to brand purchase attitudes, but only when cognitive interest is low.

For the Brand Loyalist, on the other hand, both emotional response as well as cognitive interest are positively related to brand purchase attitudes. It is not the case that high cognitive interest always yields high brand purchase attitudes irrespective of emotional response. The highest brand purchase attitudes occur when *both* cognitive interest and emotional response are high.

To summarize, these results provide at least partial support for our hypotheses concerning how people/product relationships affect people's responses to advertising. As expected, the Brand Loyalists appear more resistant to competitive advertising (in terms of brand purchase attitudes) than do the Information Seekers. More importantly, when the overall differences between the groups are controlled for, it appears that pieces of copy relate differently to positive brand purchase attitudes for different groups.

Finally, when comparing the Brand Loyalists with the Information Seekers, it was shown that perceptions about aspects of advertising relate differently to brand purchase attiitudes for each of the two groups. Specifically, for the Involved Information Seeker, cognitive interest always relates to positive brand purchase attitudes, while emotional response appears to only relate when cognitive interest is low. For the Brand Loyalists, however, both cognitive interest and emotional response seem to always relate to brand purchase attitudes.

ISSUES AND IMPLICATIONS

We need to keep in mind that this research was primarily exploratory, and used a data base that was not designed specifically to answer our questions. Also, our analyses were primarily correlational and do not demonstrate causality. Thus, a number of research issues remain.

First, the current research deals with people's perceptions about advertising, and not about the actual characteristics of the advertising that elicit these perceptions. What is needed is a way of measuring aspects of advertising itself, and relating these to consumer response.

Secondly, measures need to be developed that will allow us to look at how advertising affects the two uninvolved groups. Specifically, measures that allow us to tap into pre-conscious levels of awareness and processing need to be developed.

Also, responses to advertising need to be studied for people viewing advertising for their own brand. For example, how will the reinforcement value of

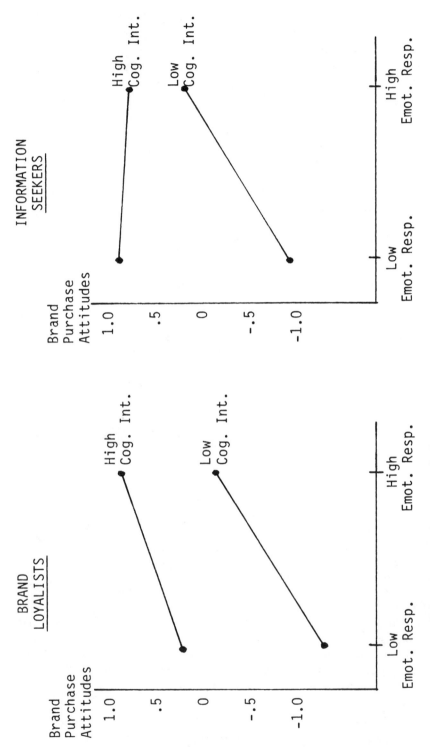

FIG. 11.2a.   Brand Purchase Attitudes vs. Emotional Response (high and low cognitive interest conditions).

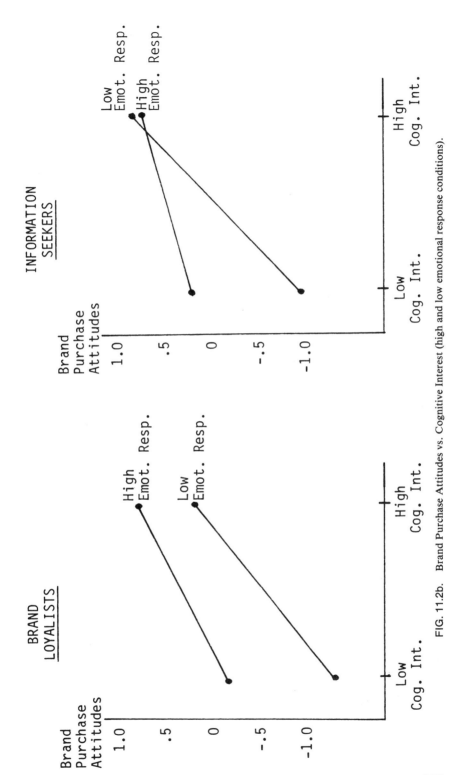

FIG. 11.2b.   Brand Purchase Attitudes vs. Cognitive Interest (high and low emotional response conditions).

257

advertising in general differ among the different groups, and what types of appeals offer the most reinforcement value for each group.

Fourthly, it should be obvious that, applying this to any particular category requires that the structure of that category, in terms of the types of relationships category users have, is well understood. Previous research has suggested that different relationships can and do exist within a single category. Further, there may be aspects of relationships that are unique to the category. These would need to be identified, as well as how they would influence advertising processing.

Finally, it is our belief that people/product relationships change over time and that many stimuli (including product experience, repeated exposures to advertising, etc.) can facilitate change. For this reason we need to study the dynamics of people/product relationships, and how advertising, through repetition, interacts with these relationships.

ACKNOWLEDGMENT

We wish to thank Daniel Romer for his invaluable assistance and thoughtful comments.

REFERENCES

Bettman, J. R., & Zins, M. A. (1979). Information format and choice task effects in decision making. *Journal of Consumer Research, 6,* 141–153.

Bloch, P. H., & Richins, M. L. (1983). A theoretical model for the study of product importance perceptions. *Journal of Maketing, 47,* 69–81.

Gutman, J. (1982). A means-end chain model based on consumer categorization processes. *Journal of Marketing, 46,* 60–72.

Hendrick, C., Mills, J., & Kiesler, C. A. (1968). Decision time as a function of the number and complexity of equally attractive alternatives. *Journal of Personality and Social Psychology, 8,* 313–318.

Houston, M. J., & Rothschild, M. L. (1978). Conceptual and methological perspectives on involvement. In S. C. Jain (Ed.), *1978 Educators' Proceedings.* Chicago: American Marketing Association, 184–187.

Hovland, C. I., Mandell, W., Campbell, E. H., Brock, T., Luchins, A., Cohen, A. R., McGuire, W. J., Janis, I. L., Feyerabend, R. L., & Anderson, N. H. (1957). *The order of presentation in persuasion.* New Haven, Conn.: Yale University Press.

Hovland, C. I., & Weiss, W. (1951). The influence of source credibility on communication effectiveness. *Public Opinion Quarterly, 15,* 635–650.

Jacoby, J., Speller, D. E., & Kohn, C. A. (1974). Brand choice behavior as a function of information load. *Journal of Marketing Research, 11,* 63–69.

Janis, I. L., & Feshbach, S. (1953). Effects of fear-arousing communications. *Journal of Abnormal and Social Psychology, 48,* 78–92.

Kahneman, D., & Tversky, A. (1979). Prospect theory: An analysis of decision under risk. *Econometrica, 47,* 263–291.

Krugman, H. E. (1965). The impact of television advertising: Learning without involvement. *Public Opinion Quarterly, 29,* 349–356.

Krugman, H. E. (1967). The Measurement of Advertising Involvement. *Public Opinion Quarterly, 30,* 583–596.

Lasswell, H. D. (1948). *Power and personality.* New York: W. W. Norton & Company.

McGuire, W. J. (1964). Inducing resistance to persuasion: Some contemporary approaches. In L. Berkowitz (Ed.), *Advances in experimental social psychology, Vol. 1.* New York: Academic Press.

Olson, J. C., & Reynolds, T. J. (1983). Understanding consumers' cognitive structures: Implications for advertising strategy. In L. Percy & A. Woodside (Eds.), *Advertising and consumer psychology.* Lexington, Mass.: Lexington Books, 77–90.

Schlinger, M. J. (1979). A profile of responses to commercials. *Journal of Advertising Research, 19,* 37–46.

Taylor, S. E., & Thompson, S. C. (1982). Stalking the elusive vividness effect. *Psychological Review, 89,* 155–181.

Tyebjee, T. T. (1979). Refinement of the involvement concept: An advertising planning point of view. In J. C. Maloney & B. Silverman (Eds.), *Attitude research plays for high stakes.* Chicago: American Marketing Association, 94–111.

Vaughn, R. (1979). How advertising works: A planning model. *Journal of advertising research, 20,* 27–33.

Wells, W. D., & Tigert, D. J. (1971). Activities, interests, and opinions. *Journal of Advertising Research, 11,* 27–35.

Wright, P. L. (1974). The harassed decision maker: Time pressures, distractions, and the use of evidence. *Journal of Applied Psychology, 59,* 555–561.

12

Understanding Consumers' Cognitive Structures: The Relationship of Levels of Abstraction to Judgments of Psychological Distance and Preference

Thomas J. Reynolds
Institute for Consumer Research and
University of Texas, Dallas

Jonathan Gutman
University of Southern California

John A. Fiedler
Ted Bates Worldwide, Inc.

INTRODUCTION

Recently, a means-end framework for conceptualizing cognitive processes has received considerable attention as an alternative to traditional attribute-based attitude measurement. The underlying concept for this approach involves understanding the levels of abstraction in product perception (Gutman & Reynolds, 1979), namely the attribute — consequence — value hierarchical content levels that serve to interpret product perceptions in meaningful ways. The approach presented in this chapter suggests a potential improvement to either attribute or benefit or other positive consequence-based models. The improvement results from the inclusion of end benefits or values into the model. Although several applications and refinements of this theoretical perspective have been offered in the recent literature (Young & Feigen, 1975; Gutman, 1982; Howard, 1977; see Olson & Reynolds, 1983 for a complete review), methodological implications of this approach, especially evaluation of the overall model have been noticeably absent.

To date, the most extensive means-end methodology offered is an in-depth interviewing technique termed "laddering" (Gutman & Reynolds, 1979). The initial step of this procedure is to elicit from the respondent the bases on which he/she distinguishes among competing products, either in terms of preference or perception. In-depth probing then attempts to trace the network of connections or associations in memory, that when completed, terminates in a personal value. This hierarchy of connections across the concepts elicited at different levels of abstraction is termed a means-end chain. Typically, the means-end chain is composed of an attribute important in distinguishing among relevant products; a reason why that attribute is important in distinguishing among relevant products, a consequence; and the reason why the consequence is relevant to one's self, the value. Values, then, refer to the ways in which one desires to see "self" or manifest other types of motivations that seem to direct behavior, e.g., achievement. The term "laddering" is derived from the sequence of directed probes which attempt to move the consumer to higher levels of abstraction, ultimately leading to personal values.

As such, this methodology reveals a perceptual framework, which the consumer uses to process and give meaning to information with respect to a product class. This perceptual framework also has a process interpretation in that the translations across levels, by way of the connections ultimately relating to self, essentially define the basis of choice. By understanding why things are meaningful to an individual, one can actually determine the underlying bases of choice.

The cognitive organization of an individual serves as the basis for receiving and assessing information. This cognitive structure serves as the key input to the choice process. The laddering approach to understanding the cognitive organization about a product allows one to understand consumer decisonmaking more than do current procedures. One benefit of the approach is that the two components of cognitive structure, content and structure, can be identified and interrelated using the laddering process. An additional benefit is that the means-end chain provides a link between perception and affect, offering a unique perspective to understanding the decision-making process. Affect is considered a specific goal-oriented cognitive process, while perception refers to the more broad, fundamental perceptual tasks of grouping and distinguishing.

Albeit exciting and interesting to consider the possibilities of such an approach for marketing, an important concern at this early stage of investigation is validity. Specifically, what is the predictive validity of this essentially qualitative research tool? How do the higher levels of abstraction relate to tasks centered on understanding perception, preference and/or their interaction? And, can consumers accurately provide importance evaluations representing the relative contribution of these higher levels with respect to their contribution for understanding preference? If consumers can do so, this would permit including higher level abstractions in more traditional attitude models. In addition, we address the issue of whether or not consumers are able to truly understand the concept of "levels of abstraction" and therefore be able to use this information to identify their most dominant orientation or "more representative" ladder with respect to preference. That is, when a respondent is presented with several "levels of abstraction" hierarchies comprised of connections between attributes, consequences, and values, can the respondent identify which hierarchy corresponds most closely to their preferred choices?

The purpose of this study is to provide some initial, and undoubtedly, tentative answers with respect to the methodological issues outlined above. The means-end framework as represented by its dominant methodology, laddering, was investigated as a way to provide additional understanding of the consumer in terms of perceptual and preference discrimination judgments. The methodological and analytical procedures used to provide this specific type of information are relatively new and thus require some additional exposition. This is done in the following section.

BACKGROUND

The methodological process of assessing the contribution of a set of descriptors or attributes to a set of discrimination judgments is typified by the procedures used to ascribe meaning to multidimensional scaling (MDS) spaces. The standard approach is to first obtain judgments reflecting the psychological distance between all pairs of stimuli ($n(n - 1)/2$; where n equals the number of stimuli). The task of assessing the psychological distances is usually done in either of two ways. Probably most common is using a 1 to 9 scale representing psychological dissimilarity, 1 representing "very similar" and 9 "very dissimilar." A second commonly used method is to have the respondent sort a deck of cards, each card containing one pair of objects, into piles representing pairs of objects of equal distance from one another. A more rigorous extension of this sorting task is to require the respondent to produce a complete rank ordering of all the cards (pairs of objects).

The result of analyzing data of this type is a spatial representation that is thought to reflect the true perceptual distances among the stimuli. The method assumes an ordered metric scale on the data which avoids an inherent biasing of the judgment task caused by research-supplied scales. The problem that arises from this type of analysis is how to interpret the resulting spatial configuration. This is accomplished by administering another judgment task to the respondent, namely, the rating or sorting of the stimulus objects by researcher-supplied attributes or benefits. These belief assessments of the stimulus objects are then individually regressed on the spatial coordinates, providing a basis to graphically position vectors representing the descriptors in the space. The descriptors are then examined to ascertain which ones (if any) the respondent used as the underlying bases of his/her judgments. This is done by evaluating the multiple correlations that quantify the goodness-of-linear fit of the respective descriptor vector to the dimensional coordinates for the stimuli which define the spatial coordinates.

Although applications of this set of procedures are relatively straightforward, two problems arise when this method is used to assess the contribution of the various content levels output from the laddering. First, judgments reflecting perceptions, such as rating of psychological distance, only represent half of the picture. Preference must also be related to the various levels if the basis of each judgment task is to be distinguished. Thus, an essentially identical methodology must be utilized to provide a comparison between perceptual differences and preference differences, in particular, with respect to the contributions of the respective levels of abstraction output from the laddering process.

The second problem stems from the metric assumptions inherent to the regression approach of relating the descriptors to the derived space. For example, the traditional ratings may not be on an interval scale, this obviously being the case if the sorting format is used. This fact is additionally troubling, in that the sorting procedures are often considered more desirable since they create a more involving task environment for the respondent and they probably mirror more closely the fundamental cognitive processes of grouping and distinguishing. What is required for this problem is a method of analysis whose assumptions are not as restrictive as regression, a non-metric regression that only requires an assumption of ordinality.

An analytic technique has been developed recently (Reynolds, 1983; Reynolds & Cliff, 1983) that has an option to treat the attribute ratings of stimulus objects ordinally. This technique, termed Cognitive Differentiation Analysis (CDA) yields an index reflecting the discriminative power of each of the descriptors.

In addition to being non-metric, CDA has another significant advantage over the traditional regression procedures. CDA operates directly on the $n(n - 1)/2$ pairwise similarity judgments, rather than on the coordinates derived from the MDS. By skipping the scaling step, CDA avoids dealing with any possible scaling distortions.

The application of CDA to judgments of psychological distance or preference yields measures of the (assumed) contribution of each of the descriptors. The indices from the analysis correspond to an ordinal measure of correlation (i.e., Kendall's tau [Kendall, 1955]) between differences among pairs of stimuli when ranked according to perceptual or preference difference and differences among pairs of stimuli when ranked according to differences on the descriptor. For each of the levels (attribute, consequence, value) derived from the laddering procedure, an index reflecting the degree of discrimination produced by that descriptor vector is computed.

A remaining issue is to formulate a preference task which corresponds to the perception task. This problem can be resolved by instructing each respondent to consider how much he/she prefers each stimulus in the pair instead of making the psychological distance the basis of discrimination. Then, having a mental picture of how much each stimulus is preferred, carry out the same sorting task as for perception but this time in terms of preference. Thus, all pairwise differences in preference, produced by forcing the respondent to make fine discriminations required by the complete sorting of these differences, can be recorded in an identical format as the psychological distances or similarities.

An interesting assumption of this procedure is that preference is not unidimensional in nature. Although this assumption is not included in most preference-based models, the logic underlying it is worth a comment. To illustrate, a consistent point of view held by many of the means-end theorists (Gutman, 1982) is that the consumption occasion provides the basis for determining which value makes a particular consequence desirable. If this is true, preference must be multidimensional in nature, which justifies the use of the type of research methodology described here.

In sum, the primary goal of this research is to determine if the means-end approach, represented by the laddering procedure, reveals additional insight into the consumer processes of evaluating perceptual differences and differences in preference among stimuli. Secondarily, research issues relating to how well consumers can deal with these higher level abstractions are investigated.

METHOD

Sample/Stimuli

The research methods applied in this study were experimental and were part of a larger study of advertising strategy. The product category was convenience restaurants. The respondents were 35 heavy users of convenience restaurants and as such, were aware and had frequented eight major competitors in the category. Half the sample were men and half women; within sex, half had children in the household.

Procedure

There were four tasks for each respondent. After a brief warm-up period, the respondent evaluated all 28 pairs of the eight restaurants with respect to psychological distance or similarity. This was accomplished in two stages. Respondents first sorted all pairs into four piles with respect to their general degree of similarity. Next, they rank-ordered all the pairs within the piles, yielding a complete rank order for all 28 pairs.

The second task involved development of the ladders. The respondent responded to 10 triads of convenience restaurants by providing distinctions as to why two were similar and different from the third. Of the distinctions elicited from this process, the respondent was asked to select the five most important distinctions he/she uses in selecting a convenience restaurant. Starting with the attribute distinction that was evaluated as most important, the respondents were "laddered," i.e., asked why that attribute was important in a series of probes until a consequence and a value were reached. As soon as a consequence and value were reached on three ladders, the respondent moved to the next task in the interview.

The third task involved having the respondent rank his ladders in terms of their overall importance in chooosing a restaurant. The interviewer summarized each of the three ladders as scenarios and asked which best seemed to represent his or her way of thinking about the category. Then the respondent was asked to rank the restaurants with respect to each of the elements in each of the three ladders, totaling nine rankings. In addition, importance ratings, in terms of selecting a restaurant, were obtained using a 7–point scale for each element in each ladder.

The last task was the preference sort to identify the relative pairwise preference discriminations between restaurants. The procedure was identical to the two-staged similarity sort used in the first task. Again, a complete rank order of the relative preference differences was obtained.

RESULTS

As a first step in the analysis, CDA was performed for each individual's data, relating the restaurant assessments on the attribute, consequence, and values levels of the each respondent's ladders to both the psychological distances and the preference discriminations separately. The result was an index for all nine elements (three attributes, three consequences, and three values) for both similarity and preference. Another result was an index for each ladder, which was created by combining the three elements of each ladder (see Reynolds, 1983, for a description of this procedure).

These indices allowed us to describe the degree to which each element contributes to similarity and preference differences in consumers' perceptions of the restaurants. As shown in Fig. 12.1, distinctions at all levels (attributes, consequences, and values) show a higher association with preference than with psychological distance. Also note that the ladder ranked as most mean-

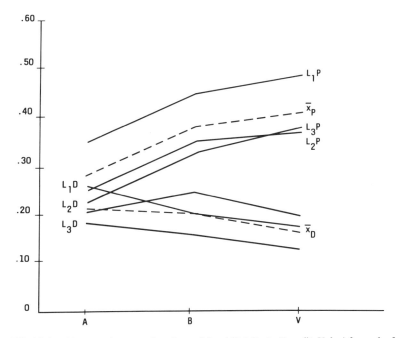

FIG. 12.1.   Non-metric tau-*r* values for each level (Attribute, Benefit, Value) for each of the three ladders (L₁, L₂, L₃).

ingful by respondents (L1) has a higher correlation with preference than do L2 and L3 for which there is no difference. Differences with respect to similarity are minimal.

More importantly, as we move up the hierarchical content structure from attribute to consequence to value, the association between preference and the ladder elements becomes stronger. The opposite pattern is seen when observing the associations between perceived similarity (e.g., psychological distances among restaurants) and the laddered constructs.

When examining patterns of association between the laddered constructs and similarity and preference, for ladders reordered so as to conform to the overall Tau index value (LI, LII, LIII), the data show an even more remarkable pattern (see Fig. 12.2). When grouped in order of their importance in choosing a restaurant, the ladders with the higher indices are associated far more with preference than with psychological distance. Here again, the degree of association between ladder elements and preference is stronger the higher the level of abstraction.

It appears that when consumers articulate and define differences between the restaurants, they operate at the level of attributes. But when consumers make a choice among restaurants, higher order elements — values — play a far more important role. It is values rather than the traditionally used product

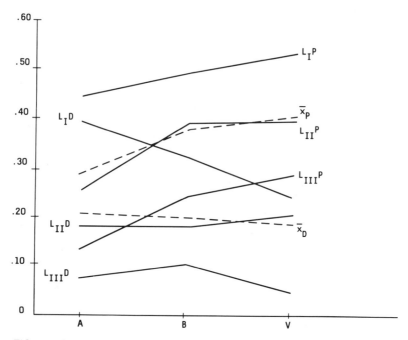

FIG. 12.2.   Non-metric tau-r values for each level (Attribute, Benefit, Value) for each of the three reordered ladders (L_I, L_{II}, L_{III}).

class attributes which provide the insights into how consumers are making their decisions.

Figure 12.3 shows the importance ratings given by respondents to the elements in their ladders. In effect, this represents what people tell us is important. It is the traditional way in which importance ratings are obtained.

As can be seen in Fig. 12.3, respondents assign greater importance to concrete attributes than they do to the somewhat more abstract benefits and values. This should not be surprising. From both the sociological and psychological perspectives, it is difficult for a consumer in a one-to-one interview situation to admit to himself, let alone an unknown interviewer, that "intangibles" influence his decision. It is far more acceptable to discuss the concrete and, at least on the surface, rational features (attributes) than to admit that values such as self-esteem or psychological well-being can effect one's purchase decisions.

Respondents were asked to identify, as described above, which of the elicited ladders was more meaningful in choosing a convenience restaurant. However, when one compares (Table 12.1A) the results of their selections (L1, L2, L3) as to the ladder which is most congruent to their expressed preferences (the reordered ladders: LI, LII, LIII), it appears that their selection is only slightly better than chance and that they are unable or unwilling to select the most dominant or representative ladder in terms of their choice behavior.

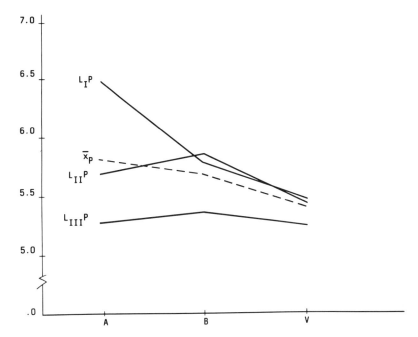

FIG. 12.3.   Self-Report Importance Weights for each level (Attribute, Benefit, Value) for the reordered ladders with respect to Preference (L_IP, $L_{II}P$, $L_{III}P$).

A similar analysis with respect to perceived similarity (Table 12.1B) shows no relationship at all between the respondent rated ordering (L1, L2, L3) of ladders and the ladders ordered by Tau values (LI, LII, LIII) with respect to psychological distance.

IMPLICATIONS

The means-end framework has been offered as an improvement over traditional attribute-based attitude models. The research presented here raises concerns regarding these models and their applications. It is worthwhile to review the assumptions of these models and methods in the light of current research.

Conjoint measurement has been extensively employed to determine optimal product or service configurations. A variety of interviewing procedures and scaling techniques have been used to develop consumers' part-worth functions for each characteristic of a set of products. These utility values, when combined, are assumed to represent the total value allocated to the product and thus to mirror preference. However, the results of the current research suggests that distinctions made at the attribute level may not be closely related to preference. Consumers may not be making choice decisions by

TABLE 12.1
Correspondence of Self
Reported Ordered Ladders
$(L_{1, 2, 3})$ to Ordinal Value
of Non-Metric Tau-r for
Entire Ladder
$(L_I = Hi, L_{III} = Lo)$

	$I\,A-PREFERENCE$		
	L_1	L_2	L_3
L_I	20	8	7
L_{II}	7	14	14
L_{III}	8	13	14

	$I\,B-DISTANCE$		
	L_1	L_2	L_3
L_I	16	6	13
L_{II}	12	13	10
L_{III}	7	16	12

searching for an optimal bundle of product attributes, but rather by attempting to satisfy personal values.

Benefit segmentation may be flawed because of other limitations. Basically, at issue here is the ability of consumers to assign appropriate importance weights to the various benefits being sought. Unfortunately, merely including values in the procedure would also appear to have little effect due to the fact that consumers assign the lowest importance weights at the highest, and often most motivating levels of abstraction.

Lifestyle research would appear to suffer less from the limitations discussed above. Consumers' values are clearly reflected in their activities, interests, and opinions (AIOs). However, only the weakest inferences can be made as to the linkages between the values inferred from AIOs and brand choice. Further, due to the aggregate nature of the analysis, lifestyle research assumes homogeneous values within a product class.

In sum, this study suggests that many of the traditional approaches to understanding a market's structure may be inadequate. Most are based upon the assumption that understanding and, ultimately, fulfilling consumers' product attribute needs (or, in rarer instances, the tangible benefits which products provide consumers) is sufficient to effect consumers' choice behavior. Market structure or market segmentation studies premised in this way may be misleading if those interpreting and using the results assume such needs are highly associated with brand preference. For, as these data suggest, attributes and benefits are associated with choice behavior to a far lesser degree than are values.

This investigation has, beyond its methodological implications, ramifications for advertising strategy development. If we accept that values can be more "motivating" to consumers' brand decisions, then they ought to be considered when developing alternative strategies for a brand. In this regard, Olson and Reynolds (1983) have shown that information regarding consumers' cognitive structures can be utilized in developing advertising strategies. They delineate five necessary components: The "Driving Force" is the value orientation of the strategy; the "Leverage Point" is the manner by which the advertising taps into or activates the end-level of the advertising's focus; the "Executional Framework" is the overall scenario whose tone and style communicate the value orientation of the advertising; the "Consumer Benefit" represents the major consequences, positive *or* negative, associated with brand usage; and finally, the "Message Elements," those specific attributes or features of the product which are to be communicated verbally or visually. This rather complete view of strategy addresses how the different levels of abstraction drawn from laddering can be understood, utilized, and evaluated directly in the development and assessment of strategic positionings.

SUMMARY

Earlier we raised several methodological issues regarding the use of the means-end framework. This study provides insights and raises many questions. While limited by the size of the sample, the scope of the study coupled with the fact that we were operating in what is likely to be a low-involvement category for most consumers suggests that the insights generated by the approach are important and have potentially dramatic implications.

Based on the study, we find:

1. Supportive evidence for the predictive validity of laddering in that the CDA indices for preference are higher at the values and consequences level than at the attribute level.
2. While the higher levels elicited by laddering are more predictive for preference, the reverse is true for psychological distance. The attribute level was more predictive when the criterion was degree of similarity.
3. Consumers cannot select their most representative ladder. The data showed that the ladder picked by respondents as being most representative of the way they make choices about convenience restaurants was not the ladder with the highest CDA index for preference.

4. Higher levels of abstraction cannot be incorporated into traditional attitude models as consumers cannot properly assign importance weights across different content categories. Because these critical content areas cannot be incorporated into attitude research, one must question the validity of these traditional models.

Understanding consumers and the basis of their decision-making strategies is essential to developing strategies and to developing effective communications. To understand the decision-making process, we must identify the cognitive structures that are brought to bear during the decision. This entails, from a means-end chain perspective, knowledge of how personal values interrelate with important consequences of consumption to provide the continuing motivation for consumer behavior.

REFERENCES

Gutman, J. (1982). A means-end chain model based on consumer categorization processes. *Journal of Marketing, 46,* (Spring), 60–72.

Gutman, J., & Reynolds, T. J. (1979). An investigation of the levels of cognitive abstraction utilized by consumers in product differentiation. In J. Eighmey (Ed.), *Attitude research under the sun.* Chicago: American Marketing Association, 128–150.

Howard, J. (1977). *Consumer behavior: Application and theory.* New York: McGraw-Hill.

Kendall, M. G. (1955). *Rank correlation method.* London: Griffin.

Olson, J. C., & Reynolds, T. J. (1983). Understanding consumers' cognitive structures: Implications for advertising strategy. In L. Percy & A. G. Woodside (Eds.), *Advertising and Consumer Psychology.* Lexington Books, 77–90.

Reynolds, T. J. (1983). A non-metric approach to determine the differentiating power of attribute ratings with respect to pairwise similarity judgments. *American Marketing Association Educator's Conference.* Sarasota, Florida.

Reynolds, T. J., & Cliff, N. (1983). True ordinal regression. *International Psychometric Meetings.* Paris, France.

Young, S., & Feigin, B. (1975). Using the benefit chain for improved strategy formulation. *Journal of Marketing,* (July), 72–74.

13 Concluding Remarks

Linda F. Alwitt
Leo Burnett U.S.A.

Andrew A. Mitchell
University of Toronto

INTRODUCTION

The chapters in this volume make a number of important contributions to our understanding of the persuasion process and have a number of implications for advertisers in developing and testing advertising campaigns. The first section of these concluding remarks contains a discussion of the contribution of the papers toward providing a better understanding of the persuasion process. The implications of the papers for advertising practitioners are discussed in the second section.

TOWARD A THEORY OF PERSUASION

As mentioned in the introduction, the dominant model of the persuasion process in the early to mid 1970s was one where individuals actively processed the content of the message in a persuasive communication. According to this model, which has been termed the high involvement/verbal response model, individuals had to go through a series of independent stages that included attention, comprehension, yielding and retention of the message in order for persuasion to occur. Since then, considerable effort has been directed at identifying alternative models of the persuasion process, the mediators that affect this process and the variables that determine which of the alternative models may be operating. The chapters in this volume provide further insights into these variables and processes. The discussion of their contribution is divided into five sections. The first and second sections review models of persuasion and persuasion effects over time. The third section discusses variables which may cause individual differences in consumers' reactions to advertisements while the fourth reviews psychological processes during exposure to advertising. An emerging model of the persuasion process is discussed in the fifth section.

Models of Persuasion

The chapters in this volume make a number of important contributions to our conceptual understanding of the cognitive processes that occur during exposure to advertising that underlie persuasion. As mentioned in the introduction, the two factors that seem to directly affect these processes are attention and processing strategy. These two factors, in turn, are affected by a number of other variables such as the content and executional elements of the message, and the individual's goal hierarchy and knowledge.

Greenwald and Leavitt (Chapter 10) emphasize the amount of attention devoted to processing the content of the message and discuss four different levels of attention. The first is the pre-attention level. Here data from the environment is monitored without the individuals' awareness. The second level is focal attention. At this level, individuals identify and categorize elements of the message. The third level is comprehension of the message, while the fourth level is elaboration. At the third level, the individual attaches meaning to the message and at the fourth level a personal verbal reaction is made to the message (e.g., the generation of counterarguments and support arguments). Greenwald and Leavitt suggest that individuals have control over the amount of attention devoted to the communication and adjust attention levels depending on their involvement with the communication.

A direct parallel between this approach and the elaboration likelihood model proposed by Petty and Cacioppo (Chapter 4) can be seen. Their model focuses on the amount of cognitive resources devoted to processing the content of the message and on the type of verbal responses that an individual makes to the persuasive communication. These responses occur primarily with the latter two stages identified by Greenwald and Leavitt, comprehension and elaboration.

In this model, if individuals put considerable effort into processing the information from the message and allocate most of their cognitive resources to this task, then persuasion is said to occur by the central route. If individuals put little effort into processing the content of the message they use other cues in the message, such as the number of message arguments, to form or change their attitudes or beliefs. In this case, persuasion is said to occur by the peripheral route.

Petty and Cacioppo (Chapter 4) use this model to explain the effect of advertising repetition. Much of the research on repetition effects has found an inverted U relationship between the amount of repetition and attitude change (e.g., Cacioppo & Petty, 1979). To explain these findings, Petty and Cacioppo hypothesize that the central route to persuasion is operating on the increasing portion of the inverted U relationship and that the peripheral route is operating on the decreasing portion of the relationship. On the increasing portion of the curve, individuals focus on the content of the message and, if the message is complex, require a number of message repetitions before they comprehend it and make a personal reaction to it. On the decreasing portion, however, individuals focus more on those executional elements of the message which, with repetition, tend to produce a negative reaction to the advertisement. This in turn reduces the amount of attitude change.

In the elaboration likelihood model, individuals either actively process the content of the message or they rely on cues in the message to form or change their attitudes. A related but somewhat different approach is taken by Lichtenstein and Srull (Chapter 5) and Beattie and Mitchell (Chapter 6), who specifically define two different information acquisition processes. With online or brand processing, individuals actively process the content of the message and form or change their attitudes toward the advertised brand. Both Lichtenstein and Srull and Beattie and Mitchell also define a second type of processing. With this processing, the individual focuses on executional aspects of the advertisement instead of the message topic. Although the individual does not actively process the information about the message topic, some information is acquired through incidental learning. Also, and perhaps more importantly, attitude formation or change does not occur during exposure to the message. Lichtenstein and Srull refer to this as a recall model and Beattie and Mitchell call this nonbrand processing.

Both Lichtenstein and Srull and Beattie and Mitchell demonstrate that a stronger relationship exists between recall and brand attitudes when individuals execute a nonbrand processing strategy than when they execute a brand processing strategy. According to their model, when individuals execute a brand processing strategy, they form an attitude toward the advertised brand and this attitude is stored in memory. When they are later asked for an evaluation of this brand, they simply retrieve the attitude that is stored in memory. Consequently, there is no relationship between recall of message information stored in memory and brand attitudes under these conditions. When individuals execute a nonbrand processing strategy, however, they do not form an attitude toward the brand. When they are later asked for an evaluation of the brand, they use whatever information is available in memory to form this attitude. Consequently, a strong relationship is found between recall and brand attitudes with a nonbrand processing strategy.

Similar effects were found in the two studies even though the methodology used in each study was different. Lichtenstein and Srull showed subjects a single advertisement and examined the relationship between the *amount* of information recalled from the advertisement and brand attitudes, while Beattie and Mitchell showed subjects a large number of advertisements and examined the relationship between recall of a particular advertisement and brand attitudes. Beattie and Mitchell also found better aided recall with a brand processing strategy than with a nonbrand processing strategy. They argued that this occurred because subjects activate a product or brand schema while executing a brand processing strategy and are, therefore, more likely to form linkages between this schema and a memory trace of the advertisement. When they execute a nonbrand processing strategy, they do not activate this schema so these linkages are less likely to be formed.

Lutz (Chapter 2) ties the processing strategy and the attention or cognitive resource dimensions together and discusses the processes underlying attitude toward the advertisement effects under four different conditions. Lutz hypothesizes that when individuals focus on the content of the message (brand processing) and put considerable effort into critically evaluating the content of the message, attitude toward the advertisement will have little effect on brand attitudes. As the amount of effort or attention devoted to evaluating the content of the message decreases, the effect of attitude toward advertisement on brand attitudes will increase; however, message thoughts (e.g., counterarguments) will still have an effect. If the individual focuses on the executional elements in the message, then, attitude toward the advertisement will have the greatest effect. The amount of thought devoted to evaluating the advertisement will determine how attitude toward the advertisement affects brand attitudes. When little thought is devoted to this task, attitude toward the advertisement effects occur through classical conditioning or "affect transfer." When considerable thought is devoted to evaluating the advertisement, these thoughts become the primary determinant of brand attitudes.

In a similar vein, Batra and Ray (Chapter 1) examine the relationship between attitude toward the advertisement, brand familiarity, purchase intentions and two different measures of affect associated with the brand. They hypothesize that two different types of processes may lead to purchase intentions. The first is a cognitive route that involves the evaluation of product attributes and the use of counterarguing and support arguing. This route appears to be similar to the central route discussed by Petty and Cacioppo and the use of a brand processing strategy as discussed by Beattie and Mitchell. The second route is based on the individuals' affective reaction to the advertisement and is hypothesized to operate through brand familiarity. Here Batra and Ray draw on the "mere exposure" research of Zajonc and suggest that as individuals become more familiar with a brand they develop more positive feelings toward it.

Batra and Ray also develop two different measures of affect based on the two routes. The first is hedonic affect, or general feelings about the brand, while the second is utilitarian affect, which is a measure of the value of the brand to the individual. They hypothesize that affective reactions to the advertisement will be strongly related to hedonic affect while counterarguing and support arguing will be related to utilitarian affect. Their analysis, however, indicates the opposite. The number of counterarguments and support arguments generated was more closely related to their measure of hedonic affect and the measure of affective feelings about the advertisement was more closely related to utilitarian affect. A causal model was then estimated which specifies the relationship between attitude toward the advertisement, brand familiarity, the two measures of brand affect and purchase intentions. According to the model, affect reactions toward the advertisement operate through brand familiarity.

In summary, the chapters in this volume provide converging evidence for a model of how individuals process information from advertisments. The two critical factors that affect these processes are the amount of attention devoted to the advertisement and the processing strategy that is used. In processing information from advertisements, individuals may devote considerable effort to processing the information in the advertisement to form or change attitudes toward the advertised brand. Alternatively, they may execute a nonbrand processing strategy and focus on the executional aspects of the advertisement.

Persuasion Effects Over Time

Two of the chapters examine persuasion effects over time. Pratkanis and Greenwald (Chapter 7) examine the conditions necessary for the "sleeper effect" to occur. Most of the research examining persuasion effects over time find that the amount of persuasion tends to decay (e.g., Cook & Flay, 1978). Some studies, however, have found an increase in persuasion over time. This finding has been termed a "sleeper effect." This effect generally occurs when individuals receive a persuasive communication from a source low in credibility. Initially, the amount of persuasion is small since the individual perceives that the message comes from a source with little credibility, and therefore, discounts the message arguments. Over time, however, persuasion increases. A number of hypotheses have been proposed to explain these effects. According to the most generally accepted hypothesis, the discounting cue hypothesis, this occurs because after a period of time the subjects disassociate the source of the message from their memory of the message.

The sleeper effect has a checkered past. The effect was initially found by Hovland, Lumsdaine, and Sheffield, (1949), however, recent attempts to replicate the effect have generally failed (Gillig & Greenwald, 1974). In a series of studies reported in their paper, Pratkanis and Greenwald investigate the conditions required to produce a reliable sleeper effect. They find, for instance, that in order to produce these effects, subjects must first receive the message, note the best arguments from the message and then learn the source of the message. As Pratkanis and Greenwald point out, if these conditions are the only ones that will cause a "sleeper effect," these effects will probably be relatively rare in natural situations.

Moore and Hutchinson (Chapter 3) present a model of the relationsip between affective reactions toward advertisements and brand attitudes over time. According to their model, attitude toward the advertisement initially has a direct effect on brand attitudes. Consequently a positive linear relationship exists between these two variables immediately after exposure to an advertisement. Relying on the discounting cue hypothesis, they argue that over time the advertisement becomes disassociated from the content of the message which means that the attitude toward the advertising effects are only transitory. They further hypothesize that affective reactions to advertisements may have an indirect effect because affectively extreme advertisements attract more attention and, therefore, increase brand awareness. This brand awareness endures over time resulting in a J-shaped relationship between attitude toward the advertisement and brand attitudes when delayed measures are used.

The results of the study reported here and their previous research (Moore & Hutchinson, 1983) provide some support for the hypothesized J-shaped relationship between attitude toward the advertisement and brand attitude over time. In addition, the results of the study reported here indicate that the relationship between these two variables declined over time and the effect of brand awareness on brand attitudes increased over time. Other aspects of the model, however, were not supported. For instance, no relationship was found between attitude toward the advertisement and brand awareness.

Individual Difference Variables

The chapter by Cushing and Douglas-Tate (Chapter 11) develops a typology for examing individual differences in response to advertising based on the consumer's involvement with a particular brand or product category. Their typology has four groups of product users: involved brand loyalists, involved information seekers, uninvolved brand switchers, and routine brand buyers. The involved brand loyalists have strong personal ties to their brand and are highly involved with the product category. It is hypothesized that they will probably ignore rational advertising appeals from competing brands. The involved information seekers have little commitment to any brand, but are highly involved with the product category. Consequently, they are constantly searching for information about alternative brands. Cushing and Douglas-Tate hypothesize that informational advertising about competitive products will be very effective with this group. The routine brand buyer is not involved with either a brand or the product category, however, he or she consistently purchases a specific brand for convenience. The uninvolved brand switcher is also not involved with either a brand or the product category. They are, however, very susceptable to promotions, and purchase whichever brand is on sale. Cushing and Douglas-Tate also present evidence that these different segments respond differently to the same advertisements.

Reynolds, Gutman, and Fiedler (Chapter 12) discuss a hierarchical model of memory that links product attributes, product benefits and the values or goals of the individual and a procedure for measuring these linkages. Previously, they have discussed how the model could be used to determine which level of the hierarchy to emphasize in developing advertising strategy (e.g., Olson & Reynolds, 1983). In this paper, they examine how well the different levels of the hierarchy predict preferences for fast food restaurants and find that preferences are most closely related to values or goals. These results are important since in marketing it has generally been assumed that product attributes provide the best prediction of preferences.

Psychological Processes During Viewing

The papers by Anderson (Chapter 8) and Alwitt (Chapter 9) examine the psychological processes that occur while individuals view television commercials, however, the two papers examine these processes at different levels. Alwitt examines how different elements of television commercials affect brain wave activity. Episodes in television commercials are coded into four categories of events: cinematic techniques, brand and message events, audiovisual modes of communication and cognitive-emotional events. A moderate proportion of EEG activity is accounted for by these events, however, some events account for more EEG activity than others. The EEGs measured in this study tend to be influenced more by the brand or message related content of advertising than by cognitive-emotional events or by simple reactions to cinematic devices such as cuts or closeups. Alwitt, however, cautions that the usefulness of EEGs in elucidating psychological processes which occur while people view television commercials will depend on the EEG methodology, availability of basic data which relate EEG to various psychological processes, and evaluation of those aspects of television commercials which elicit various EEG responses.

Anderson examines attentional processes while individuals watch television. His paper discusses four important findings. First, the amount of time spent looking at television peaks around eight years of age. Second, individuals pay attention to television when they are able to understand it and when it is *not* predictable. When it becomes predictable they tend to focus attention on other stimuli. Third, once individuals start watching television there is an inertia to continue watching even when scenes change. Finally, individuals may still attend to television even though they are not looking at it by monitoring the audio portion. When the audio indicates that something of interest is occuring on the screen, individuals shift their visual attention to the television screen.

An Emerging Model of the Persuasion Process

A reasonably consistent model of the persuasion process is emerging based on the papers in this volume and other research. The focus of this model is on the cognitive processes that occur during exposure to a persuasive message since these processes affect what information is acquired from the persuasive message and the attitudes that are formed or changed. A number of variables control these processes. The most important of these appear to be attention and processing strategy. Attention has two critical dimensions — focus and capacity. The first dimension, focus, refers to where the individual directs his or her attention, while capacity refers to the amount of attention used in a particular task (Kahneman, 1973; Navon & Gopher, 1979; Eysenck, 1982).

Anderson's paper (Chapter 8) examines factors which affect the focus of attention. His research indicates that two of the factors which affect the focus of attention are the ability to understand the message and the extent to which it is predictable. Both of these factors will be determined by the knowledge that the individual has about the message topic and the executional elements in the message. For instance, an advertisement for a particular brand of beer may contain scenes of a sailboat race. In order to understand this commercial, an individual would need to have knowledge about both beer and sailing. Presumably, individuals have schemata for both the message topic (e.g. beer) and the executional elements (e.g., sailboats). The content of these schemata may determine how much attention is focused on the message as opposed to other elements in the environment, and the interconnections between these schemata may determine how well the message is comprehended and whether it is persuasive.

Different stimuli in the environment constantly compete for an individual's focus of attention. Current models of attention indicate that individuals constantly monitor information from the different senses at a preattentive level (e.g. Kahneman, 1973). Anderson's research (Chapter 8), for instance, indicates that individuals may focus attention on other objects in the environment while the television set is on, while, at the same time they monitor the audio portion of the message. When the audio indicates that something interesting is occuring, they will focus their attention back to the screen.

Somewhat more controversial is whether affective feelings for stimuli can develop at the preattentive stage. Zajonc (1980), based on his "mere exposure" research and more recent studies (e.g., Moreland & Zajonc, 1979; Wilson, 1979), suggests that affect can develop at this stage. Wilson (1979), for instance, demonstrated that individuals can have positive feelings toward objects they have seen, but cannnot recognize. A number of recent articles, however, have challenged this position on both theoretical and methodological grounds (e.g., Birnbaum & Mellers, 1979; Birnbaum, 1981; Lazarus, 1982).

After focusing attention on the message, the next two levels of attention identified by Greenwald and Leavitt are comprehension and elaboration. At the comprehension level, individuals assign meaning to the entire message while at the elaboration stage they make a personal response to the message. This personal response may involve the generation of counterarguments or support arguments. Research within the distraction paradigm (e.g., Petty, Wells, & Brock, 1976) indicates that these latter two stages require an increasing amount of attention. Since individuals have some control over the amount of attention devoted to a message, Greenwald and Leavitt argue that an individual's involvement with the message topic determines the amount of attention devoted to it.

The second dimension affecting the processing that occurs during exposure to a persuasion message is processing strategy. This dimension primarily affects the comprehension and elaboration stages. Here two different processing strategies have been identified. The first occurs when individuals use the information in the advertisement to evaluate the advertised brand (brand processing strategy) and the second occurs when individuals focus on the executional elements in the advertisement (nonbrand processing strategy). Both Lichtenstein and Srull (Chapter 5) and Beattie and Mitchell (Chapter 6) demonstrate that there is a closer relationship beteween recall and evaluation when individuals execute a nonbrand processing strategy than when they execute a brand processing strategy. This apparently occurs because individuals form an attitude toward the brand while executing a brand processing strategy, but do not when executing a nonbrand processing strategy. In addition, the study by Beattie and Mitchell found that with aided recall, subjects remembered more advertisements when executing a brand processing strategy than with a nonbrand processing strategy. They argued that this occurred because the subjects activated a brand or product schema when executing a brand processing strategy, however, when they execute a nonbrand processing strategy they are less likely to activate this schema.

Current research also indicates that as individuals increase the amount of attentional resources or elaboration while executing a brand processing strategy, attitude toward the advertisement has less of an effect on brand attitudes (e.g., Mitchell, 1984). This is consistent with Lutz's hypothesis (Chapter 2). Lutz, however, also suggests that different processes may determine attitude toward the advertisement with differing amounts of elaboration when individuals execute a nonbrand processing strategy. If there is little elaboration, attitude toward the advertisement will affect brand attitudes directly through classical conditioning or "affect transfer." When the amount of elaboration about the advertisement increases, these elaborations will affect both attitude toward the advertisement and brand attitudes.

There is a critical difference between the approach suggested here, which considers both the amount of attention devoted to the advertisement and the processing strategy that is used, and the elaboration likelihood model developed by Petty and Cacioppo (1981). The latter considers only one dimension to be important, the amount of elaboration concerning message content, while the approach discussed here considers two dimensions to be important. Further research needs to be directed at determining whether this conceptual difference is important.

Two factors that will affect the amount of attention devoted to the persuasive message and the processing strategy that is used are involvement with the advertised product or brand and the amount of knowledge about the product or brand. Douglas-Tate and Cushing (Chapter 11) examine involvement with the product or brand. They identify four groups of consumers that differ along these dimensions and find that they react to the same advertisements differently.

Gutman, Reynolds, and Fiedler suggest that an individual's knowledge about a product category affects how they process information from an advertisement. They present a hierarchical model of knowledge that contains three types of knowledge: product attribute information, perceived benefits, and values. Theoretically, if individual differences exist in the relationship among attributes, benefits, and values, these differences may affect how individuals process information from advertisements.

Three other factors also affect the amount of attention devoted to the advertisement and the processing strategy that is used. The first is the individual's goal hierarchy (e.g., Schank & Abelson, 1977) while exposed to the advertisement. Individuals' goals change over time. At one point in time, an individual may be considering the purchase of an automobile and, therefore, may actively search for information about automobiles. Consequently, whenever they are exposed to an advertisement for automobiles, they may actively process the information from the advertisement (e.g., execute a brand processing strategy). When they are not considering an automobile purchase the individual may decide to expend little effort in processing the information contained in the advertisement. When this happens they may either execute a nonbrand processing strategy or devote little attentional resources to the advertisement.

The executional elements of the advertisement may also affect the amount of attention devoted to the advertisement and the processing strategy that is used. If the advertisement contains a strong attention getting device (e.g., a famous personality) or a scene of interest to the individual (e.g., sailing), the individual may focus his or her attention on the executional elements of the advertisement and execute a nonbrand processing strategy.

Finally, the modality of the message will effect the opportunity to process the information in the message. With both radio and television, only a limited amount of time is available to process the information contained in the message; however, with print, the individual can spend as much time as he or she would like in processing the message related information. Consequently, with radio and television, the individual may not have enough time to think about the contents of the message (e.g., Wright, 1973) and, therefore, may not be able to execute a brand processing strategy.

In summary, then, a number of variables will affect how much attention is devoted to the advertisement and the processing strategy that is used. These include the personal relationship between the individual and the topic of the message, the individual's goal hierarchy, the individual's knowledge about the message topic, the modality of the message and the executional elements of the advertisement.

A model of these variables and their effect on the information acquisition processes is shown in Fig. 13.1. In the model, the amount of attention devoted to the message and the processing strategy that is used affect what information is acquired from the advertisement and whether attitudes are formed or changed. A number of variables affect these processes. These can be categorized into message, environmental and individual factors. The topic of message (e.g., brand and/or product advertised), the modality of the message, and the executional elements in the advertisement affect both the amount of attention devoted to the message and the processing strategy that is used. Environmental factors will affect the amount of attention devoted to the message. For instance, while watching a television commercial an individual may also try to monitor a conversation that is taking place in the room. This monitoring of the conversation will reduce the amount of attention available for processing the information in the commercial. Finally, the individual's relationship to the brand and the amount of knowledge about the product and brand will affect both the amount of attention devoted to the brand and the processing strategy that is used.

Although a number of different mediators of advertising effects have been identified, the three that have received the most attention recently are (1) salient beliefs about the advertised brand (e.g., Fishbein & Ajzen, 1975; Lutz, 1975), (2) verbal thoughts during exposure to the advertisement (e.g., Greenwald, 1968; Wright, 1973), and attitude toward the advertisement (e.g., Mitchell & Olson, 1981). The chapters in this volume help to clarify the relationship among these different mediators (See Fig. 13.2). The relationship between exposure to advertisements, verbal product thoughts, and atti-

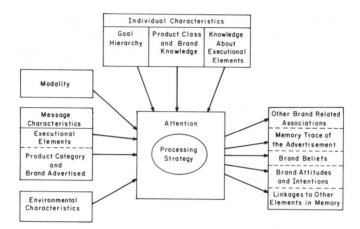

FIG. 13.1.   Variables affecting individual response to advertising.

tude formation and change (links 3 and 5) has been demonstrated many times (e.g., Wright, 1973; Olson, Toy, & Dover, 1982), as have the links between exposure to advertisement, belief formation and change, and attitude formation and change (links 2 and 8) (e.g., Lutz, 1975; Mitchell & Olson, 1981). The link between verbal product thoughts and belief formation and change (link 7) has been demonstrated by Olson, Toy, and Dover (1982) and the link between attitude toward the advertisement and brand attitudes (links 2 and 6) has been demonstrated by Mitchell and Olson (1981).

In most previous academic advertising research, only product related verbal thoughts have been used as mediators of advertising effects (e.g., Wright, 1973). Batra and Ray (Chapter 1) also coded the verbal thoughts that occur during exposure to an advertisement thoughts into advertisement-related thoughts and show that a relationship exists between these thoughts and attitude toward the advertisement (link 4). This link has also been demonstrated by Lutz, MacKenzie, and Belch (1983) and Mitchell (1983b).

The final link (link 9) is between attitudes and behavior. In marketing, our thinking about this link has relied heavily on the conceptualization provided by Fishbein and Ajzen (1975). Under this conceptualization, the relationship between attitudes and a specific behavior (e.g., purchasing a brand) will be strongest when attitudes toward performing the specific behavior are measured and when the measurement of the attitudes and the performance of the behavior are contiguous. Recently, however, other researchers have suggested that other factors may mediate this relationship. For instance, Fazio and Zanna (1981) suggest that attitude accessibility and confidence may be positively related to attitude behavior consistency. More research is needed in this area to understand this relationship.

Finally, it should be noted that two of the mediators discussed here are verbal mediators of attitude formation and change (e.g., verbal thoughts and beliefs). Currently, we do not have a clear understanding of how nonverbal responses to advertisements, such as the feelings generated while viewing an emotional television commercial, may effect persuasion. There is some indication that attitude toward the advertisement may capture some of these effects (e.g., Lutz, Chapter 2; Mitchell, 1984), however, more research is needed in this area.

In summary, then, significant relationships have been demonstrated among the three different mediators of advertising effects as shown in Fig. 13.2. These links, however, have only been demonstrated with pairs of mediators. For instance, Mitchell and Olson (1981) examined these links using only attitude toward the advertisement and belief formation and change, Lutz, MacKenzie, and Belch (1983) examined only verbal thoughts and attitude toward the advertisement, and Olson, Toy, and Dover (1982) examined only verbal thoughts and belief formation and change. Future research needs to examine the relationship among all three mediators simultaneously.

Batra and Ray (Chapter 1) develop a somewhat different model. As discussed earlier, their model makes a conceptual distinction between two types of affect, hedonic and utilitarian. The former is a general measure of the feelings someone has about a brand while the latter is a measure of the value of the brand to the individual. In addition, their model contains a construct called brand familiarity. Conceptually, this construct may be viewed as picking up the affective feelings generated through the "mere exposure" effect, or alternatively, it might be viewed as a measure of the amount of information that the individual has about the brand. The latter interpretation suggests that familiarity might be similar to the belief formation and change construct, however, it is not clear conceptually, why attitude toward advertisement would operate through this construct under this interpretation of brand familiarity. More research is clearly needed to determine if the conceptual distinction between the two types of affect is important and to clarify the brand familiarity construct and its mediating role in the persuasion process.

The relationship between these different mediators also needs to be examined when different models of persuasion are operating. Batra and Ray, for instance, find that under low involvement conditions, persuasion occurs

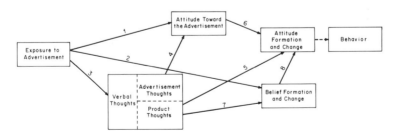

FIG. 13.2.   Relationship between some of the mediators of persuasion.

through attitude toward the advertisement and brand familiarity. Lutz, MacKenzie, and Belch (1983), find that only attitude toward the advertisement has an effect on brand attitudes under low involvement conditions, however, under high involvement conditions both attitude toward the advertisement and verbal product thoughts have an effect on brand attitudes. Unfortunately, it will be difficult to compare the results of different studies until we clarify our conceptual definitions of the relevant variables. Batra and Ray, for instance, use the relative amount of product related verbal thoughts as a measure of involvement while Lutz, MacKenzie and Belch (1983), use the amount of interest and knowledge about the advertised brand as a measure of involvement.

It is also important to consider the relationship between these variables over time. As mentioned previously, most of the previous research on persuasion effects indicates that the amount of persuasion decays over time. In some situations, however, persuasion has been found to increase. The research by Pratkanis and Greenwald (Chapter 7) indicates that this will probably rarely happen outside of the laboratory if the conditions that they identify are the only ones that will produce this effect.

Moore and Hutchinson (Chapter 3) examine alternative theoretical models of the relationship between attitude toward the advertisement, recall of the advertisement, and brand awareness over time. They find no relationship between attitude toward the advertisement and brand awareness and some support for a J-shaped relationship between attitude toward the advertisement and brand attitudes after a week delay. In addition, with the delay measures, attitude toward the advertisement had an effect on brand attitudes only if the advertisement was recalled and an increase in the effect of brand awareness on brand attitudes over time. Although they examined a number of different models to explain these relationships, the pattern of the data did not fit any of the models.

A related issue involves the effect of advertising repetition. Petty and Cacioppo (Chapter 4) present a model to explain the inverted-U relationship frequently found between attitude change and repetition. The generally accepted reason why attitude change initially increases with repetition (e.g., increasing portion of the inverted U relationship) is that repetition facilitates the comprehension and acquisition of information from the message. Somewhat less well understood is the reason why attitude change eventually starts to decrease with additional repetition. Petty and Cacioppo hypothesize that this may be due to mood effects or reactance. Their study provides some support for this explanation, since both attitudes and attitude toward the advertisement decreased with repetition of the same advertisement under low involvement conditions.

Although the papers in this volume make a significant contribution to understanding persuasion effects over time and repetition effects, more research in this area is clearly needed. Ideally, we would like to understand the factors that affect the rate of decay of persuasion over time and the factors that determine the point at which repetition will have a decreasing or negative effect, so we can determine how frequently to repeat a given message. In their paper, Petty and Cacioppo have provided an indication of what these factors might be for repetition. Finally, more research needs to be directed at combining persuasion effects over time and repetition so we can understand how advertising repetition should be spaced over time. In order to do this, we will probably need to develop a theoretical model of the cognitive mechanisms that determine persuasive effects over time. The paper by Moore and Hutchinson (Chapter 2) discusses some of these mechanisms.

In summary, the papers in this volume present converging evidence concerning an emerging model of persuasion. The papers, also, however, indicate important areas where further research is necessary. Among these areas are: (1) whether a single dimension — amount of cognitive resources (e.g., attention) devoted to processing the information from the message — or whether two dimensions — cognitive resources and processing strategy — are required to obtain an understanding of advertising effects; (2) whether a single or multiple measures of affect toward a brand are required to explain advertising effects; (3) the role of brand familiarity and brand awarenesss in the persuasion process; (4) examination of other mediators of the attitude behavior relationship; (5) the effect of nonverbal responses to advertisements on persuasion; (6) the cognitive mechanisms underlying persuasion effects over time; and (7) the cognitive mechanisms underlying the decline in persuasion frequently found after a large number of repetitions.

IMPLICATIONS FOR ADVERTISERS

For advertisers, persuasion ultimately means increased sales in the marketplace. The role of advertising in influencing sales is notoriously difficult to isolate, and the role of particular advertising executions is even more difficult to evaluate. As discussed earlier, theories of persuasion that emphasize recall and comprehension of the advertising message have been the basis for theories of how advertising persuades consumers to buy the advertised brand. They are part of the reason that many advertisements stress the news value ("new, improved!"), the product attributes ("smooth, mellow taste"), or demonstrations, and that procedures for evaluating advertising effectiveness emphasize recall.

The chapters of this volume suggest that the traditional view of how advertising works may apply to only a limited amount of the advertising in print and on the air. They suggest that: (1) while message comprehension may be necessary, it is certainly not sufficient for advertising to be persuasive, and

(2) message comprehension interacts with executional aspects of advertising and consumer attitudes and values in its effect on persuasion. The executional aspects of advertising which mediate the role of the message in persuading a consumer to buy a brand seem to operate through attitude toward the advertisement (Chapters 1, 2, 3), and their effect on brand attitudes is greatest with nonbrand processing (Chapter 6) and the peripheral route to persuasion (Chapter 4). The consumer characteristics that interact with advertising to direct buyer decisions include the way people relate products to their lives (Chapters 11 and 12), the strategies they use when they view advertising (Chapters 8, 9, 10), and the strategies they use when they make purchase decisions (Chapters 5, 6, 7).

In sum, theories from the 1960s and 1970s justified rational, message-evaluated advertising. The thinking represented by the chapters in this volume argue also for the effectiveness of advertising that is liked, executions (as well as messages) that are well comprehended, relevance of the advertising message to underlying values, and sensitivity of advertising to the prevalent person-product relationship of a product category.

As all seminal research does, many of the chapters raise as many questions as they answer. However, several specific implications can be drawn from these chapters for the development of advertising strategies, for executional considerations and for the ways advertising can be evaluated. Some of these implications are discussed in the following section.

Implications for the Development of Advertising Strategies

Reynolds, Gutman, and Fiedler (Chapter 12) presented evidence that the values that motivate people to carry on their life activities are more closely related to brand preferences than are brand attributes or benefits. Consequently, their research supports the idea that advertising strategies should be based on knowledge of how our motivating life values are related to the consequences that products have for our lives, and how these consequences are derived from product attributes. Once we know more about how a product category is represented within the experience, knowledge, and value framework of its potential consumers, advertising strategies can be developed which both distinguish a brand from its competitors and also appeal to consumers at the level at which they make purchase decisions. Furthermore, this research suggests that the product attributes that discriminate among brands of a product category may only be effective as selling points if consumers are clearly able to associate the consequences of those attributes to their own lives.

Not only do advertising strategies depend on what a consumer knows, thinks, and feels about the product category, but also on his or her relationship to the brands in that category. Cushing and Douglas-Tate (Chapter 11) point out that how people relate to brands in a product category may influence the way those consumers react to the advertising for those brands. Their typology, which combines brand loyalty and involvement with a product category, suggests that different types of appeals will be most effective for each category. As we learn more about the relationship between consumers and brands, we will obtain a better understanding of the types of appeals that are most effective for different brands.

The results of Lichenstein and Srull (Chapter 5) and Beattie and Mitchell (Chapter 6) imply that it is important to know *when* a purchase decision is made relative to exposure of advertising. They report that recall is less related to judgment when the judgment is made at the time the advertising is seen than when the judgment is made at a later time.

This implies that advertising strategies and executional styles for different product categories should take into account when the purchase decision is likely to be made. If the purchase decision for a product is made at the point of purchase—in the supermarket, at the store or at the travel agent, for example—then the decision may be partially based on the consumer's memory for the advertising for brands of that product category if the individual has not already formed an evaluation of the brand. However, if the purchase decision for a product is made at the time the advertising is seen, then later *recall* of the advertising may not be directly related to the decision because the advertising has directly and immediately influenced that purchase decision. One might hypothesize that consumers would have enough interest in a new product or a new perception of an established brand to make a purchase decision about it at the time the advertising is viewed. However, purchase decisions about established brands or line extensions may be more likely to be made at the point of purchase. What is said in an ad and how the message and execution is designed to be remembered should take into account when the purchase decision is made.

Implications for Executional and Media Considerations

Evidence for the influence of positive attitudes toward the advertising on positive attitudes to the advertised brand is discussed in many of the chapters. They generally concur that advertising that is liked should result in more positive brand attitudes. Although there is some evidence for the effectiveness of "ads you love to hate" as sales vehicles (cf. Moore & Hutchinson, Chapter 3), this appears to be the more risky route to persuasion.

Batra & Ray, in Chapter 1, offer evidence that the major impact of the attitude toward the advertisement on brand attitudes works through brand familiarity. This result implies that one can capitalize on advertising which the audience likes by exposing it often and thereby increasing familiarity with the brand. To the extent that mood and image advertising is liked better than demonstrations, comparative advertising, and hard sell product-attribute advertising, this result suggests that mood and image advertising should receive more media weight than the other types of advertising. However, we do not know the relative importance of the attitude toward the advertisement on purchase decisions, compared to product-related aspects of advertising and previously-acquired product attitudes of the consumer. From the evidence presented in this volume, it appears that the relative importance of the attitude toward the advertisement in influencing consumer purchase decisions depends on their allocation of attention and processing strategies they use. Attention and processing strategies, in turn, are influenced by the product category of the advertised brand, and with consumer involvement with the category, the brand, and the advertising.

The executional style adopted for advertising for a brand should also depend on the purpose of the advertising, as suggested by Greenwald and Leavitt in Chapter 10. All advertising does not require a level of cognitive involvement that will result in total recall of the brand, message, and executional elements. Rather, they argue, advertising that reminds consumers of the brand name can be executed so that consumers absorb it with less cognitive effort. This point of view also implies that advertising effectiveness should be copy-tested by a method which matches the intent of the advertising.

An issue of concern to advertisers is how long to expose an advertising execution before consumers become tired of it, before it "wears out." Lutz in Chapter 2 suggests that attitude toward the advertisment is an important construct for understanding advertising wearout. Cacioppo and Petty (Chapter 4) also address the issue of wearout. Their results indicate that repetition of advertising (within the limited time frame of a laboratory experiment) initially leads to more rational consideration of the advertising and uses the central route to persuasion. Repetition leads to more consideration of the message rather than of the execution and also to more counterargument. The advantages afforded by an attention-catching or message-distracting execution is that it may delay consideration of the message. In the same way, pools of advertising executions rather than a single execution may also delay consideration of the message.

Media planners are aware of the importance of matching consumers with the differing appeals of different magazines, television, or radio shows. Anderson's results suggest that another factor might be considered, program context. Anderson, discussing attention to television in Chapter 8, implies that the attentional appeal of the program or advertising which immediately precedes an advertisement can determine whether or not the viewer will continue to attend to that advertisement. If the preceding television content is sufficiently absorbing, it should keep the viewer glued to the screen despite the attention-distracting presence of a change in continuity from program to commercial or from one commercial to another. Not only does the overall appeal of the program context influence viewer attention but the format of the program also influences patterns of viewer attention. Krugman (1983), for instance, has observed that commercials have the greatest impact on viewers when the commercials are embedded in programs that have continuity in their format, such as a drama rather than a talk show.

Anderson also points out the importance of the audio portion of television for viewers to monitor whether or not they should look at the television. A typical "commercial voice" may be a cue to the viewer to leave the room while a "watch this demonstration" may be a cue to look up at the screen.

Implications for the Evaluation of Advertising

When is it appropriate to use recall of advertising in order to try to predict its eventual effectiveness in the marketplace? Lichtenstein and Srull's results (Chapter 5) imply that it depends on whether the purchase decision is made when the advertising is seen or at the point of purchase. Beattie and Mitchell (Chapter 6) suggest that not all commercials that are attended to are recalled, but that aided recall is better when the consumer executes a brand processing strategy. Beattie and Mitchell also report that advertising recall is closely related to brand attitudes if advertisements are recalled by consumers who are less involved with the product or brand and, therefore, use a nonbrand strategy. Since their evidence is correlational, we cannot be sure of the direction of causality, however, if brand attitudes are not formed during exposure to the advertisements with a nonbrand processing strategy, as argued by Beattie and Mitchell, then the direction of causality should flow from recall to evaluation.

Anderson's (Chapter 8) research on the moment-by-moment viewing of television offers evidence that people look at television when the content is at an optimal level of comprehension for them and look away when the level is too high. When viewers have seen a commercial enough times so that they understand the message, the storyline, and anything else they wish to extract from it, they are no longer attracted to it because it presents no new information and too little of a challenge. This implies that a measure of moment-by-moment attention to commercials might be used as a measure of the wearout of advertising executions.

In recent years, measures of "brain waves" have been marketed to advertisers as another way to assess their advertising copy. The attraction of a measure which tracks reactions to advertising as they occur and which purports to reflect nonverbalizable reactions has intrigued some advertisers. The chapter by Alwitt suggests that the electrical activity of the brain reflects aspects of commercials which may be useful to know about. However, the state of knowledge about how to interpret EEG responses is too meager to render these reactions as either diagnostically or evaluatively meaningful for a particular advertising execution. Further, although the distinction between "left and right brains" may be an interesting and useful metaphor for advertisers, its usefulness as a physiological indicator of viewer reactions is limited. It seems premature for advertisers to consider evaluation of advertising based on EEG responses because these responses cannot be interpreted yet in terms of the psychological processes they reflect, let alone how those processes influence purchase decisions.

Although a number of the chapters use methods that might be translated into measures for evaluating advertising, Batra and Ray specifically (Chapter 1) developed a coding scheme for thought protocols which includes various affective reactions to advertising. The two affective codes they found to be the most closely related to other reactions to advertising and to the brand were the measure of SEVA (surgency, elation, vigor, and activation) and the measure of social affection (references to the ad being warm, touching, etc.). This way of analyzing reactions to advertising may be one more way to assess its emotional appeal.

In sum, the chapters in this volume offer implications for the development of advertising strategies, advertising executions and media plans, and copy-testing methods. The emerging theory of persuasion and research on advertising effect will hopefully generate new research on persuasion, and will lead to fresh approaches to the development of advertising strategies, executional vehicles, and copy testing approaches.

REFERENCES

Birnbaum, M. H. (1981). Thinking and feeling: A skeptical review. *American Psychologist, 36,* 99–101.

Birnbaum, M. H., & Mellers, B. A. (1979). One mediator model of exposure effects is still viable. *Journal of Personality and Social Psychology, 37,* 1090–1096.

Cacioppo, J. T., & Petty, R. E. (1979). Effects of message repetition and position on cognitive responses, recall and persuasion. *Journal of Personality and Social Psychology, 37,* 97–109.

Cook, T. D., & Flay, B. R. (1978). The persistence of experimentally induced attitude change. In L. Berkowitz (Ed.), *Advances in experimental social psychology.* New York: Academic Press, 1–5.

Eysenck, M. W. (1982). *Attention and arousal.* New York: Springer-Verlag.

Fazio, R. H., & Zanna, M. P. (1981). Direct experience and attitude-behavior consistency. In R. Berkowitz (Ed.), *Advances in experimental social psychology, Vol. 14.* New York: Academic Press, 161–202.

Fishbein, M., & Ajzen, I. (1975). *Belief, attitude, intention and behavior.* Reading, MA: Addison-Wesley Publishing Co.

Gillig, P. M., & Greenwald, A. G. (1974). Is it time to lay the sleeper effect to rest? *Journal of Personality and Social Psychology, 29,* 132–139.

Greenwald, A. G. (1968). Cognitive learning, cognitive response to persuasion and attitude change. In A. G. Greenwald, T. C. Brock, & T. M. Ostrom (Eds.), *Psychological Foundations of Attitudes.* New York: Academic Press, 147–170.

Hovland, C. I., Lumsdaine, A. A., & Sheffield, F. D. (1949). *Experiments on mass communication*. Princeton, NJ: Princeton University Press.

Kahneman, D. (1973). *Attention and effort*. Englewood Cliffs, NJ: Prentice-Hall.

Krugman, H. E. (1983). Television program interest and commercial interruption. *Journal of Advertising Research, 23,* 21-23.

Lazarus, R. S. (1982). Thoughts on the relations between emotion and cognition. *American Psychologist, 37,* 1019-1024.

Lutz, R. J. (1975). Changing brand attitudes through modifications of cognitive structure. *Journal of Consumer Research, 1,* 49-59.

Lutz, R. J., MacKenzie, S. B., & Belch, B. E. (1983). Attitude toward the advertisement as a mediator of advertising effectiveness: determinants and consequences. In R. P. Bagozzi & A. M. Tybout (Eds.), *Advances in consumer research, Vol. 10.* Ann Arbor: Association for Consumer Research, 523-537.

Mitchell, A. A. (1984). *The effect of visual and verbal components in advertisements on attitude toward the advertisement and brand attitudes.* Working Paper, Graduate School of Industrial Administration, Carnegie-Mellon University, Pittsburgh, PA 15213.

Mitchell, A. A. (1983a). Cognitive processes initiated by exposure to advertising. In R. Harris (Ed.), *Information Processing Research in Advertising.* Hillsdale, NJ: Lawrence Erlbaum Associates.

Mitchell, A. A. (1983b). The effect of visual and emotional advertising: An information processing approach. In L. Percy & A. Woodside (Eds.), *Advertising and consumer psychology.* Lexington, MA: Lexington Books.

Mitchell, A. A., & Olson, J. C. (1981). Are product attribute beliefs the only mediator of advertising effects on brand attitudes. *Journal of Marketing Research, 18,* 318-332.

Moore, D. L., & Hutchinson, J. W. (1983). The effects of ad affect on advertising effectiveness. In R. P. Bagozzi & A. M. Tybout (Eds.), *Advances in consumer research: Volume X.* Ann Arbor: Association for Consumer Research, 526-531.

Moreland, R. C., & Zajonc, R. B. (1979). Exposure effects may not depend on stimulus recognition. *Journal of Personality and Social Psychology, 37,* 1085-1089.

Navon, D., & Gopher, D. (1979). On the economy of the human processing system. *Psychological Review, 86,* 214-255.

Olson, J. C., & Reynolds, T. C. (1983). Understanding consumers' cognitive structures: Implications for advertising strategy. In L. Percy & A. Woodside (Eds.), *Advertising and consumer psychology.* Lexington, MA: Lexington Books.

Olson, J. C., Toy, D. R., & Dover, P. A. (1982). Do cognitive responses mediate the effects of advertising content on cognitive structure? *Journal of Consumer Research, 9,* 245-262.

Petty, R. E., & Cacioppo, J. T. (1981). *Attitudes and Persuasion: Classic and Contemporary Approaches.* Dubuque, IA: Wm. C. Brown Company.

Petty, R. E., Cacioppo, J. T., & Schumann, D. (1983). Central and peripheral routes to advertising effectiveness: The moderating role of involvement. *Journal of Consumer Research, 10,* 135-146.

Petty, R. E., Wells, G. L., & Brock, T. C. (1976). Distraction can enhance or reduce yielding to propaganda: Thought disruption versus effort justification. *Journal of Personality and Social Psychology, 34,* 874-884.

Schank, R., & Abelson, R. (1977). *Scripts, plans, goals and understanding.* Hillsdale, NJ: Lawrence Erlbaum Associates.

Wilson, W. R. (1979). Feeling more than we can know: Exposure effects without learning. *Journal of Personality and Social Psychology, 37,* 811-821.

Wright, P. L. (1973). Cognitive processes mediating acceptance of advertising. *Journal of Marketing Research, 4,* 53-62.

Zajonc, R. B. (1980). Feeling and thinking: Preferences need no inferences. *American Psychologist, 35,* 151-175.

Author Index

Subject Index

301